MALCOLM X SPEAKS

Pathfinder

New York • London • Montreal • Sydney

Edited by George Breitman

Copyright © 1965, 1989 by Betty Shabazz and Pathfinder Press
All rights reserved

ISBN 978-0-87348-546-3
Library of Congress Catalog Card Number 90-64058
Manufactured in the United States of America

First cloth edition, 1965
Second cloth edition, 1989
Fifteenth printing, 2020

COVER PHOTO: Malcolm X during 1963 civil rights demonstration in
New York City. Frontispiece photo: Malcolm X at news conference
announcing break with Nation of Islam, March 12, 1964 (Robert
Parent).

COVER DESIGN: Eva Braiman

All correspondence concerning rights and permissions should be
addressed to:

PATHFINDER
www.pathfinderpress.com
E-mail: pathfinder@pathfinderpress.com

Contents

the man/Mercenaries and hostages/The little
black goat/Dick Gregory/The revolution in
Zanzibar/President Nyerere in Cairo/Message from
Che Guevara/Muhammad Babu of Tanzania/All
those fine decorations/Reward for a sheriff

for moral reasons / Pressure from outside / Seeds of division / Greatest accomplishments of 1964 / Not alone in Mississippi / Not trying to incite / Like a knot on the wall / What preceding generation did / Stay radical long enough / Not hate, but sense / No interpretation necessary

Foreword

Malcolm Little was born in Omaha, Nebraska, on May 19, 1925. A dropout from school at 15, he was convicted of burglary and sent to prison in his twenty-first year. There he was converted to the Nation of Islam (Black Muslims). When he left prison in 1952, he dedicated himself to building the Black Muslims, and adopted the name Malcolm X. He withdrew from that movement in March, 1964, organizing first the Muslim Mosque, Inc., and later the non-religious Organization of Afro-American Unity. He made two trips to Africa and the Middle East during 1964. Three months after his return to the United States, he was assassinated in New York on February 21, 1965. His own story of his life is recounted in *The Autobiography of Malcolm X* (Grove Press, 1965).

This book is a selection of speeches by Malcolm X. All of them were made during the last year of his life (except for the first selection, made shortly before his departure from the Black Muslim movement). With that exception, it ranges in time from his declaration of independence on March 12, 1964, to his death. It represents only a small portion of the speeches and interviews he gave during that period in the United States, Africa, the Middle East and Europe. It does not attempt to deal with Malcolm's assassination.

The aim of this book is to present, in his own words, the major ideas Malcolm expounded and defended during his last year. We feel that this aim is largely fulfilled by the speeches and other material included here, even though not all of his speeches were available to us. Convinced that Malcolm will be the subject of much study and many controversies in the years to come—by activists in the black freedom struggle as well as historians, scholars and students—we believe that the present book will serve as an invaluable source of material for their studies and disputes, and that it will correct, at least partially, some misconceptions about one of the most misunderstood and misrepresented men of our time.

Malcolm was primarily a speaker, not a writer. The only things in this book written by him are his memorandum to the Organization of African Unity in Cairo and some letters. The printed speeches do not convey adequately his remarkable qualities as a speaker, their effect on his audiences and the interplay between him and them. We would have preferred to publish a series of long-playing record albums presenting this material in his own voice, with its tones of indignation and anger, with its chuckles, and with the interruptions of applause and laughter from the audience. (We counted almost 150 such interruptions by the audience in the tape of a single speech, "The Ballot or the Bullet.") Since we lack the resources and time to publish and distribute such recordings and since the cost would limit the number of people who could buy them, we are doing the next best thing.

In editing, we have made only such changes as any speaker would make in preparing his speeches for print, and such as we believe Malcolm would have made himself. That is, we have corrected slips of the tongue and minor grammatical lapses which are unavoidable in most speeches given extemporaneously or from brief notes. Since we sought to avoid repetitions, common to speakers who speak as often as Malcolm did, we have omitted sections that were repeated or paraphrased in other speeches included here. Omissions of this kind are indicated by three periods (. . .).

The explanatory notes accompanying the speeches are intended primarily to indicate where and when they were given, with a minimum of interpretative or editorial comment. The reader is urged to bear in mind throughout the book that Malcolm's ideas were developing with rapidity and that certain positions he took in the first two months after his break with the Black Muslims underwent further change in the last months of his life.

G.B.

1

Message to the grass roots

In late 1963, the Detroit Council for Human Rights announced a Northern Negro Leadership Conference to be held in Detroit on November 9 and 10. When the council's chairman, Rev. C.L. Franklin, sought to exclude black nationalists and Freedom Now Party advocates from the conference, Rev. Albert B. Cleage, Jr., resigned from the council and, in collaboration with the Group On Advanced Leadership (GOAL), arranged for a Northern Negro Grass Roots Leadership Conference. This was held in Detroit at the same time as the more conservative gathering, which was addressed by Congressman Adam Clayton Powell among others. The two-day Grass Roots conference was climaxed by a large public rally at the King Solomon Baptist Church, with Rev. Cleage, journalist William Worthy and Malcolm X as the chief speakers. The audience, almost all black and with non-Muslims in the great majority, interrupted Malcolm with applause and laughter so often that he asked it to desist because of the lateness of the hour.

A few weeks after the conference, President Kennedy was

assassinated and Elijah Muhammad silenced Malcolm X. This is, therefore, one of the last speeches Malcolm gave before leaving Muhammad's organization. It is the only specimen of his speeches as a Black Muslim included in this book. But it is not a typical Black Muslim speech. Even though Malcolm continued to preface certain statements with the phrase, "The Honorable Elijah Muhammad says," he was increasingly, in the period before the split, giving his own special stamp to the Black Muslims' ideas, including the idea of separation. The emphasis of this speech is considerably different from earlier ones of the type included in Louis E. Lomax's book, *When the Word Is Given*. . . .

The following selection consists of about one-half of the speech. The long-playing record, "Message to the Grass Roots by Malcolm X," published by the Afro-American Broadcasting and Recording Company, Detroit, is vastly superior to the written text in conveying the style and personality of Malcolm at his best—when he was speaking to a militant black audience.

We want to have just an off-the-cuff chat between you and me, us. We want to talk right down to earth in a language that everybody here can easily understand. We all agree tonight, all of the speakers have agreed, that America has a very serious problem. Not only does America have a very serious problem, but our people have a very serious problem. America's problem is us. We're her problem. The only reason she has a problem is she doesn't want us here. And every time you look at yourself, be you black, brown, red or yellow, a so-called Negro, you represent a person who poses such a serious problem for America because you're not wanted. Once you face this as a fact, then you can start plotting a course that will make you appear intelligent, instead of unintelligent.

What you and I need to do is learn to forget our differences. When we come together, we don't come together as Baptists or Methodists. You don't catch hell because you're a Baptist, and you don't catch hell because you're a Methodist. You don't catch hell because you're a Methodist or Baptist, you don't catch hell because you're a Democrat or a Republican, you don't catch hell because you're a Mason or an Elk, and you sure don't catch hell because you're an American; because if you were an American, you wouldn't catch hell. You catch hell because you're a black man. You catch hell, all of us catch hell, for the same reason.

So we're all black people, so-called Negroes, second-class citizens, ex-slaves. You're nothing but an ex-slave. You don't like to be told that. But what else are you? You are ex-slaves. You didn't come here on the "Mayflower." You came here on a slave ship. In chains, like a horse, or a cow, or a chicken. And you were brought here by the people who came here on the "Mayflower," you were brought here by the so-called Pilgrims, or Founding Fathers. They were the ones who brought you here.

We have a common enemy. We have this in common: We have a common oppressor, a common exploiter, and a common discriminator. But once we all realize that we have a common enemy, then we unite—on the basis of what we have in common. And what we have foremost in common is that enemy—the white man. He's an enemy to all of us. I know some of you all think that some of them aren't enemies. Time will tell.

In Bandung back in, I think, 1954, was the first unity meeting in centuries of black people. And once you study what happened at the Bandung conference, and the results of the Bandung conference, it actually serves as a model for the same procedure you and I can use to get our problems solved. At Bandung all the nations came together, the dark nations from Africa and Asia. Some of them were Buddhists, some of them were Muslims, some of them were Christians, some were Confucianists, some were atheists. Despite their religious differences, they came together. Some were communists, some were socialists, some were capitalists—despite their economic and political differences, they came together. All of them were black, brown, red or yellow.

The number-one thing that was not allowed to attend the Bandung conference was the white man. He couldn't come. Once they excluded the white man, they found that they could get together. Once they kept him out, everybody else fell right in and fell in line. This is the thing that you and I have to understand. And these people who came together didn't have nuclear weapons, they didn't have jet planes, they didn't have all of the heavy armaments that the white man has. But they had unity.

They were able to submerge their little petty differences and agree on one thing: That there one African came from Kenya and was being colonized by the Englishman, and another African came from the Congo and was being colonized by the Belgian, and another African came from Guinea and was being colonized by the French, and another came from Angola and was being colonized by the Portuguese. When they came to the Bandung conference, they looked at the Portuguese, and at the Frenchman, and at the Englishman, and at the Dutchman, and learned or realized the one thing that all of them had in common— they were all from Europe, they were all Europeans, blond, blue-eyed and white skins. They began to recognize who their enemy was. The same man that was colonizing our people in Kenya was colonizing our people in the Congo. The same one in the Congo was colonizing our people in South Africa, and in Southern Rhodesia, and in Burma, and in India, and in Afghanistan, and in Pakistan. They realized all over the world where the dark man was being oppressed, he was being oppressed by the white man; where the dark man was being exploited, he was being exploited by the white man. So they got together on this basis—that they had a common enemy.

And when you and I here in Detroit and in Michigan and in America who have been awakened today look around us, we too realize here in America we all have a common enemy, whether he's in Georgia or Michigan, whether he's in California or New York. He's the same man—blue eyes and blond hair and pale skin—the same man. So what we have to do is what they did. They agreed to stop quarreling among themselves. Any little spat that they had, they'd settle it among themselves, go into a huddle—don't let the enemy know that you've got a disagreement.

Instead of airing our differences in public, we have to realize we're all the same family. And when you have a family squabble, you don't get out on the sidewalk. If you do, everybody calls you uncouth, unrefined, uncivilized, savage. If you don't make it at home, you settle it at home; you get in the closet, argue it out behind closed doors, and then when you come out on the street, you pose a common front, a united front. And this is what we need to do in the community, and in the city, and in the state. We need to stop airing our differences in front of the white man, put the white man out of our meetings, and then sit down and talk shop with each other. That's what we've got to do.

I would like to make a few comments concerning the difference between the black revolution and the Negro revolution. Are they both the same? And if they're not, what is the difference? What is the difference between a black revolution and a Negro revolution? First, what is a revolution? Sometimes I'm inclined to believe that many of our people are using this word "revolution" loosely, without taking careful consideration of what this word actually means, and what its historic characteristics are. When you study the historic nature of revolutions, the motive of a revolution, the objective of a revolution, the result of a revolution, and the methods used in a revolution, you may change words. You may devise another program, you may change your goal and you may change your mind.

Look at the American Revolution in 1776. That revolution was for what? For land. Why did they want land? Independence. How was it carried out? Bloodshed. Number one, it was based on land, the basis of independence. And the only way they could get it was bloodshed. The French Revolution—what was it based on? The landless against the landlord. What was it for? Land. How did they get it? Bloodshed. Was no love lost, was no compromise, was no negotiation. I'm telling you—you don't know what a revolution is. Because when you find out what it is, you'll get back in the alley, you'll get out of the way.

The Russian Revolution—what was it based on? Land; the landless against the landlord. How did they bring it about? Bloodshed. You haven't got a revolution that doesn't involve bloodshed. And you're afraid to bleed. I said, you're afraid to bleed.

As long as the white man sent you to Korea, you bled. He sent you to Germany, you bled. He sent you to the South Pacific to fight the Japanese, you bled. You bleed for white people, but when it comes to seeing your own churches being bombed and little black girls murdered, you haven't got any blood. You bleed when the white man says bleed; you bite when the white man says bite; and you bark when the white man says bark. I hate to say this about us, but it's true. How are you going to be nonviolent in Mississippi, as violent as you were in Korea? How can you justify being nonviolent in Mississippi and Alabama, when your churches are being bombed, and your little girls are being murdered, and at the same time you are going to get violent with Hitler, and Tojo, and somebody else you don't even know?

If violence is wrong in America, violence is wrong abroad. If it is wrong to be violent defending black women and black children and black babies and black men, then it is wrong for America to draft us and make us violent abroad in defense of her. And if it is right for America to draft us, and teach us how to be violent in defense of her, then it is right for you and me to do whatever is necessary to defend our own people right here in this country.

The Chinese Revolution—they wanted land. They threw the British out, along with the Uncle Tom Chinese. Yes, they did. They set a good example. When I was in prison, I read an article—don't be shocked when I say that I was in prison. You're still in prison. That's what America means: prison. When I was in prison, I read an article in *Life* magazine showing a little Chinese girl, nine years old; her father was on his hands and knees and she was pulling the trigger because he was an Uncle Tom Chinaman. When they had the revolution over there, they took a whole generation of Uncle Toms and just wiped them out. And within ten years that little girl became a full-grown woman. No more Toms in China. And today it's one of the toughest, roughest, most feared countries on this earth—by the white man. Because there are no Uncle Toms over there.

Of all our studies, history is best qualified to reward our research. And when you see that you've got problems, all you have to do is examine the historic method used all over the world by others who have problems similar to yours. Once you see how they got theirs straight, then you know how you can get yours straight. There's been a revolution, a black revolution, going on in Africa. In Kenya, the Mau Mau were revolutionary; they were the ones who brought the word "Uhuru" to the fore. The Mau Mau, they were revolutionary, they believed in scorched earth, they knocked everything aside that got in their way, and their revolution also was based on land, a desire for land. In Algeria, the northern part of Africa, a revolution took place. The Algerians were revolutionists, they wanted land. France offered to let them be integrated into France. They told France, to hell with France, they wanted some land, not some France. And they engaged in a bloody battle.

So I cite these various revolutions, brothers and sisters, to show you that you don't have a peaceful revolution. You don't have a turn-the-other-cheek revolution. There's no such thing as a nonviolent revolution. The only kind of revolution that is nonviolent is the Negro revolution. The only revolution in which the goal is loving your enemy is the Negro revolution. It's the only revolution in which the goal is a desegregated lunch counter, a desegregated theater, a desegregated park, and a desegregated public toilet; you can sit down next to white folks—on the toilet. That's no revolution. Revolution is based on land. Land is the basis of all independence. Land is the basis of freedom, justice, and equality.

The white man knows what a revolution is. He knows that the black revolution is world-wide in scope and in nature. The black revolution is sweeping Asia, is sweeping Africa, is rearing its head in Latin America. The Cuban Revolution—that's a revolution. They overturned the system. Revolution is in Asia, revolution is in Africa, and the white man is screaming because he sees revolution in Latin America. How do you think he'll react to you when you learn what a real revolution is? You don't know what a revolution is. If you did, you wouldn't use that word.

Revolution is bloody, revolution is hostile, revolution knows no compromise, revolution overturns and destroys everything that gets in its way. And you, sitting around here like a knot on the wall, saying, "I'm going to love these folks no matter how much they hate me." No, you need a revolution. Whoever heard of a revolution where they lock arms, as Rev. Cleage was pointing out beautifully, singing "We Shall Overcome"? You don't do that in a revolution. You don't do any singing, you're too busy swinging. It's based on land. A revolutionary wants land so he can set up his own nation, an independent nation. These Negroes aren't asking for any nation—they're trying to crawl back on the plantation.

When you want a nation, that's called nationalism. When the white man became involved in a revolution in this country against England, what was it for? He wanted this land so he could set up another white nation. That's white nationalism. The American Revolution was white nationalism. The French Revolution was white nationalism. The Russian Revolution too—yes, it was—white nationalism. You don't think so? Why do you think Khrushchev and Mao can't get their heads together? White nationalism. All the revolutions that are going on in Asia and Africa today are based on what?—black nationalism. A revolutionary is a black nationalist. He wants a nation. I was reading some beautiful words by Rev. Cleage, pointing out why he couldn't get together with someone else in the city because all of them were afraid of being identified with black nationalism. If you're afraid of black nationalism, you're afraid of revolution. And if you love revolution, you love black nationalism.

To understand this, you have to go back to what the young brother here referred to as the house Negro and the field Negro back during slavery. There were two kinds of slaves, the house Negro and the field Negro. The house Negroes—they lived in the house with master, they dressed pretty good, they ate good because they ate his food— what he left. They lived in the attic or the basement, but still they lived near the master; and they loved the master more than the master loved himself. They would give their life to save the master's house—quicker than the master would. If the master said, "We got a good house here," the house Negro would say, "Yeah, we got a good house here." Whenever the master said "we," he said "we." That's how you can tell a house Negro.

If the master's house caught on fire, the house Negro would fight harder to put the blaze out than the master would. If the master got sick, the house Negro would say, "What's the matter, boss, *we* sick?" *We* sick! He identified himself with his master, more than his master identified with himself. And if you came to the house Negro and said, "Let's run away, let's escape, let's separate," the house Negro would look at you and say, "Man, you crazy. What you mean, separate? Where is there a better house than this? Where can I wear better clothes than this? Where can I eat better food than this?" That was that house Negro. In those days he was called a "house nigger." And that's what we call them today, because we've still got some house niggers running around here.

This modern house Negro loves his master. He wants to live near him. He'll pay three times as much as the house is worth just to live near his master, and then brag about "I'm the only Negro out here." "I'm the only one on my job." "I'm the only one in this school." You're nothing but a house Negro. And if someone comes to you right now and says, "Let's separate," you say the same thing that the house Negro said on the plantation. "What you mean, separate? From America, this good white man? Where you going to get a better job than you get here?" I mean, this is what you say. "I ain't left nothing in Africa," that's what you say. Why, you left your mind in Africa.

On that same plantation, there was the field Negro. The field Negroes—those were the masses. There were always more Negroes in the field than there were Negroes in the house. The Negro in the field caught hell. He ate leftovers. In the house they ate high up on the hog. The Negro in the field didn't get anything but what was left of the insides of the hog. They call it "chitt'lings" nowadays. In those days they called them what they were—guts. That's what you were—gut-eaters. And some of you are still gut-eaters.

The field Negro was beaten from morning to night; he lived in a shack, in a hut; he wore old, castoff clothes. He hated his master. I say he hated his master. He was intelligent. That house Negro loved his master, but that field Negro—remember, they were in the majority, and they hated the master. When the house caught on fire, he didn't try to put it out; that field Negro prayed for a wind, for a breeze. When the master got sick, the field Negro prayed that he'd die. If someone came to the field Negro and said, "Let's separate, let's run," he didn't say "Where we going?" He'd say, "Any place is better than here." You've got field Negroes in America today. I'm a field Negro. The masses are the field Negroes. When they see this man's house on fire, you don't hear the little Negroes talking about *"our* government is in trouble." They say, *"The* government is in trouble." Imagine a Negro: *"Our* government"! I even heard one say *"our* astronauts." They won't even let him near the plant—and *"our* astronauts"! *"Our* Navy"—that's a Negro that is out of his mind, a Negro that is out of his mind.

Just as the slavemaster of that day used Tom, the house

Negro, to keep the field Negroes in check, the same old slavemaster today has Negroes who are nothing but modern Uncle Toms, twentieth-century Uncle Toms, to keep you and me in check, to keep us under control, keep us passive and peaceful and nonviolent. That's Tom making you nonviolent. It's like when you go to the dentist, and the man's going to take your tooth. You're going to fight him when he starts pulling. So he squirts some stuff in your jaw called novocaine, to make you think they're not doing anything to you. So you sit there and because you've got all of that novocaine in your jaw, you suffer—peacefully. Blood running all down your jaw, and you don't know what's happening. Because someone has taught you to suffer—peacefully.

The white man does the same thing to you in the street, when he wants to put knots on your head and take advantage of you and not have to be afraid of your fighting back. To keep you from fighting back, he gets these old religious Uncle Toms to teach you and me, just like novocaine, to suffer peacefully. Don't stop suffering—just suffer peacefully. As Rev. Cleage pointed out, they say you should let your blood flow in the streets. This is a shame. You know he's a Christian preacher. If it's a shame to him, you know what it is to me.

There is nothing in our book, the Koran, that teaches us to suffer peacefully. Our religion teaches us to be intelligent. Be peaceful, be courteous, obey the law, respect everyone; but if someone puts his hand on you, send him to the cemetery. That's a good religion. In fact, that's that old-time religion. That's the one that Ma and Pa used to talk about: an eye for an eye, and a tooth for a tooth, and a head for a head, and a life for a life. That's a good religion. And nobody resents that kind of religion being taught but a wolf, who intends to make you his meal.

This is the way it is with the white man in America. He's a wolf—and you're sheep. Any time a shepherd, a pastor, teaches you and me not to run from the white man and, at the same time, teaches us not to fight the white man, he's a traitor to you and me. Don't lay down a life all by itself. No, preserve your life, it's the best thing you've got. And if you've got to give it up, let it be even-steven.

The slavemaster took Tom and dressed him well, fed him well and even gave him a little education—a *little* education; gave him a long coat and a top hat and made all the other slaves look up to him. Then he used Tom to control them. The same strategy that was used in those days is used today, by the same white man. He takes a Negro, a so-called Negro, and makes him prominent, builds him up, publicizes him, makes him a celebrity. And then he becomes a spokesman for Negroes—and a Negro leader.

I would like to mention just one other thing quickly, and that is the method that the white man uses, how the white man uses the "big guns," or Negro leaders, against the Black revolution. They are not a part of the Black revolution. They are used against the Black revolution.

When Martin Luther King failed to desegregate Albany, Georgia, the civil-rights struggle in America reached its low point. King became bankrupt almost, as a leader. The Southern Christian Leadership Conference was in financial trouble; and it was in trouble, period, with the people when they failed to desegregate Albany, Georgia. Other Negro civil-rights leaders of so-called national stature became fallen idols. As they became fallen idols, began to lose their prestige and influence, local Negro leaders began to stir up the masses. In Cambridge, Maryland, Gloria Richardson; in Danville, Virginia, and other parts of the country, local leaders began to stir up our people at the grass-roots level. This was never done by these Negroes of national stature. They control you, but they have never incited you or excited you. They control you, they contain you, they have kept you on the plantation.

As soon as King failed in Birmingham, Negroes took to the streets. King went out to California to a big rally and raised I don't know how many thousands of dollars. He came to Detroit and had a march and raised some more thousands of dollars. And recall, right after that Roy Wilkins attacked King. He accused King and CORE [Congress Of Racial Equality] of starting trouble everywhere and then making the NAACP [National Association for the Advancement of Colored People] get them out of jail and spend a lot of money; they accused King and CORE of raising all the money and not paying it back. This happened; I've got it in documented evidence in the newspaper. Roy started attacking King, and King started attacking Roy, and Farmer started attacking both of them. And as these Negroes of national stature began to attack each other, they began to lose their control of the Negro masses.

The Negroes were out there in the streets. They were talking about how they were going to march on Washington. Right at that time Birmingham had exploded, and the Negroes in Birmingham—remember, they also exploded. They began to stab the crackers in the back and bust them up 'side their head—yes, they did. That's when Kennedy sent in the troops, down in Birmingham. After that, Kennedy got on the television and said "this is a moral issue." That's when he said he was going to put out a civil-rights bill. And when he mentioned civil-rights bill and the Southern crackers started talking about how they were going to boycott or filibuster it, then the Negroes started talking—about what? That they were going to march on Washington, march on the Senate, march on the White House, march on the Congress, and tie it up, bring it to a halt, not let the government proceed. They even said they were going out to the airport and lay down on the runway and not let any airplanes land. I'm telling you what they said. That was revolution. That was revolution. That was the black revolution.

It was the grass roots out there in the street. It scared the white man to death, scared the white power structure in Washington, D.C., to death; I was there. When they found out that this black steamroller was going to come down on the capital, they called in Wilkins, they called in Randolph, they called in these national Negro leaders that you respect and told them, "Call it off." Kennedy said, "Look, you all are letting this thing go too far." And Old Tom said, "Boss, I can't stop it, because I didn't start it." I'm telling you what they said. They said, "I'm not even in it, much less at the head of it." They said, "These Negroes are doing things on their own. They're running ahead of us." And that old shrewd fox, he said, "If you all aren't in it, I'll put you in it. I'll put you at the head of it. I'll endorse it. I'll welcome it. I'll help it. I'll join it."

A matter of hours went by. They had a meeting at the Carlyle Hotel in New York City. The Carlyle Hotel is owned by the Kennedy family; that's the hotel Kennedy spent the night at, two nights ago; it belongs to his family. A philanthropic society headed by a white man named Stephen Currier called all the top civil-rights leaders together at the Carlyle Hotel. And he told them, "By you all fighting each other, you are destroying the civil-rights movement. And since you're fighting over money from white liberals, let us set up what is known as the Council for United Civil Rights Leadership. Let's form this council, and all the civil-rights organizations will belong to it, and we'll use it for, fund-raising purposes." Let me show you how tricky the white man is. As soon as they got it formed, they elected

Whitney Young as its chairman, and who do you think became the co-chairman? Stephen Currier, the white man, a millionaire. Powell was talking about it down at Cobo Hall today. This is what he was talking about. Powell knows it happened. Randolph knows it happened. Wilkins knows it happened. King knows it happened. Every one of that Big Six—they know it happened.

Once they formed it, with the white man over it, he promised them and gave them $800,000 to split up among the Big Six; and told them that after the march was over they'd give them $700,000 more. A million and a half dollars—split up between leaders that you have been following, going to jail for, crying crocodile tears for. And they're nothing but Frank James and Jesse James and the what-do-you-call-'em brothers.

As soon as they got the setup organized, the white man made available to them top public-relations experts; opened the news media across the country at their disposal, which then began to project these Big Six as the leaders of the march. Originally they weren't even in the march. You were talking this march talk on Hastings Street, you were talking march talk on Lenox Avenue, and on Fillmore Street, and on Central Avenue, and 32nd Street and 63rd Street. That's where the march talk was being talked. But the white man put the Big Six at the head of it; made them the march. They became the march. They took it over. And the first move they made after they took it over, they invited Walter Reuther, a white man; they invited a priest, a rabbi, and an old white preacher, yes, an old white preacher. The same white element that put Kennedy into power—labor, the Catholics, the Jews, and liberal Protestants; the same clique that put Kennedy in power, joined the march on Washington.

It's just like when you've got some coffee that's too black, which means it's too strong. What do you do? You integrate it with cream, you make it weak. But if you pour too much cream in it, you won't even know you ever had coffee. It used to be hot, it becomes cool. It used to be strong, it becomes weak. It used to wake you up, now it puts you to sleep. This is what they did with the march on Washington. They joined it. They didn't integrate it, they infiltrated it. They joined it, became a part of it, took it over. And as they took it over, it lost its militancy. It ceased to be angry, it ceased to be hot, it ceased to be uncompromising. Why, it even ceased to be a march. It became a picnic, a circus. Nothing but a circus, with clowns and all. You had one right here in Detroit—I saw it on television—with clowns leading it, white clowns and black clowns. I know you don't like what I'm saying, but I'm going to tell you anyway. Because I can prove what I'm saying. If you think I'm telling you wrong, you bring me Martin Luther King and A. Philip Randolph and James Farmer and those other three, and see if they'll deny it over a microphone.

No, it was a sellout. It was a takeover. When James Baldwin came in from Paris, they wouldn't let him talk, because they couldn't make him go by the script. Burt Lancaster read the speech that Baldwin was supposed to make; they wouldn't let Baldwin get up there, because they know Baldwin is liable to say anything. They controlled it so tight, they told those Negroes what time to hit town, how to come, where to stop, what signs to carry, what song to sing, what speech they could make, and what speech they couldn't make; and then told them to get out of town by sundown. And every one of those Toms was out of town by sundown. Now I know you don't like my saying this. But I can back it up. It was a circus, a performance that beat anything Hollywood could ever do, the performance of the year. Reuther and those other three devils should get an Academy Award for the best actors because they acted like they really loved Negroes and fooled a whole lot of Negroes. And the six Negro leaders should get an award too, for the best supporting cast.

2

A declaration of independence

Elijah Muhammad suspended Malcolm X on December 4, 1963, ostensibly for making an unauthorized remark about the assassination of President Kennedy. Actually, differences had been developing for some time between Malcolm and the more conservative elements in the Black Muslim leadership. The only hint of these, in the subsequent three months when Malcolm made no public statements, came when he was interviewed by Louis E. Lomax in December, 1963. While denying differences with Muhammad and expressing continued loyalty to him, Malcolm stated that "the younger Black Muslims," lacking Muhammad's "divine patience" with the enemy, "want to see some action." The implication was that they were being restrained by the leadership.

On March 8, 1964, Malcolm announced that he was leaving the Nation of Islam and was organizing a new movement. He said that the Black Muslim movement had "gone as far as it can" because it was too narrowly sectarian and too inhibited. He also said: "I am prepared to cooperate in local civil-rights actions in the South and elsewhere and shall do so because every campaign for specific objectives can only heighten the political consciousness of the Negroes and intensify their identification against white society. . . . There is no use deceiving ourselves. Good education, housing and jobs are imperatives for the Negroes, and I shall support them in their fight to win these objectives, but I shall tell the Negroes that while these are necessary, they cannot solve the main Negro problem."

On March 12, he held a formal press conference at the Park Sheraton Hotel in New York in order to explain his new position in greater detail. Before opening the floor to questions by reporters, he read the following prepared statement. It is included here as an index to Malcolm's thinking at that time, which was to undergo further changes in the remaining eleven months of his life.

Malcolm said in this statement that he was and would remain a Muslim; and he did. But a few weeks later he was to go to Mecca and return with a different understanding of Islam, particularly in the sphere of race.

Hoping and trying to avoid conflict with the Black Muslims, he still praised Muhammad in this statement for his analysis and program, and declined to discuss the "internal differences" that had "forced" him out of the Nation of Islam. Later, after Muhammad began to assail him publicly, he was to regret this: "I made an error, I know now, in not speaking out the full truth when I was first 'suspended.'"

Previously, Malcolm had held that "separation" was the only solution. Now, on March 12, he called separation into a separate nation or a return to Africa "the best solution," and he weakened this further by calling it "still a long-range program." By May, 1964, he was to discontinue altogether any advocacy of a separate nation, and to say he thought Negroes should stay in the United States and fight for what was rightfully theirs.

As a Black Muslim, he had equated "black nationalism" and

"separation." In the press statement proclaiming himself to be a black nationalist, however, he differentiated the two concepts, defining black nationalism in such a way as to include non-separatists too. In the final months of his life he was seeking for a term to describe his philosophy that would be more precise and more complete than black nationalism.

The press statement expressed Malcolm's intention to organize the Muslim Mosque, Inc., "in such manner [as] to provide for the active participation of all Negroes . . . despite their religious or non-religious beliefs." Three months later he was to decide that the achievement of this aim required the formation of another group, the broader, secular Organization of Afro-American Unity.

This March 12 statement, therefore, should be read as a transitional phase in the development of Malcolm's ideas, marking important changes from his Black Muslim past, but not representing all the conclusions he reached before his death.

Because 1964 threatens to be a very explosive year on the racial front, and because I myself intend to be very active in every phase of the American Negro struggle for *human rights,* I have called this press conference this morning in order to clarify my own position in the struggle—especially in regard to politics and nonviolence.

I am and always will be a Muslim. My religion is Islam. I still believe that Mr. Muhammad's analysis of the problem is the most realistic, and that his solution is the best one. This means that I too believe the best solution is complete separation, with our people going back home, to our own African homeland.

But separation back to Africa is still a long-range program, and while it is yet to materialize, 22 million of our people who are still here in America need better food, clothing, housing, education and jobs *right now.* Mr. Muhammad's program does point us back homeward, but it also contains within it what we could and should be doing to help solve many of our own problems while we are still here.

Internal differences within the Nation of Islam forced me out of it. I did not leave of my own free will. But now that it has happened, I intend to make the most of it. Now that I have more independence of action, I intend to use a more flexible approach toward working with others to get a solution to this problem.

I do not pretend to be a divine man, but I do believe in divine guidance, divine power, and in the fulfillment of divine prophecy. I am not educated, nor am I an expert in any particular field—but I am sincere, and my sincerity is my credentials.

I'm not out to fight other Negro leaders or organizations. We must find a common approach, a common solution, to a common problem. As of this minute, I've forgotten everything bad that the other leaders have said about me, and I pray they can also forget the many bad things I've said about them.

The problem facing our people here in America is bigger than all other personal or organizational differences. Therefore, as leaders, we must stop worrying about the threat that we seem to think we pose to each other's personal prestige, and concentrate our united efforts toward solving the unending hurt that is being done daily to our people here in America.

I am going to organize and head a new mosque in New York City, known as the Muslim Mosque, Inc. This gives us a religious base, and the spiritual force necessary to rid our people of the vices that destroy the moral fiber of our community.

Our political philosophy will be black nationalism. Our economic and social philosophy will be black nationalism.

Our cultural emphasis will be black nationalism.

Many of our people aren't religiously inclined, so the Muslim Mosque, Inc., will be organized in such manner to provide for the active participation of all Negroes in our political, economic, and social programs, despite their religious or non-religious beliefs.

The political philosophy of black nationalism means: we must control the politics and the politicians of our community. They must no longer take orders from outside forces. We will organize, and sweep out of office all Negro politicians who are puppets for the outside forces.

Our accent will be upon youth: we need new ideas, new methods, new approaches. We will call upon young students of political science throughout the nation to help us. We will encourage these young students to launch their own independent study, and then give us their analysis and their suggestions. We are completely disenchanted with the old, adult, established politicians. We want to see some new faces—more militant faces.

Concerning the 1964 elections: we will keep our plans on this a secret until a later date—but we don't intend for our people to be the victims of a political sellout again in 1964.

The Muslim Mosque, Inc., will remain wide open for ideas and financial aid from all quarters. Whites can help us, but they can't join us. There can be no black-white unity until there is first some black unity. There can be no workers' solidarity until there is first some racial solidarity. We cannot think of uniting with others, until after we have first united among ourselves. We cannot think of being acceptable to others until we have first proven acceptable to ourselves. One can't unite bananas with scattered leaves.

Concerning nonviolence: it is criminal to teach a man

not to defend himself when he is the constant victim of brutal attacks. It is legal and lawful to own a shotgun or a rifle. We believe in obeying the law.

In areas where our people are the constant victims of brutality, and the government seems unable or unwilling to protect them, we should form rifle clubs that can be used to defend our lives and our property in times of emergency, such as happened last year in Birmingham; Plaquemine, Louisiana; Cambridge, Maryland; and Danville, Virginia. When our people are being bitten by dogs, they are within their rights to kill those dogs.

We should be peaceful, law-abiding—but the time has come for the American Negro to fight back in self-defense whenever and wherever he is being unjustly and unlawfully attacked.

If the government thinks I am wrong for saying this, then let the government start doing its job.

3

The ballot or the bullet

Ten days after Malcolm X's declaration of independence, the Muslim Mosque, Inc., held the first of a series of four Sunday night public rallies in Harlem, at which Malcolm began the job of formulating the ideology and philosophy of a new movement. In the opinion of many who heard these talks, they were the best he ever gave. Unfortunately, taped recordings of these meetings were not available in the preparation of this book. Simultaneously, however, Malcolm began to accept speaking engagements outside of New York—at Chester, Pennsylvania; Boston; Cleveland; Detroit; etc.—and tapes of some of these were available.

In the Cleveland talk, given at Cory Methodist Church on April 3, 1964, Malcolm presented many of the themes he had been developing in the Harlem rallies. The meeting, sponsored by the Cleveland chapter of the Congress of Racial Equality, took the form of a symposium entitled "The Negro Revolt—What Comes Next?" The first speaker was Louis E. Lomax, whose talk was in line with CORE doctrine and was well received by the large, predominantly Negro audience. Malcolm's talk got even more applause, although it differed in fundamental respects from anything ever said at a CORE meeting.

"The Ballot or the Bullet," Malcolm's own title for his speech, was notable, among other things, for its statement that elements of black nationalism were present and growing in such organizations as the NAACP and CORE. For various reasons, the black nationalist convention which in this talk he projected for August, 1964, was not held.

Mr. Moderator, Brother Lomax, brothers and sisters, friends and enemies: I just can't believe everyone in here is a friend and I don't want to leave anybody out. The question tonight, as I understand it, is "The Negro Revolt, and Where Do We Go From Here?" or "What Next?" In my little humble way of understanding it, it points toward either the ballot or the bullet.

Before we try and explain what is meant by the ballot or the bullet, I would like to clarify something concerning myself. I'm still a Muslim, my religion is still Islam. That's my personal belief. Just as Adam Clayton Powell is a Christian minister who heads the Abyssinian Baptist Church in New York, but at the same time takes part in the political struggles to try and bring about rights to the black people in this country; and Dr. Martin Luther King is a Christian minister down in Atlanta, Georgia, who heads another organization fighting for the civil rights of black people in this country; and Rev. Galamison, I guess you've heard of him, is another Christian minister in New York who has been deeply involved in the school boycotts to eliminate segregated education; well, I myself am a minister, not a Christian minister, but a Muslim minister; and I believe in action on all fronts by whatever means necessary.

Although I'm still a Muslim, I'm not here tonight to

discuss my religion. I'm not here to try and change your religion. I'm not here to argue or discuss anything that we differ about, because it's time for us to submerge our differences and realize that it is best for us to first see that we have the same problem, a common problem—a problem that will make you catch hell whether you're a Baptist, or a Methodist, or a Muslim, or a nationalist. Whether you're educated or illiterate, whether you live on the boulevard or in the alley, you're going to catch hell just like I am. We're all in the same boat and we all are going to catch the same hell from the same man. He just happens to be a white man. All of us have suffered here, in this country, political oppression at the hands of the white man, economic exploitation at the hands of the white man, and social degradation at the hands of the white man.

Now in speaking like this, it doesn't mean that we're anti-white, but it does mean we're anti-exploitation, we're anti-degradation, we're anti-oppression. And if the white man doesn't want us to be anti-him, let him stop oppressing and exploiting and degrading us. Whether we are Christians or Muslims or nationalists or agnostics or atheists, we must first learn to forget our differences. If we have differences, let us differ in the closet; when we come out in front, let us not have anything to argue about until we get finished arguing with the man. If the late President Kennedy could get together with Khrushchev and exchange some wheat, we certainly have more in common with each other than Kennedy and Khrushchev had with each other.

If we don't do something real soon, I think you'll have to agree that we're going to be forced either to use the ballot or the bullet. It's one or the other in 1964. It isn't that time is running out—time has run out! 1964 threatens to be the most explosive year America has ever witnessed. The most explosive year. Why? It's also a political year. It's the year when all of the white politicians will be back in the so-called Negro community jiving you and me for some votes. The year when all of the white political crooks will be right back in your and my community with their false promises, building up our hopes for a letdown, with their trickery and their treachery, with their false promises which they don't intend to keep. As they nourish these dissatisfactions, it can only lead to one thing, an explosion; and now we have the type of black man on the scene in America today—I'm sorry, Brother Lomax—who just doesn't intend to turn the other cheek any longer.

Don't let anybody tell you anything about the odds are against you. If they draft you, they send you to Korea and make you face 800 million Chinese. If you can be brave over there, you can be brave right here. These odds aren't as great as those odds. And if you fight here, you will at least know what you're fighting for.

I'm not a politician, not even a student of politics; in fact, I'm not a student of much of anything. I'm not a Democrat, I'm not a Republican, and I don't even consider myself an American. If you and I were Americans, there'd be no problem. Those Hunkies that just got off the boat, they're already Americans; Polacks are already Americans; the Italian refugees are already Americans. Everything that came out of Europe, every blue-eyed thing, is already an American. And as long as you and I have been over here, we aren't Americans yet.

Well, I am one who doesn't believe in deluding myself. I'm not going to sit at your table and watch you eat, with nothing on my plate, and call myself a diner. Sitting at the table doesn't make you a diner, unless you eat some of what's on that plate. Being here in America doesn't make you an American. Being born here in America doesn't make you an American. Why, if birth made you American, you wouldn't need any legislation, you wouldn't need any amendments to the Constitution, you wouldn't be faced with civil-rights filibustering in Washington, D.C., right now. They don't have to pass civil-rights legislation to make a Polack an American.

No, I'm not an American. I'm one of the 22 million black people who are the victims of Americanism. One of the 22 million black people who are the victims of democracy, nothing but disguised hypocrisy. So, I'm not standing here speaking to you as an American, or a patriot, or a flag-saluter, or a flag-waver—no, not I. I'm speaking as a victim of this American system. And I see America through the eyes of the victim. I don't see any American dream; I see an American nightmare.

These 22 million victims are waking up. Their eyes are coming open. They're beginning to see what they used to only look at. They're becoming politically mature. They are realizing that there are new political trends from coast to coast. As they see these new political trends, it's possible for them to see that every time there's an election the races are so close that they have to have a recount. They had to recount in Massachusetts to see who was going to be governor, it was so close. It was the same way in Rhode Island, in Minnesota, and in many other parts of the country. And the same with Kennedy and Nixon when they ran for president. It was so close they had to count all over again. Well, what does this mean? It means that when white people are evenly divided, and black people have a bloc of votes of their own, it is left up to them to determine who's going to sit in the White House and who's going to be in the dog house.

It was the black man's vote that put the present administration in Washington, D.C. Your vote, your dumb vote,

your ignorant vote, your wasted vote put in an administration in Washington, D.C., that has seen fit to pass every kind of legislation imaginable, saving you until last,
then filibustering on top of that. And your and my leaders
have the audacity to run around clapping their hands and
talk about how much progress we're making. And what
a good president we have. If he wasn't good in Texas, he
sure can't be good in Washington, D.C. Because Texas is a
lynch state. It is in the same breath as Mississippi, no different; only they lynch you in Texas with a Texas accent
and lynch you in Mississippi with a Mississippi accent.
And these Negro leaders have the audacity to go and have
some coffee in the White House with a Texan, a Southern
cracker—that's all he is—and then come out and tell you
and me that he's going to be better for us because, since
he's from the South, he knows how to deal with the South-
erners. What kind of logic is that? Let Eastland be president, he's from the South too. He should be better able to
deal with them than Johnson.

In this present administration they have in the House
of Representatives 257 Democrats to only 177 Republicans. They control two-thirds of the House vote. Why
can't they pass something that will help you and me? In
the Senate, there are 67 senators who are of the Democratic Party. Only 33 of them are Republicans. Why, the
Democrats have got the government sewed up, and you're
the one who sewed it up for them. And what have they
given you for it? Four years in office, and just now getting
around to some civil-rights legislation. Just now, after everything else is gone, out of the way, they're going to sit
down now and play with you all summer long—the same
old giant con game that they call filibuster. All those are
in cahoots together. Don't you ever think they're not in
cahoots together, for the man that is heading the civil-

rights filibuster is a man from Georgia named Richard Russell. When Johnson became president, the first man he asked for when he got back to Washington, D.C., was "Dicky"—that's how tight they are. That's his boy, that's his pal, that's his buddy. But they're playing that old con game. One of them makes believe he's for you, and he's got it fixed where the other one is so tight against you, he never has to keep his promise.

So it's time in 1964 to wake up. And when you see them coming up with that kind of conspiracy, let them know your eyes are open. And let them know you got something else that's wide open too. It's got to be the ballot or the bullet. The ballot or the bullet. If you're afraid to use an expression like that, you should get on out of the country, you should get back in the cotton patch, you should get back in the alley. They get all the Negro vote, and after they get it, the Negro gets nothing in return. All they did when they got to Washington was give a few big Negroes big jobs. Those big Negroes didn't need big jobs, they already had jobs. That's camouflage, that's trickery, that's treachery, window-dressing. I'm not trying to knock out the Democrats for the Republicans, we'll get to them in a minute. But it is true—you put the Democrats first and the Democrats put you last.

Look at it the way it is. What alibis do they use, since they control Congress and the Senate? What alibi do they use when you and I ask, "Well, when are you going to keep your promise?" They blame the Dixiecrats. What is a Dixiecrat? A Democrat. A Dixiecrat is nothing but a Democrat in disguise. The titular head of the Democrats is also the head of the Dixiecrats, because the Dixiecrats are a part of the Democratic Party. The Democrats have never kicked the Dixiecrats out of the party. The Dixiecrats bolted themselves once, but the Democrats didn't put them out. Imagine, these lowdown Southern segregationists put the Northern Democrats down. But the Northern Democrats have never put the Dixiecrats down. No, look at that thing the way it is. They have got a con game going on, a political con game, and you and I are in the middle. It's time for you and me to wake up and start looking at it like it is, and trying to understand it like it is; and then we can deal with it like it is.

The Dixiecrats in Washington, D.C., control the key committees that run the government. The only reason the Dixiecrats control these committees is because they have seniority. The only reason they have seniority is because they come from states where Negroes can't vote. This is not even a government that's based on democracy. It is not a government that is made up of representatives of the people. Half of the people in the South can't even vote. Eastland is not even supposed to be in Washington. Half of the senators and congressmen who occupy these key positions in Washington, D.C., are there illegally, are there unconstitutionally.

I was in Washington, D.C., a week ago Thursday, when they were debating whether or not they should let the bill come onto the floor. And in the back of the room where the Senate meets, there's a huge map of the United States, and on that map it shows the location of Negroes throughout the country. And it shows that the Southern section of the country, the states that are most heavily concentrated with Negroes, are the ones that have senators and congressmen standing up filibustering and doing all other kinds of trickery to keep the Negro from being able to vote. This is pitiful. But it's not pitiful for us any longer; it's actually pitiful for the white man, because soon now, as the Negro awakens a little more and sees the vise that he's in, sees the bag that he's in, sees the real game that he's in, then the Negro's going to develop a new tactic.

These senators and congressmen actually violate the constitutional amendments that guarantee the people of that particular state or county the right to vote. And the Constitution itself has within it the machinery to expel any representative from a state where the voting rights of the people are violated. You don't even need new legislation. Any person in Congress right now, who is there from a state or a district where the voting rights of the people are violated, that particular person should be expelled from Congress. And when you expel him, you've removed one of the obstacles in the path of any real meaningful legislation in this country. In fact, when you expel them, you don't need new legislation, because they will be replaced by black representatives from counties and districts where the black man is in the majority, not in the minority.

If the black man in these Southern states had his full voting rights, the key Dixiecrats in Washington, D.C., which means the key Democrats in Washington, D.C., would lose their seats. The Democratic Party itself would lose its power. It would cease to be powerful as a party. When you see the amount of power that would be lost by the Democratic Party if it were to lose the Dixiecrat wing, or branch, or element, you can see where it's against the interests of the Democrats to give voting rights to Negroes in states where the Democrats have been in complete power and authority ever since the Civil War. You just can't belong to that party without analyzing it.

I say again, I'm not anti-Democrat, I'm not anti-Republican, I'm not anti-anything. I'm just questioning their sincerity, and some of the strategy that they've been using on our people by promising them promises that they don't intend to keep. When you keep the Democrats in power, you're keeping the Dixiecrats in power. I doubt that my good Brother Lomax will deny that. A vote for a Democrat is a vote for a Dixiecrat. That's why, in 1964, it's time now for you and me to become more politically mature and realize what the ballot is for; what we're supposed to get when we cast a ballot; and that if we don't cast a ballot, it's going to end up in a situation where we're going to have to cast a bullet. It's either a ballot or a bullet.

In the North, they do it a different way. They have a system that's known as gerrymandering, whatever that means. It means when Negroes become too heavily concentrated in a certain area, and begin to gain too much political power, the white man comes along and changes the district lines. You may say, "Why do you keep saying white man?" Because it's the white man who does it. I haven't ever seen any Negro changing any lines. They don't let him get near the line. It's the white man who does this. And usually, it's the white man who grins at you the most, and pats you on the back, and is supposed to be your friend. He may be friendly, but he's not your friend.

So, what I'm trying to impress upon you, in essence, is this: You and I in America are faced not with a segregationist conspiracy, we're faced with a government conspiracy. Everyone who's filibustering is a senator—that's the government. Everyone who's finagling in Washington, D.C., is a congressman—that's the government. You don't have anybody putting blocks in your path but people who are a part of the government. The same government that you go abroad to fight for and die for is the government that is in a conspiracy to deprive you of your voting rights, deprive you of your economic opportunities, deprive you of decent housing, deprive you of decent education. You don't need to go to the employer alone, it is the government itself, the government of America, that is responsible for the oppression and exploitation and degradation of black people in this country. And you should drop it in their lap. This government has failed the Negro. This so-called democracy has failed the Negro. And all these white liberals have definitely failed the Negro. So, where do we go from here? First, we need some friends. We need some new allies. The entire civil-rights struggle needs a new interpretation, a broader interpretation. We need to look at this civil-rights thing from another angle—from the inside as well as from the outside. To those of us whose philosophy is black nationalism, the only way you can get involved in the civil-rights struggle is give it a new interpretation. That old interpretation excluded us. It kept us out. So, we're giving a new interpretation to the civil-rights struggle, an interpretation that will enable us to come into it, take part in it. And these handkerchief-heads who have been dillydallying and pussyfooting and compromising—we don't intend to let them pussyfoot and dillydally and compromise any longer.

How can you thank a man for giving you what's already yours? How then can you thank him for giving you only part of what's already yours? You haven't even made progress, if what's being given to you, you should have had already. That's not progress. And I love my Brother Lomax, the way he pointed out we're right back where we were in 1954. We're not even as far up as we were in 1954. We're behind where we were in 1954. There's more segregation now than there was in 1954. There's more racial animosity, more racial hatred, more racial violence today in 1964, than there was in 1954. Where is the progress?

And now you're facing a situation where the young Negro's coming up. They don't want to hear that "turn-the-other-cheek" stuff, no. In Jacksonville, those were teenagers, they were throwing Molotov cocktails. Negroes have never done that before. But it shows you there's a new deal coming in. There's new thinking coming in. There's new strategy coming in. It'll be Molotov cocktails this month, hand grenades next month, and something else next month. It'll be ballots, or it'll be bullets. It'll be liberty, or it will be death. The only difference about this kind of death—it'll be reciprocal. You know what is meant by "reciprocal"? That's one of Brother Lomax's words, I stole it from him. I don't usually deal with those big words because I don't usually deal with big people. I deal with small people. I find you can get a whole lot of small people and whip hell out of a whole lot of big people. They haven't got anything to lose, and they've got everything to gain. And they'll let you know in a minute: "It takes two to tango; when I go, you go."

The black nationalists, those whose philosophy is black nationalism, in bringing about this new interpretation of the entire meaning of civil rights, look upon it as meaning, as Brother Lomax has pointed out, equality of opportunity. Well, we're justified in seeking civil rights, if it means equality of opportunity, because all we're doing there is trying to collect for our investment. Our mothers and fathers invested sweat and blood. Three hundred and ten years we worked in this country without a dime in return—I mean without a *dime* in return. You let the white man walk around here talking about how rich this country is, but you never stop to think how it got rich so quick. It got rich because you made it rich.

You take the people who are in this audience right now. They're poor, we're all poor as individuals. Our weekly salary individually amounts to hardly anything. But if you take the salary of everyone in here collectively it'll fill up a whole lot of baskets. It's a lot of wealth. If you can collect the wages of just these people right here for a year, you'll be rich—richer than rich. When you look at it like that, think how rich Uncle Sam had to become, not with this handful, but millions of black people. Your and my mother and father, who didn't work an eight-hour shift, but worked from "can't see" in the morning until "can't see" at night, and worked for nothing, making the white man rich, making Uncle Sam rich.

This is our investment. This is our contribution—our blood. Not only did we give of our free labor, we gave of our blood. Every time he had a call to arms, we were the first ones in uniform. We died on every battlefield the white man had. We have made a greater sacrifice than anybody who's standing up in America today. We have made a greater contribution and have collected less. Civil rights, for those of us whose philosophy is black nationalism, means: "Give it to us now. Don't wait for next year. Give it to us yesterday, and that's not fast enough."

I might stop right here to point out one thing. Whenever you're going after something that belongs to you, anyone who's depriving you of the right to have it is a criminal. Understand that. Whenever you are going after something that is yours, you are within your legal rights to lay claim to it. And anyone who puts forth any effort to deprive you of that which is yours, is breaking the law, is a criminal. And this was pointed out by the Supreme Court decision. It outlawed segregation. Which means segregation is against the law. Which means a segregationist is breaking the law. A segregationist is a criminal. You can't label him as anything other than that. And when you demonstrate against segregation, the law is on your side. The Supreme Court is on your side.

Now, who is it that opposes you in carrying out the law? The police department itself. With police dogs and clubs. Whenever you demonstrate against segregation, whether it is segregated education, segregated housing, or anything else, the law is on your side, and anyone who stands in the way is not the law any longer. They are breaking the law, they are not representatives of the law. Any time you demonstrate against segregation and a man has the audacity to put a police dog on you, kill that dog, kill him, I'm telling you, kill that dog. I say it, if they put me in jail tomorrow, kill—that—dog. Then you'll put a stop to it. Now, if these white people in here don't want to see that kind of action, get down and tell the mayor to tell the police department to pull the dogs in. That's all you have to do. If you don't do it, someone else will.

If you don't take this kind of stand, your little children will grow up and look at you and think "shame." If you don't take an uncompromising stand—I don't mean go out and get violent; but at the same time you should never be nonviolent unless you run into some nonviolence. I'm nonviolent with those who are nonviolent with me. But when you drop that violence on me, then you've made me go insane, and I'm not responsible for what I do. And that's the way every Negro should get. Any time you know you're within the law, within your legal rights, within your moral rights, in accord with justice, then die for what you believe in. But don't die alone. Let your dying be reciprocal. This is what is meant by equality. What's good for the goose is good for the gander.

When we begin to get in this area, we need new friends, we need new allies. We need to expand the civil-rights struggle to a higher level—to the level of human rights. Whenever you are in a civil-rights struggle, whether you know it or not, you are confining yourself to the jurisdiction of Uncle Sam. No one from the outside world can speak out in your behalf as long as your struggle is a civil-rights struggle. Civil rights comes within the domestic affairs of this country. All of our African brothers and our Asian brothers and our Latin-American brothers cannot open their mouths and interfere in the domestic affairs of the United States. And as long as it's civil rights, this comes under the jurisdiction of Uncle Sam.

But the United Nations has what's known as the charter of human rights, it has a committee that deals in human rights. You may wonder why all of the atrocities that have been committed in Africa and in Hungary and in Asia and in Latin America are brought before the UN, and the Negro problem is never brought before the UN. This is part of the conspiracy. This old, tricky, blue-eyed liberal who is supposed to be your and my friend, supposed to be in our corner, supposed to be subsidizing our struggle, and supposed to be acting in the capacity of an adviser, never tells you anything about human rights. They keep you wrapped up in civil rights. And you spend so much time barking up the civil-rights tree, you don't even know there's a human-rights tree on the same floor.

When you expand the civil-rights struggle to the level of human rights, you can then take the case of the black man in this country before the nations in the UN. You can take it before the General Assembly. You can take Uncle Sam before a world court. But the only level you can do it on is the level of human rights. Civil rights keeps you under his restrictions, under his jurisdiction. Civil rights keeps you in his pocket. Civil rights means you're asking Uncle Sam to treat you right. Human rights are something you were born with. Human rights are your God-given rights. Human rights are the rights that are recognized by all nations of this earth. And any time anyone violates your human rights, you can take them to the world court. Uncle Sam's hands are dripping with blood, dripping with the blood of the black man in this country. He's the earth's number-one hypocrite. He has the audacity—yes, he has—imagine him posing as the leader of the free world. The free world!—and you over here singing "We Shall Overcome." Expand the civil-rights struggle to the level of human rights, take it into the United Nations, where our African brothers can throw their weight on our side, where our Asian brothers can throw their weight on our side, where our Latin-American brothers can throw their weight on our side, and where 800 million Chinamen are sitting there waiting to throw their weight on our side.

Let the world know how bloody his hands are. Let the world know the hypocrisy that's practiced over here. Let it be the ballot or the bullet. Let him know that it must be the ballot or the bullet.

When you take your case to Washington, D.C., you're taking it to the criminal who's responsible; it's like running from the wolf to the fox. They're all in cahoots together. They all work political chicanery and make you look like a chump before the eyes of the world. Here you are walking around in America, getting ready to be drafted and sent abroad, like a tin soldier, and when you get over there, people ask you what are you fighting for, and you have to stick your tongue in your cheek. No, take Uncle Sam to court, take him before the world.

By ballot I only mean freedom. Don't you know—I disagree with Lomax on this issue—that the ballot is more important than the dollar? Can I prove it? Yes. Look in the UN. There are poor nations in the UN; yet those poor nations can get together with their voting power and keep the rich nations from making a move. They have one nation—one vote, everyone has an equal vote. And when those brothers from Asia, and Africa and the darker parts of this earth get together, their voting power is sufficient to hold Sam in check. Or Russia in check. Or some other section of the earth in check. So, the ballot is most important.

Right now, in this country, if you and I, 22 million African-Americans—that's what we are—Africans who are in America. You're nothing but Africans. Nothing but Africans. In fact, you'd get farther calling yourself African instead of Negro. Africans don't catch hell. You're the only one catching hell. They don't have to pass civil-rights bills for Africans. An African can go anywhere he wants right now. All you've got to do is tie your head up. That's right, go anywhere you want. Just stop being a Negro. Change your name to Hoogagagooba. That'll show you how silly the white man is. You're dealing with a silly man. A friend of mine who's very dark put a turban on his head and went into a restaurant in Atlanta before they called themselves desegregated. He went into a white restaurant, he sat down, they served him, and he said, "What would happen if a Negro came in here?" And there he's sitting, black as night, but because he had his head wrapped up the waitress looked back at him and says, "Why, there wouldn't no nigger dare come in here."

So, you're dealing with a man whose bias and prejudice are making him lose his mind, his intelligence, every day. He's frightened. He looks around and sees what's taking place on this earth, and he sees that the pendulum of time is swinging in your direction. The dark people are waking up. They're losing their fear of the white man. No place where he's fighting right now is he winning. Everywhere he's fighting, he's fighting someone your and my complexion. And they're beating him. He can't win any more. He's won his last battle. He failed to win the Korean War. He couldn't win it. He had to sign a truce. That's a loss. Any time Uncle Sam, with all his machinery for warfare, is held to a draw by some rice-eaters, he's lost the battle. He had to sign a truce. America's not supposed to sign a truce. She's supposed to be bad. But she's not bad any more. She's bad as long as she can use her hydrogen bomb, but she can't use hers for fear Russia might use hers. Russia can't use hers, for fear that Sam might use his. So, both of them are weaponless. They can't use the weapon because each's weapon nullifies the other's. So the only place where action can take place is on the ground. And the white man can't win another war fighting on the ground. Those days are over. The black man knows it, the brown man knows it, the red man knows it, and the yellow man knows it. So they engage him in guerrilla warfare. That's not his style. You've got to have heart to be a guerrilla warrior, and he hasn't got any heart. I'm telling you now.

I just want to give you a little briefing on guerrilla warfare because, before you know it, before you know it—It takes heart to be a guerrilla warrior because you're on your own. In conventional warfare you have tanks and a whole lot of other people with you to back you up, planes over your head and all that kind of stuff. But a guerrilla is on his own. All you have is a rifle, some sneakers and a bowl of rice, and that's all you need—and a lot of heart. The Japanese on some of those islands in the Pacific, when the American soldiers landed, one Japanese sometimes could hold the whole army off. He'd just wait until the sun went down, and when the sun went down they were all equal. He would take his little blade and slip from bush to bush, and from American to American. The white soldiers couldn't cope with that. Whenever you see a white soldier that fought in the Pacific, he has the shakes, he has a nervous condition, because they scared him to death.

The same thing happened to the French up in French Indochina. People who just a few years previously were rice farmers got together and ran the heavily-mechanized French army out of Indochina. You don't need it—modern warfare today won't work. This is the day of the guerrilla.

They did the same thing in Algeria. Algerians, who were nothing but Bedouins, took a rifle and sneaked off to the hills, and de Gaulle and all of his highfalutin' war machinery couldn't defeat those guerrillas. Nowhere on this earth does the white man win in a guerrilla warfare. It's not his speed. Just as guerrilla warfare is prevailing in Asia and in parts of Africa and in parts of Latin America, you've got to be mighty naive, or you've got to play the black man cheap, if you don't think some day he's going to wake up and find that it's got to be the ballot or the bullet.

I would like to say, in closing, a few things concerning the Muslim Mosque, Inc., which we established recently in New York City. It's true we're Muslims and our religion is Islam, but we don't mix our religion with our politics and our economics and our social and civil activities—not any more. We keep our religion in our mosque. After our religious services are over, then as Muslims we become involved in political action, economic action and social and civic action. We become involved with anybody, anywhere, any time and in any manner that's designed to eliminate the evils, the political, economic and social evils that are afflicting the people of our community.

The political philosophy of black nationalism means that the black man should control the politics and the politicians in his own community; no more. The black man in the black community has to be re-educated into the science of politics so he will know what politics is supposed to bring him in return. Don't be throwing out any ballots. A ballot is like a bullet. You don't throw your ballots until you see a target, and if that target is not within your reach, keep your ballot in your pocket. The political philosophy of black nationalism is being taught in the Christian church. It's being taught in the NAACP. It's being taught in CORE meetings. It's being taught in SNCC [Student Nonviolent

Coordinating Committee] meetings. It's being taught in Muslim meetings. It's being taught where nothing but atheists and agnostics come together. It's being taught everywhere. Black people are fed up with the dillydallying, pussyfooting, compromising approach that we've been using toward getting our freedom. We want freedom *now*, but we're not going to get it saying "We Shall Overcome." We've got to fight until we overcome.

The economic philosophy of black nationalism is pure and simple. It only means that we should control the economy of our community. Why should white people be running all the stores in our community? Why should white people be running the banks of our community? Why should the economy of our community be in the hands of the white man? Why? If a black man can't move his store into a white community, you tell me why a white man should move his store into a black community. The philosophy of black nationalism involves a re-education program in the black community in regards to economics. Our people have to be made to see that any time you take your dollar out of your community and spend it in a community where you don't live, the community where you live will get poorer and poorer, and the community where you spend your money will get richer and richer. Then you wonder why where you live is always a ghetto or a slum area. And where you and I are concerned, not only do we lose it when we spend it out of the community, but the white man has got all our stores in the community tied up; so that though we spend it in the community, at sundown the man who runs the store takes it over across town somewhere. He's got us in a vise.

So the economic philosophy of black nationalism means in every church, in every civic organization, in every fraternal order, it's time now for our people to become conscious of the importance of controlling the economy of our community. If we own the stores, if we operate the businesses, if we try and establish some industry in our own community, then we're developing to the position where we are creating employment for our own kind. Once you gain control of the economy of your own community, then you don't have to picket and boycott and beg some cracker downtown for a job in his business.

The social philosophy of black nationalism only means that we have to get together and remove the evils, the vices, alcoholism, drug addiction, and other evils that are destroying the moral fiber of our community. We ourselves have to lift the level of our community, the standard of our community to a higher level, make our own society beautiful so that we will be satisfied in our own social circles and won't be running around here trying to knock our way into a social circle where we're not wanted.

So I say, in spreading a gospel such as black nationalism, it is not designed to make the black man re-evaluate the white man—you know him already—but to make the black man re-evaluate himself. Don't change the white man's mind—you can't change his mind, and that whole thing about appealing to the moral conscience of America—America's conscience is bankrupt. She lost all conscience a long time ago. Uncle Sam has no conscience. They don't know what morals are. They don't try and eliminate an evil because it's evil, or because it's illegal, or because it's immoral; they eliminate it only when it threatens their existence. So you're wasting your time appealing to the moral conscience of a bankrupt man like Uncle Sam. If he had a conscience, he'd straighten this thing out with no more pressure being put upon him. So it is not necessary to change the white man's mind. We have to change our own mind. You can't change his mind about us. We've got to change our own minds about each other. We have to see each other with new eyes. We have to see each other as brothers and sisters. We have to come together with warmth so we can develop unity and harmony that's necessary to get this problem solved ourselves. How can we do this? How can we avoid jealousy? How can we avoid the suspicion and the divisions that exist in the community? I'll tell you how.

I have watched how Billy Graham comes into a city, spreading what he calls the gospel of Christ, which is only white nationalism. That's what he is. Billy Graham is a white nationalist; I'm a black nationalist. But since it's the natural tendency for leaders to be jealous and look upon a powerful figure like Graham with suspicion and envy, how is it possible for him to come into a city and get all the cooperation of the church leaders? Don't think because they're church leaders that they don't have weaknesses that make them envious and jealous—no, everybody's got it. It's not an accident that when they want to choose a cardinal [as Pope] over there in Rome, they get in a closet so you can't hear them cussing and fighting and carrying on.

Billy Graham comes in preaching the gospel of Christ, he evangelizes the gospel, he stirs everybody up, but he never tries to start a church. If he came in trying to start a church, all the churches would be against him. So, he just comes in talking about Christ and tells everybody who gets Christ to go to any church where Christ is; and in this way the church cooperates with him. So we're going to take a page from his book.

Our gospel is black nationalism. We're not trying to threaten the existence of any organization, but we're spreading the gospel of black nationalism. Anywhere there's a church that is also preaching and practicing the gospel of black nationalism, join that church. If the NAACP is preaching and practicing the gospel of black nationalism, join the NAACP. If CORE is spreading and practicing the gospel of black nationalism, join CORE. Join any organization that has a gospel that's for the uplift of the black man. And when you get into it and see them pussyfooting or compromising, pull out of it because that's not black nationalism. We'll find another one.

And in this manner, the organizations will increase in number and in quantity and in quality, and by August, it is then our intention to have a black nationalist convention which will consist of delegates from all over the country who are interested in the political, economic and social philosophy of black nationalism. After these delegates convene, we will hold a seminar, we will hold discussions, we will listen to everyone. We want to hear new ideas and new solutions and new answers. And at that time, if we see fit then to form a black nationalist party, we'll form a black nationalist party. If it's necessary to form a black nationalist army, we'll form a black nationalist army. It'll be the ballot or the bullet. It'll be liberty or it'll be death.

It's time for you and me to stop sitting in this country, letting some cracker senators, Northern crackers and Southern crackers, sit there in Washington, D.C., and come to a conclusion in their mind that you and I are supposed to have civil rights. There's no white man going to tell me anything about *my* rights. Brothers and sisters, always remember, if it doesn't take senators and congressmen and presidential proclamations to give freedom to the white man, it is not necessary for legislation or proclamation or Supreme Court decisions to give freedom to the black man. You let that white man know, if this is a country of freedom, let it be a country of freedom; and if it's not a country of freedom, change it.

We will work with anybody, anywhere, at any time, who is genuinely interested in tackling the problem head-on, nonviolently as long as the enemy is nonviolent, but violent when the enemy gets violent. We'll work with you on the voter-registration drive, we'll work with you on rent strikes, we'll work with you on school boycotts—I don't believe in any kind of integration; I'm not even worried about it because I know you're not going to get it anyway; you're not going to get it because you're afraid to die; you've got to be ready to die if you try and force yourself on the white man, because he'll get just as violent as those crackers in Mississippi, right here in Cleveland. But we will still work with you on the school boycotts because we're against a segregated school system. A segregated school system produces children who, when they graduate, graduate with crippled minds. But this does not mean that a school is segregated because it's all black. A segregated school means a school that is controlled by people who have no real interest in it whatsoever.

Let me explain what I mean. A segregated district or community is a community in which people live, but outsiders control the politics and the economy of that community. They never refer to the white section as a segregated community. It's the all-Negro section that's a segregated community. Why? The white man controls his own school, his own bank, his own economy, his own politics, his own everything, his own community—but he also controls yours. When you're under someone else's control, you're segregated. They'll always give you the lowest or the worst that there is to offer, but it doesn't mean you're segregated just because you have your own. You've got to *control* your own. Just like the white man has control of his, you need to control yours.

You know the best way to get rid of segregation? The

white man is more afraid of separation than he is of integration. Segregation means that he puts you away from him, but not far enough for you to be out of his jurisdiction; separation means you're gone. And the white man will integrate faster than he'll let you separate. So we will work with you against the segregated school system because it's criminal, because it is absolutely destructive, in every way imaginable, to the minds of the children who have to be exposed to that type of crippling education.

Last but not least, I must say this concerning the great controversy over rifles and shotguns. The only thing that I've ever said is that in areas where the government has proven itself either unwilling or unable to defend the lives and the property of Negroes, it's time for Negroes to defend themselves. Article number two of the constitutional amendments provides you and me the right to own a rifle or a shotgun. It is constitutionally legal to own a shotgun or a rifle. This doesn't mean you're going to get a rifle and form battalions and go out looking for white folks, although you'd be within your rights—I mean, you'd be justified; but that would be illegal and we don't do anything illegal. If the white man doesn't want the black man buying rifles and shotguns, then let the government do its job. That's all. And don't let the white man come to you and ask you what you think about what Malcolm says—why, you old Uncle Tom. He would never ask you if he thought you were going to say, "Amen!" No, he is making a Tom out of you.

So, this doesn't mean forming rifle clubs and going out looking for people, but it is time, in 1964, if you are a man, to let that man know. If he's not going to do his job in running the government and providing you and me with the protection that our taxes are supposed to be for, since he spends all those billions for his defense budget, he certainly can't begrudge you and me spending $12 or $15 for a single-shot, or double-action. I hope you understand. Don't go out shooting people, but any time, brothers and sisters, and especially the men in this audience—some of you wearing Congressional Medals of Honor, with shoulders this wide, chests this big, muscles that big—any time you and I sit around and read where they bomb a church and murder in cold blood, not some grownups, but four little girls while they were praying to the same god the white man taught them to pray to, and you and I see the government go down and can't find who did it.

Why, this man—he can find Eichmann hiding down in Argentina somewhere. Let two or three American soldiers, who are minding somebody else's business way over in South Vietnam, get killed, and he'll send battleships, sticking his nose in their business. He wanted to send troops down to Cuba and make them have what he calls free elections—this old cracker who doesn't have free elections in his own country. No, if you never see me another time in your life, if I die in the morning, I'll die saying one thing: the ballot or the bullet, the ballot or the bullet.

If a Negro in 1964 has to sit around and wait for some cracker senator to filibuster when it comes to the rights of black people, why, you and I should hang our heads in shame. You talk about a march on Washington in 1963, you haven't seen anything. There's some more going down in '64. And this time they're not going like they went last year. They're not going singing "We Shall Overcome." They're not going with white friends. They're not going with placards already painted for them. They're not going with round-trip tickets. They're going with one-way tickets.

And if they don't want that non-nonviolent army going down there, tell them to bring the filibuster to a halt. The black nationalists aren't going to wait. Lyndon B. Johnson is the head of the Democratic Party. If he's for civil rights, let him go into the Senate next week and declare himself. Let him go in there right now and declare himself. Let him go in there and denounce the Southern branch of his party. Let him go in there right now and take a moral stand—right now, not later. Tell him, don't wait until election time. If he waits too long, brothers and sisters, he will be responsible for letting a condition develop in this country which will create a climate that will bring seeds up out of the ground with vegetation on the end of them looking like something these people never dreamed of. In 1964, it's the ballot or the bullet. Thank you.

4

The black revolution

On April 8, 1964, Malcolm X gave a speech on "The Black Revolution" at a meeting sponsored by the Militant Labor Forum
at Palm Gardens in New York. This forum is connected with
The Militant, a socialist weekly, which Malcolm considered "one
of the best newspapers anywhere." The audience was around
three-quarters white. Most of it responded favorably to the
talk. There were some sharp exchanges during the discussion
period between the speaker and white liberals who resented
his attacks on liberalism and the Democratic Party and tried to
pin the label of hatemonger on him.

The talk gave Malcolm an opportunity for a fuller presenta-
tion of his arguments for internationalizing the black struggle
by indicting the United States government before the United
Nations for racism. It is notable also for his statement that a
"bloodless revolution" was still possible in the United States under certain circumstances.

Friends and enemies: Tonight I hope that we can have
a little fireside chat with as few sparks as possible being

tossed around. Especially because of the very explosive condition that the world is in today. Sometimes, when a person's house is on fire and someone comes in yelling fire, instead of the person who is awakened by the yell being thankful, he makes the mistake of charging the one who awakened him with having set the fire. I hope that this little conversation tonight about the black revolution won't cause many of you to accuse us of igniting it when you find it at your doorstep. . . .

During recent years there has been much talk about a population explosion. Whenever they are speaking of the population explosion, in my opinion they are referring primarily to the people in Asia or in Africa—the black, brown, red, and yellow people. It is seen by people of the West that, as soon as the standard of living is raised in Africa and Asia, automatically the people begin to reproduce abundantly. And there has been a great deal of fear engendered by this in the minds of the people of the West, who happen to be, on this earth, a very small minority.

In fact, in most of the thinking and planning of whites in the West today, it's easy to see the fear in their minds, conscious minds and subconscious minds, that the masses of dark people in the East, who already outnumber them, will continue to increase and multiply and grow until they eventually overrun the people of the West like a human sea, a human tide, a human flood. And the fear of this can be seen in the minds, in the actions, of most of the people here in the West in practically everything that they do. It governs their political views and it governs their economic views and it governs most of their attitudes toward the present society.

I was listening to Dirksen, the senator from Illinois, in Washington, D.C., filibustering the civil-rights bill; and one thing that he kept stressing over and over and over was that if this bill is passed, it will change the social structure of America. Well, I know what he's getting at, and I think that most other people today, and especially our people, know what is meant when these whites, who filibuster these bills, express fears of changes in the social structure. Our people are beginning to realize what they mean.

Just as we can see that all over the world one of the main problems facing the West is race, likewise here in America today, most of your Negro leaders as well as the whites agree that 1964 itself appears to be one of the most explosive years yet in the history of America on the racial front, on the racial scene. Not only is this racial explosion probably to take place in America, but all of the ingredients for this racial explosion in America to blossom into a world-wide racial explosion present themselves right here in front of us. America's racial powder keg, in short, can actually fuse or ignite a world-wide powder keg.

There are whites in this country who are still complacent when they see the possibilities of racial strife getting out of hand. You are complacent simply because you think you outnumber the racial minority in this country; what you have to bear in mind is wherein you might outnumber us in this country, you don't outnumber us all over the earth.

Any kind of racial explosion that takes place in this country today, in 1964, is not a racial explosion that can be confined to the shores of America. It is a racial explosion that can ignite the racial powder keg that exists all over the planet that we call earth. I think that nobody would disagree that the dark masses of Africa and Asia and Latin America are already seething with bitterness, animosity, hostility, unrest, and impatience with the racial intolerance that they themselves have experienced at the hands of the white West.

And just as they have the ingredients of hostility toward the West in general, here we also have 22 million African-Americans, black, brown, red, and yellow people, in this country who are also seething with bitterness and impatience and hostility and animosity at the racial intolerance not only of the white West but of white America in particular.

And by the hundreds of thousands today we find our own people have become impatient, turning away from your white nationalism, which you call democracy, toward the militant, uncompromising policy of black nationalism. I point out right here that as soon as we announced we were going to start a black nationalist party in this country, we received mail from coast to coast, especially from young people at the college level, the university level, who expressed complete sympathy and support and a desire to take an active part in any kind of political action based on black nationalism, designed to correct or eliminate immediately evils that our people have suffered here for 400 years.

The black nationalists to many of you may represent only a minority in the community. And therefore you might have a tendency to classify them as something insignificant. But just as the fuse is the smallest part or the smallest piece in the powder keg, it is yet that little fuse that ignites the entire powder keg. The black nationalists to you may represent a small minority in the so-called Negro community. But they just happen to be composed of the type of ingredient necessary to fuse or ignite the entire black community.

And this is one thing that whites—whether you call yourselves liberals or conservatives or racists or whatever else you might choose to be—one thing that you have to realize is, where the black community is concerned, although the large majority you come in contact with may impress you as being moderate and patient and loving and long-suffering and all that kind of stuff, the minority who you consider to be Muslims or nationalists happen to be made of the type of ingredient that can easily spark the black community. This should be understood. Because to me a powder keg is nothing without a fuse.

1964 will be America's hottest year; her hottest year yet; a year of much racial violence and much racial bloodshed. But it won't be blood that's going to flow only on one side. The new generation of black people that have grown up in this country during recent years are already forming the opinion, and it's a just opinion, that if there is to be bleeding, it should be reciprocal—bleeding on both sides.

It should also be understood that the racial sparks that are ignited here in America today could easily turn into a flaming fire abroad, which means it could engulf all the people of this earth into a giant race war. You cannot confine it to one little neighborhood, or one little community, or one little country. What happens to a black man in America today happens to the black man in Africa. What happens to a black man in America and Africa happens to the black man in Asia and to the man down in Latin America. What happens to one of us today happens to all of us. And when this is realized, I think that the whites— who are intelligent even if they aren't moral or aren't just or aren't impressed by legalities—those who are intelligent will realize that when they touch this one, they are touching all of them, and this in itself will have a tendency to be a checking factor.

The seriousness of this situation must be faced up to. I was in Cleveland last night, Cleveland, Ohio. In fact I was there Friday, Saturday and yesterday. Last Friday the warning was given that this is a year of bloodshed, that the black man has ceased to turn the other cheek, that he has ceased to be nonviolent, that he has ceased to feel that he must be confined by all these restraints that are put upon him by white society in struggling for what white society says he was supposed to have had a hundred years ago.

So today, when the black man starts reaching out for what America says are his rights, the black man feels that he is within his rights—when he becomes the victim of brutality by those who are depriving him of his rights—to do whatever is necessary to protect himself. An example of this was taking place last night at this same time in Cleveland, where the police were putting water hoses on our people there and also throwing tear gas at them—and they met a hail of stones, a hail of rocks, a hail of bricks. A couple of weeks ago in Jacksonville, Florida, a young teenage Negro was throwing Molotov cocktails.

Well, Negroes didn't do this ten years ago. But what you should learn from this is that they are waking up. It was stones yesterday, Molotov cocktails today; it will be hand grenades tomorrow and whatever else is available the next day. The seriousness of this situation must be faced up to. You should not feel that I am inciting someone to violence. I'm only warning of a powder-keg situation. You can take it or leave it. If you take the warning, perhaps you can still save yourself. But if you ignore it or ridicule it, well, death is already at your doorstep. There are 22 million African-Americans who are ready to fight for independence right here. When I say fight for independence right here, I don't mean any nonviolent fight, or turn-the-other-cheek fight. Those days are gone. Those days are over.

If George Washington didn't get independence for this country nonviolently, and if Patrick Henry didn't come up with a nonviolent statement, and you taught me to look upon them as patriots and heroes, then it's time for you to realize that I have studied your books well. . . .

1964 will see the Negro revolt evolve and merge into the world-wide black revolution that has been taking place on this earth since 1945. The so-called revolt will become a real black revolution. Now the black revolution has been taking place in Africa and Asia and Latin America; when I say black, I mean non-white—black, brown, red or yellow. Our brothers and sisters in Asia, who were colonized by the Europeans, our brothers and sisters in Africa, who were colonized by the Europeans, and in Latin America, the peasants, who were colonized by the Europeans, have been involved in a struggle since 1945 to get the colonialists, or the colonizing powers, the Europeans, off their land, out of their country.

This is a real revolution. Revolution is always based on land. Revolution is never based on begging somebody for an integrated cup of coffee. Revolutions are never fought by turning the other cheek. Revolutions are never based upon love-your-enemy and pray-for-those-who-spitefully-use-you. And revolutions are never waged singing "We Shall Overcome." Revolutions are based upon bloodshed. Revolutions are never compromising. Revolutions are never based upon negotiations. Revolutions are never based upon any kind of tokenism whatsoever. Revolutions are never even based upon that which is begging a corrupt society or a corrupt system to accept us into it. Revolutions overturn systems. And there is no system on this earth which has proven itself more corrupt, more criminal, than this system that in 1964 still colonizes 22 million African-Americans, still enslaves 22 million Afro-Americans.

There is no system more corrupt than a system that represents itself as the example of freedom, the example of democracy, and can go all over this earth telling other people how to straighten out their house, when you have citizens of this country who have to use bullets if they want to cast a ballot.

The greatest weapon the colonial powers have used in the past against our people has always been divide-and-conquer. America is a colonial power. She has colonized 22 million Afro-Americans by depriving us of first-class citizenship, by depriving us of civil rights, actually by depriving us of human rights. She has not only deprived us of the right to be a citizen, she has deprived us of the right to be human beings, the right to be recognized and respected as men and women. In this country the black can be fifty years old and he is still a "boy."

I grew up with white people. I was integrated before they even invented the word and I have never met white people yet—if you are around them long enough—who won't refer to you as a "boy" or a "gal," no matter how old you are or what school you came out of, no matter what your intellectual or professional level is. In this society we remain "boys."

So America's strategy is the same strategy as that which was used in the past by the colonial powers: divide and conquer. She plays one Negro leader against the other. She plays one Negro organization against the other. She makes us think we have different objectives, different goals. As soon as one Negro says something, she runs to this Negro and asks him, "What do you think about what he said?" Why, anybody can see through that today—except some of the Negro leaders.

All of our people have the same goals, the same objective. That objective is freedom, justice, equality. All of us want recognition and respect as human beings. We don't want to be integrationists. Nor do we want to be separationists. We want to be human beings. Integration is only a method that is used by some groups to obtain freedom, justice, equality and respect as human beings. Separation is only a method that is used by other groups to obtain freedom, justice, equality or human dignity.

Our people have made the mistake of confusing the methods with the objectives. As long as we agree on objectives, we should never fall out with each other just because we believe in different methods or tactics or strategy to reach a common objective.

We have to keep in mind at all times that we are not fighting for integration, nor are we fighting for separation. We are fighting for recognition as human beings. We are fighting for the right to live as free humans in this society. In fact, we are actually fighting for rights that are even greater than civil rights and that is human rights. . . .

Among the so-called Negroes in this country, as a rule the civil-rights groups, those who believe in civil rights, spend most of their time trying to prove they are Americans. Their thinking is usually domestic, confined to the boundaries of America, and they always look upon themselves as a minority. When they look upon themselves upon the American stage, the American stage is a white stage. So a black man standing on that stage in America automatically is in the minority. He is the underdog, and in his struggle he always uses an approach that is a begging, hat-in-hand, compromising approach.

Whereas the other segment or section in America, known as the black nationalists, are more interested in human rights than they are in civil rights. And they place more stress on human rights than they do on civil rights. The difference between the thinking and the scope of the Negroes who are involved in the human-rights struggle and those who are involved in the civil-rights struggle is that those so-called Negroes involved in the human-rights struggle don't look upon themselves as Americans.

They look upon themselves as a part of dark mankind. They see the whole struggle not within the confines of the American stage, but they look upon the struggle on the world stage. And, in the world context, they see that the dark man outnumbers the white man. On the world stage the white man is just a microscopic minority.

So in this country you find two different types of Afro-Americans—the type who looks upon himself as a minority and you as the majority, because his scope is limited to the American scene; and then you have the type who looks upon himself as part of the majority and you as part of a microscopic minority. And this one uses a different approach in trying to struggle for his rights. He doesn't beg. He doesn't thank you for what you give him, because you are only giving him what he should have had a hundred years ago. He doesn't think you are doing him any favors.

He doesn't see any progress that he has made since the Civil War. He sees not one iota of progress because, number one, if the Civil War had freed him, he wouldn't need civil-rights legislation today. If the Emancipation Proclamation, issued by that great shining liberal called Lincoln, had freed him, he wouldn't be singing "We Shall Overcome" today. If the amendments to the Constitution had solved his problem, his problem wouldn't still be here today. And if the Supreme Court desegregation decision of 1954 was genuinely and sincerely designed to solve his problem, his problem wouldn't be with us today.

So this kind of black man is thinking. He can see where every maneuver that America has made, supposedly to solve this problem, has been nothing but political trickery and treachery of the worst order. Today he doesn't have any confidence in these so-called liberals. (I know that all that have come in here tonight don't call yourselves liberals. Because that's a nasty name today. It represents hypocrisy.) So these two different types of black people exist in the so-called Negro community and they are beginning to wake up and their awakening is producing a very dangerous situation.

You have whites in the community who express sincerity when they say they want to help. Well, how can they help? How can a white person help the black man solve his problem? Number one, you can't solve it for him. You can help him solve it, but you can't solve it for him today. One of the best ways that you can help him solve it is to let the so-called Negro, who has been involved in the civil-rights struggle, see that the civil-rights struggle must be expanded beyond the level of civil rights to human rights. Once it is expanded beyond the level of civil rights to the level of human rights, it opens the door for all of our brothers and sisters in Africa and Asia, who have their independence, to come to our rescue.

When you go to Washington, D.C., expecting those crooks down there—and that's what they are—to pass some kind of civil-rights legislation to correct a very criminal situation, what you are doing is encouraging the black man, who is the victim, to take his case into the court that's controlled by the criminal that made him the victim. It will never be solved in that way. . . .

The civil-rights struggle involves the black man taking his case to the white man's court. But when he fights it at the human-rights level, it is a different situation. It opens the door to take Uncle Sam to the world court. The black man doesn't have to go to court to be free. Uncle Sam should be taken to court and made to tell why the black man is not free in a so-called free society. Uncle Sam should be taken into the United Nations and charged with violating the UN charter of human rights.

You can forget civil rights. How are you going to get civil rights with men like Eastland and men like Dirksen and men like Johnson? It has to be taken out of their hands and taken into the hands of those whose power and authority exceed theirs. Washington has become too corrupt. Uncle Sam has become bankrupt when it comes to a conscience—it is impossible for Uncle Sam to solve the problem of 22 million black people in this country. It is absolutely impossible to do it in Uncle Sam's courts— whether it is the Supreme Court or any other kind of court that comes under Uncle Sam's jurisdiction.

The only alternative that the black man has in America today is to take it out of Senator Dirksen's and Senator Eastland's and President Johnson's jurisdiction and take it downtown on the East River and place it before that body of men who represent international law, and let them know that the human rights of black people are being violated in a country that professes to be the moral leader of the free world.

Any time you have a filibuster in America, in the Senate, in 1964 over the rights of 22 million black people, over the citizenship of 22 million black people, or that will affect the freedom and justice and equality of 22 million black people, it's time for that government itself to be taken before a world court. How can you condemn South Africa? There are only 11 million of our people in South Africa, there are 22 million of them here. And we are receiving an injustice which is just as criminal as that which is being done to the black people of South Africa.

So today those whites who profess to be liberals—and as far as I am concerned it's just lip-profession—you understand why our people don't have civil rights. You're white.

You can go and hang out with another white liberal and see how hypocritical they are. A lot of you sitting right here know that you've seen whites up in a Negro's face with flowery words, and as soon as that Negro walks away you listen to how your white friend talks. We have black people who can pass as white. We know how you talk.

We can see that it is nothing but a governmental conspiracy to continue to deprive the black people in this country of their rights. And the only way we will get these rights restored is by taking it out of Uncle Sam's hands. Take him to court and charge him with genocide, the mass murder of millions of black people in this country—political murder, economic murder, social murder, mental murder. This is the crime that this government has committed, and if you yourself don't do something about it in time, you are going to open the doors for something to be done about it from outside forces.

I read in the paper yesterday where one of the Supreme Court justices, Goldberg, was crying about the violation of human rights of three million Jews in the Soviet Union. Imagine this. I haven't got anything against Jews, but that's their problem. How in the world are you going to cry about problems on the other side of the world when you haven't got the problems straightened out here? How can the plight of three million Jews in Russia be qualified to be taken to the United Nations by a man who is a justice in this Supreme Court, and is supposed to be a liberal, supposed to be a friend of black people, and hasn't opened up his mouth one time about taking the plight of black people down here to the United Nations? . . .

If Negroes could vote south of the—yes, if Negroes could vote south of the Canadian border—south South, if Negroes could vote in the southern part of the South, Ellender wouldn't be the head of the Agricultural and

Forestry Committee, Richard Russell wouldn't be head of the Armed Services Committee, Robertson of Virginia wouldn't be head of the Banking and Currency Committee. Imagine that, all of the banking and currency of the government is in the hands of a cracker.

In fact, when you see how many of these committee men are from the South, you can see that we have nothing but a cracker government in Washington, D.C. And their head is a cracker president. I said a cracker president. Texas is just as much a cracker state as Mississippi. . . .

The first thing this man did when he came in office was invite all the big Negroes down for coffee. James Farmer was one of the first ones, the head of CORE. I have nothing against him. He's all right—Farmer, that is. But could that same president have invited James Farmer to Texas for coffee? And if James Farmer went to Texas, could he have taken his white wife with him to have coffee with the president? Any time you have a man who can't straighten out Texas, how can he straighten out the country? No, you're barking up the wrong tree.

If Negroes in the South could vote, the Dixiecrats would lose power. When the Dixiecrats lost power, the Democrats would lose power. A Dixiecrat lost is a Democrat lost. Therefore the two of them have to conspire with each other to stay in power. The Northern Dixiecrat puts all the blame on the Southern Dixiecrat. It's a con game, a giant political con game. The job of the Northern Democrat is to make the Negro think that he is our friend. He is always smiling and wagging his tail and telling us how much he can do for us if we vote for him. But at the same time that he's out in front telling us what he's going to do, behind the door he's in cahoots with the Southern Democrat setting up the machinery to make sure he'll never have to keep his promise.

This is the conspiracy that our people have faced in this country for the past hundred years. And today you have a new generation of black people who have come on the scene, who have become disenchanted with the entire system, who have become disillusioned over the system, and who are ready now and willing to do something about it.

So, in my conclusion, in speaking about the black revolution, America today is at a time or in a day or at an hour where she is the first country on this earth that can actually have a bloodless revolution. In the past, revolutions have been bloody. Historically you just don't have a peaceful revolution. Revolutions are bloody, revolutions are violent, revolutions cause bloodshed and death follows in their paths. America is the only country in history in a position to bring about a revolution without violence and bloodshed. But America is not morally equipped to do so.

Why is America in a position to bring about a bloodless revolution? Because the Negro in this country holds the balance of power, and if the Negro in this country were given what the Constitution says he is supposed to have, the added power of the Negro in this country would sweep all of the racists and the segregationists out of office. It would change the entire political structure of the country. It would wipe out the Southern segregationism that now controls America's foreign policy, as well as America's domestic policy.

And the only way without bloodshed that this can be brought about is that the black man has to be given full use of the ballot in every one of the fifty states. But if the black man doesn't get the ballot, then you are going to be faced with another man who forgets the ballot and starts using the bullet.

Revolutions are fought to get control of land, to remove the absentee landlord and gain control of the land and the institutions that flow from that land. The black man has been in a very low condition because he has had no control whatsoever over any land. He has been a beggar economically, a beggar politically, a beggar socially, a beggar even when it comes to trying to get some education. The past type of mentality, that was developed in this colonial system among our people, today is being overcome. And as the young ones come up, they know what they want. And as they listen to your beautiful preaching about democracy and all those other flowery words, they know what they're supposed to have.

So you have a people today who not only know what they want, but also know what they are supposed to have. And they themselves are creating another generation that is coming up that not only will know what it wants and know what it should have, but also will be ready and willing to do whatever is necessary to see that what they should have materializes immediately. Thank you.

5

Letters from abroad

On April 13, 1964, Malcolm X left the United States on his first extended trip abroad in 1964. Before returning on May 21, he visited Egypt, Lebanon, Saudi Arabia, Nigeria, Ghana, Morocco and Algeria. He made the pilgrimage to Mecca that every Muslim seeks to complete, which entitled him to the use of "El Hajj" in his name, and he became known in the Muslim world as El Hajj Malik El Shabazz. Besides consolidating his relations with orthodox Islam, he met with students, journalists, members of parliament, ambassadors and government leaders, and "never stopped talking about the race problem in America."

Through this first trip Malcolm made a number of contacts that were to prove important in his later efforts to "internationalize" the American Negro struggle. But its main impact seems to have been on him. "I never would have believed possible—it shocked me when I considered it—the impact of the Muslim world's influence on my previous thinking," he said later. Two days after his return, he said in a speech in Chicago:

"In the past, I have permitted myself to be used to make

sweeping indictments of all white people, and these generalizations have caused injuries to some white people who did not deserve them. Because of the spiritual rebirth which I was blessed to undergo as a result of my pilgrimage to the Holy City of Mecca, I no longer subscribe to sweeping indictments of one race. My pilgrimage to Mecca . . . served to convince me that perhaps American whites can be cured of the rampant racism which is consuming them and about to destroy this country. In the future, I intend to be careful not to sentence anyone who has not been proven guilty. I am not a racist and do not subscribe to any of the tenets of racism. In all honesty and sincerity it can be stated that I wish nothing but freedom, justice and equality: life, liberty and the pursuit of happiness—for all people. My first concern is with the group of people to which I belong, the Afro-Americans, for we, more than any other people, are deprived of these inalienable rights."

The following excerpts, describing Malcolm's reactions, are taken from letters written from abroad.

JEDDA, SAUDI ARABIA

APRIL 20, 1964

Never have I witnessed such sincere hospitality and the overwhelming spirit of true brotherhood as is practiced by people *of all colors and races* here in this ancient holy land, the home of Abraham, Muhammad and all the other prophets of the Holy Scriptures. For the past week I have been utterly speechless and spellbound by the graciousness I see displayed all around me by people *of all colors.*

Last night, April 19, I was blessed to visit the Holy City of Mecca, and complete the "Omra" part of my pilgrimage. Allah willing, I shall leave for Mina tomorrow, April 21, and be back in Mecca to say my prayers from Mt. Arafat on Tuesday, April 22. Mina is about twenty miles from Mecca.

Last night I made my seven circuits around the Kaaba, led by a young Mutawif named Muhammad. I drank water from the well of Zem Zem, and then ran back and forth seven times between the hills of Mt. Al-Safa and Al-Marwah.

There were tens of thousands of pilgrims from all over the world. They were *of all colors,* from blue-eyed blonds to black-skinned Africans, but were all participating in the same ritual, displaying a spirit of unity and brotherhood that my experiences in America had led me to believe could never exist between the white and non-white.

America needs to understand Islam, because this is the one religion that erases the race problem from its society. Throughout my travels in the Muslim world, I have met, talked to, and even eaten with, people who would have been considered "white" in America, but the religion of Islam in their hearts has removed the "white" from their minds. They practice sincere and true brotherhood with other people irrespective of their color.

Before America allows herself to be destroyed by the "cancer of racism" she should become better acquainted with the religious philosophy of Islam, a religion that has already molded people of all colors into one vast family, a nation or brotherhood of Islam that leaps over all "obstacles" and stretches itself into almost all the Eastern countries of this earth.

The whites as well as the non-whites who accept true Islam become a changed people. I have eaten from the same plate with people whose eyes were the bluest of blue, whose hair was the blondest of blond, and whose skin was the whitest of white—all the way from Cairo to Jedda and even in the Holy City of Mecca itself—and I felt the same sincerity in the words and deeds of these "white" Muslims that I felt among the African Muslims of Nigeria, Sudan and Ghana.

True Islam removes racism, because people of all colors and races who accept its religious principles and bow down to the one God, Allah, also automatically accept each other as brothers and sisters, regardless of differences in complexion.

You may be shocked by these words coming from me, but I have always been a man who tries to face facts, and to accept the reality of life as new experiences and knowledge unfold it. The experiences of this pilgrimage have taught me much, and each hour here in the Holy Land opens my eyes even more. If Islam can place the spirit of true brotherhood in the hearts of the "whites" whom I have met here in the Land of the Prophets, then surely it can also remove the "cancer of racism" from the heart of the white American, and perhaps in time to save America from imminent racial disaster, the same destruction brought upon Hitler by his racism that eventually destroyed the Germans themselves. . . .

LAGOS, NIGERIA

MAY 10, 1964

Each place I have visited, they have insisted that I don't leave. Thus I have been forced to stay longer than I originally intended in each country. In the Muslim world they loved me once they learned I was an American Muslim, and here in Africa they love me as soon as they learn that I am Malcolm X of the militant American Muslims. Africans in general and Muslims in particular love militancy.

I hope that my Hajj to the Holy City of Mecca will officially establish the religious affiliation of the Muslim Mosque, Inc., with the 750 million Muslims of the world of Islam once and for all—and that my warm reception here in Africa will forever repudiate the American white man's propaganda that the black man in Africa is not interested in the plight of the black man in America.

The Muslim world is forced to concern itself, from the moral point of view in its own religious concepts, with the fact that our plight clearly involves the violation of our *human rights.*

The Koran compels the Muslim world to take a stand on the side of those whose human rights are being violated, no matter what the religious persuasion of the victims is. Islam is a religion which concerns itself with the human rights of all mankind, despite race, color, or creed. It recognizes all (everyone) as part of one human family.

Here in Africa, the 22 million American blacks are looked upon as the long-lost brothers of Africa. Our people here are interested in every aspect of our plight, and they study our struggle for freedom from every angle. Despite Western propaganda to the contrary, our African brothers and sisters love us, and are happy to learn that we also are awakening from our long "sleep" and are developing strong love for them.

ACCRA, GHANA
MAY 11, 1964

I arrived in Accra yesterday from Lagos, Nigeria. The natural beauty and wealth of Nigeria and its people are indescribable. It is full of Americans and other whites who are well aware of its untapped natural resources. The same whites, who spit in the faces of blacks in America and sic their police dogs upon us to keep us from "integrating" with them, are seen throughout Africa, bowing, grinning and smiling in an effort to "integrate" with the Africans—they want to "integrate" into Africa's wealth and beauty. This is ironical.

This continent has such great fertility and the soil is so

profusely vegetated that with modern agricultural methods it could easily become the "breadbasket" of the world.

I spoke at Ibadan University in Nigeria, Friday night, and gave the *true* picture of our plight in America, and of the necessity of the independent African nations helping us bring our case before the United Nations. The reception of the students was tremendous. They made me an honorary member of the "Muslim Students Society of Nigeria," and renamed me "Omowale," which means "the child has come home" in the Yoruba language.

The people of Nigeria are strongly concerned with the problems of their African brothers in America, but the U.S. information agencies in Africa create the impression that progress is being made and the problem is being solved. Upon close study, one can easily see a gigantic design to keep Africans here and the African-Americans from getting together. An African official told me, "When one combines the number of peoples of *African descent* in South, Central and North America, they total well over 80 million. One can easily understand the attempts to keep the Africans from ever uniting with the African-Americans." Unity between the Africans of the West and the Africans of the fatherland will well change the course of history.

Being in Ghana now, the fountainhead of Pan-Africanism, the last days of my tour should be intensely interesting and enlightening.

Just as the American Jew is in harmony (politically, economically and culturally) with world Jewry, it is time for all African-Americans to become an integral part of the world's Pan-Africanists, and even though we might remain in America physically while fighting for the benefits the Constitution guarantees us, we must "return" to Africa philosophically and culturally and develop a working unity in the framework of Pan-Africanism.

6

The Harlem 'hate-gang' scare

In May, 1964, the New York daily newspapers began to increase circulation with lurid stories about the alleged existence of a band of young Negroes, calling themselves "Blood Brothers," who had been organized by "dissident Black Muslims" to maim and kill whites. In response to the newspaper incitation against black militants and black nationalists, the Militant Labor Forum of New York organized a symposium on "What's Behind the 'Hate-Gang' Scare?"

Invitations to speak were accepted by Junius Griffin, *New York Times* reporter who had written a series of articles claiming that such a "hate gang" did exist in Harlem; Clifton DeBerry, presidential candidate of the Socialist Workers Party; Quentin Hand, assistant executive director of the Harlem Action Group; William Reed, of New York CORE; and James Shabazz, secretary to Malcolm X.

Two last-minute changes were made in the panel of speakers. Griffin decided that journalistic ethics did not permit him to speak at the symposium and withdrew. Malcolm X, who had recently returned from his first trip abroad, asked permission to substitute for James Shabazz and replaced him at the symposium, which was held on May 29 at the Militant Labor Forum Hall. His remarks on this occasion made it plain that his trip abroad, while broadening his views on race, had in no way altered his militancy against racial oppression; and that, in addition, it had deepened his identification with the colonial revolution and introduced new elements into his thinking about capitalism and socialism.

Mr. Chairman, fellow speakers, friends: I didn't know until this afternoon about the forum this evening. But one of my co-workers, who is very able and capable, Brother James [Shabazz], told me about it, and I couldn't resist the opportunity to come. Some writer said one of my weaknesses is that I can't resist a platform. Well, that's perhaps true. Whenever you have something to say and you're not afraid to say it, I think you should go ahead and say it, and let the chips fall where they may. So I take advantage of all platforms to get off my mind what's on it.

Also, they say travel broadens your scope, and recently I've had an opportunity to do a lot of it in the Middle East and Africa. While I was traveling I noticed that most of the countries that had recently emerged into independence have turned away from the so-called capitalistic system in the direction of socialism. So out of curiosity, I can't resist the temptation to do a little investigating wherever that particular philosophy happens to be in existence or an attempt is being made to bring it into existence.

Thirdly, the first time I ever heard about the "Blood Brothers," I happened to be in Nigeria, in West Africa. And someone, a doctor, a Nigerian but who had spent too much time in Europe, was the first one to bring it to my attention, and ask me about it. It didn't make me sad

at all. And I don't see why anybody should be sad or re-
gretful in any way, shape or form—if such does exist. I
recall in 1959 when everybody began to talk about the
Black Muslims, all the Negro leaders said no such group
existed. In fact, I recall, on the Mike Wallace show Roy
Wilkins was asked about the Black Muslims; he said he
never heard of it—and then they flashed a picture of him
on the screen shaking hands with me.

And I think one of the mistakes that our people make—
they're too quick to apologize for something that might
exist that the power structure finds deplorable or finds
difficult to digest. And without even realizing it, sometimes we try and prove it doesn't exist. And if it doesn't,
sometimes it should. I am one person who believes that
anything the black man in this country needs to get his
freedom right now, that thing should exist.

As far as I'm concerned, everybody who has caught the
same kind of hell that I have caught is my blood brother.
And I have plenty of them. Because all of us have caught the
same hell. So the question is, if they don't exist, should they
exist? Not do they exist, should they exist? Do they have a
right to exist? And since when must a man deny the existence of his blood brother? It's like denying his family. . . .

If we're going to talk about police brutality, it's because
police brutality exists. Why does it exist? Because our people in this particular society live in a police state. A black
man in America lives in a police state. He doesn't live in
any democracy, he lives in a police state. That's what it is,
that's what Harlem is. . . .

I visited the Casbah in Casablanca and I visited the
one in Algiers, with some of the brothers—blood brothers. They took me down into it and showed me the suffering, showed me the conditions that they had to live under
while they were being occupied by the French. . . . They

showed me the conditions that they lived under while they were colonized by these people from Europe. And they also showed me what they had to do to get those people off their back. The first thing they had to realize was that all of them were brothers; oppression made them brothers; exploitation made them brothers; degradation made them brothers; discrimination made them brothers; segregation made them brothers; humiliation made them brothers.

And once all of them realized that they were blood brothers, they also realized what they had to do to get that man off their back. They lived in a police state; Algeria was a police state. Any occupied territory is a police state; and this is what Harlem is. Harlem is a police state; the police in Harlem, their presence is like occupation forces, like an occupying army. They're not in Harlem to protect us; they're not in Harlem to look out for our welfare; they're in Harlem to protect the interests of the businessmen who don't even live there.

The same conditions that prevailed in Algeria that forced the people, the noble people of Algeria, to resort eventually to the terrorist-type tactics that were necessary to get the monkey off their backs, those same conditions prevail today in America in every Negro community.

And I would be other than a man to stand up and tell you that the Afro-Americans, the black people who live in these communities and in these conditions, are ready and willing to continue to sit around nonviolently and patiently and peacefully looking for some good will to change the conditions that exist. No! . . .

Police Commissioner Murphy is a dangerous man. He's dangerous because either he lacks understanding or he has too much understanding and knows what he's doing. If he's functioning as he is from lack of knowledge and understanding, he's dangerous; and then if he's doing as he is from understanding, he's dangerous. Because what he's doing is creating a situation that can lead to nothing but bloodshed. Almost every public statement he makes is designed to give the police in Harlem courage to resort to tactics that are inhuman.

And in my opinion this type of incitement on the part of the police commissioner to make these policemen act other than they should, stems from a lack of understanding of the true spirit that exists among the young generation in Harlem. He must have been misinformed by some of that old generation who have been ready and willing to suffer brutality at the hands of someone just because he has on a uniform. Nowadays, our people don't care who the oppressor is; whether he has a sheet or whether he has on a uniform, he's in the same category.

You will find that there is a growing tendency among us, among our people, to do whatever is necessary to bring this to a halt. You have a man like Police Commissioner Murphy—and I'm not against the law; I'm not against law enforcement. You need laws to survive and you need law enforcement to have an intelligent, peaceful society; but we have to live in these places and suffer the type of conditions that exist from officers who lack understanding and who lack any human feeling, or lack any feeling for their fellow human being. . . . I'm not here to apologize for the existence of any blood brothers. I'm not here to minimize the factors that hint toward their existence. I'm here to say that if they don't exist, it's a miracle. . . .

If those of you who are white have the good of the black people in this country at heart, my suggestion is that you have to realize now that the day of nonviolent resistance is over; that the day of passive resistance is over. . . .

The next thing you'll see here in America—and please

don't blame it on me when you see it—you will see the same things that have taken place among other people on this earth whose condition was parallel to the 22 million Afro-Americans in this country.

The people of China grew tired of their oppressors and the people rose up against their oppressors. They didn't rise up nonviolently. It was easy to say that the odds were against them, but eleven of them started out and today those eleven control 800 million. They would have been told back then that the odds were against them. As the oppressor always points out to the oppressed, "The odds are against you."

When Castro was up in the mountains of Cuba, they told him the odds were against him. Today he's sitting in Havana and all the power this country has can't remove him.

They told the Algerians the same thing: "What do you have to fight with?" Today they have to bow down to Ben Bella. He came out of the jail that they put him in, and today they have to negotiate with him because he knew that the one thing he had on his side was truth and time. Time is on the side of the oppressed today, it's against the oppressor. Truth is on the side of the oppressed today, it's against the oppressor. You don't need anything else.

I would just like to say this in my conclusion. You'll see terrorism that will terrify you, and if you don't think you'll see it, you're trying to blind yourself to the historic development of everything that's taking place on this earth today. You'll see other things.

Why will you see them? Because people will realize that it's impossible for a chicken to produce a duck egg—even though they both belong to the same family of fowl. A chicken just doesn't have it within its system to produce a duck egg. It can't do it. It can only produce according to what that particular system was constructed to produce.

The system in this country cannot produce freedom for an Afro-American. It is impossible for this system, this economic system, this political system, this social system, this system, period. It's impossible for this system, as it stands, to produce freedom right now for the black man in this country.

And if ever a chicken did produce a duck egg, I'm quite sure you would say it was certainly a revolutionary chicken!

From the question period

QUESTION: What political and economic system does Malcolm X want?

ANSWER: I don't know. But I'm flexible. . . . As was stated earlier, all of the countries that are emerging today from under the shackles of colonialism are turning toward socialism. I don't think it's an accident. Most of the countries that were colonial powers were capitalist countries, and the last bulwark of capitalism today is America. It's impossible for a white person to believe in capitalism and not believe in racism. You can't have capitalism without racism. And if you find one and you happen to get that person into a conversation and they have a philosophy that makes you sure they don't have this racism in their outlook, usually they're socialists or their political philosophy is socialism.

QUESTION: Do you think it's possible for an integrated organization working within a country like this to succeed, with the Caucasian members of the organization conspicuous in the organization?

ANSWER: That's a very important question. Because it

boils right down to the basic tactics that have been employed by the various groups during the past ten years when the freedom struggle has gotten so much publicity. If you notice, the outstanding characteristic of the freedom struggle that is participated in by integrated groups has always been nonviolence. Any time you have an integrated group the emphasis is always on nonviolence. Because it has been substantiated, when you study these integrated groups, that usually the whites, who get involved in the action where the Negro is supposed to benefit if they're successful, are more inclined toward taking a nonviolent approach. That is what is causing the black people to become suspicious. And the groups that are ready to fight are usually not integrated. So all we say is this: We feel we've waited long enough. And we feel that all this crawling and sitting-in and crying-in and praying-in and begging-in hasn't gotten any meaningful results.

In my recent travels into the African countries and others, it was impressed upon me the importance of having a working unity among all peoples, black as well as white. But the only way this is going to be brought about is that the black ones have to be in unity first. Then those whites who want to help cannot help by joining and leading in the struggle which they've tried to do in the past. If the whites are genuinely interested in the freedom of the black people in this country, you don't need to give us a crutch. The black man has to be shown how to free himself, and the white one who is sincerely interested has to back whatever that black group decides upon to do. . . .

QUESTION: [About his letter from Mecca on religion.]
ANSWER: Travel broadens one's scope. Any time you do any travel, your scope will be broadened. It doesn't mean you change—you broaden. No religion will ever make me

forget the condition of our people in this country. No religion will ever make me forget the continued fighting with dogs against our people in this country. No religion will make me forget the police clubs that come up 'side our heads. No God, no religion, no nothing will make me forget it until it stops, until it's finished, until it's eliminated. I want to make that point clear. . . .

We will work with anyone, with any group, no matter what their color is, as long as they are genuinely interested in taking the type of steps necessary to bring an end to the injustices that black people in this country are afflicted by. No matter what their color is, no matter what their political, economic or social philosophy is, as long as their aims and objectives are in the direction of destroying the vulturous system that has been sucking the blood of black people in this country, they're all right with us. But if they're in any way that compromising, dangerous type of person, then we think they should be dealt with.

When the Algerians were struggling for their freedom, some Frenchmen came and said, "We're with you." Okay, the Algerians accepted them, but they first tested them. They said, "Prove it." I won't tell you what the test was, but they put them to the test. Nowadays, as our people begin to wake up, they're going to realize, they've been talking about Negro revolt, Negro revolution—You can't talk that stuff to me unless you're really for one. I don't even want to hear it unless you're really for one. And most of you aren't. When the deal goes down, you back out every time.

From the summary

So in essence, the summary is that there's a problem that is confronting the black people. And until the problem of the black people in this country is solved, the white people have a problem that's going to cause an end to this society, system and race as you know it. The best way to solve your problem is to help us solve our problem. I'm not a racist. I've never been a racist. I believe in indicting the system and the person that is responsible for our condition.

And the only defense that the people, who are in control of the power structure and system that's exploiting us, have had is to label those who indict it without compromise as racists and extremists. Now if there are white people who are genuinely and sincerely fed up with the condition that black people are in, in America, then they have to take a stand, but not a compromising stand, not a tongue-in-cheek stand, not a nonviolent stand. . . .

7

Appeal to African heads of state

Throughout June, 1964, Malcolm X spoke, agitated, educated and organized to create a new, non-religious movement to promote black unity and work for freedom "by any means necessary." On June 28, this new movement was born under the name of the Organization of Afro-American Unity, its "statement of basic aims and objectives" was released to the public, and Malcolm was designated chairman.

Shortly thereafter, on July 9, Malcolm again left the United States for Africa and the Middle East. His immediate objective was to attend the "African Summit"—the second meeting of the Organization of African Unity, which had been formed in 1963 to bring about joint action by the independent African governments.

The OAU conference was held in Cairo July 17–21, and was attended by nearly all the heads of the thirty-four member states. The welcoming address was made by President Gamal Abdel Nasser of the United Arab Republic who, while reviewing the events of the previous year, hailed the Civil

Rights Act of 1964 that had recently been enacted in the United States.

Malcolm was accepted as an observer at the conference. In this capacity he was permitted to submit to the delegates an eight-page memorandum urging their support of the Negro struggle in the United States and their help in bringing the plight of the American Negro before the United Nations. The memorandum, which follows, was delivered to the delegates on July 17, one day before the events that came to be called "the Harlem riots."

Your Excellencies:

The Organization of Afro-American Unity has sent me to attend this historic African summit conference as an observer to represent the interests of 22 million African-Americans whose *human rights* are being violated daily by the racism of American imperialists.

The Organization of Afro-American Unity (OAAU) has been formed by a cross-section of America's African-American community, and is patterned after the letter and spirit of the Organization of African Unity (OAU).

Just as the Organization of African Unity has called upon all African leaders to submerge their differences and unite on common objectives for the common good of all Africans—in America the Organization of Afro-American Unity has called upon Afro-American leaders to submerge their differences and find areas of agreement wherein we can work in unity for the good of the entire 22 million African-Americans.

Since the 22 million of us were originally Africans, who are now in America not by choice but only by a cruel accident in our history, we strongly believe that African problems are our problems and our problems are African problems.

Your Excellencies:

We also believe that as heads of the Independent African states you are the shepherd of *all* African peoples everywhere, whether they are still at home on the mother continent or have been scattered abroad.

Some African leaders at this conference have implied that they have enough problems here on the mother continent without adding the Afro-American problem.

With all due respect to your esteemed positions, I must remind all of you that the good shepherd will leave ninety-nine sheep, who are safe at home, to go to the aid of the one who is lost and has fallen into the clutches of the imperialist wolf.

We, in America, are your long-lost brothers and sisters, and I am here only to remind you that our problems are your problems. As the African-Americans "awaken" today, we find ourselves in a strange land that has rejected us, and, like the prodigal son, we are turning to our elder brothers for help. We pray our pleas will not fall upon deaf ears.

We were taken forcibly in chains from this mother continent and have now spent over 300 years in America, suffering the most inhuman forms of physical and psychological tortures imaginable.

During the past ten years the entire world has witnessed our men, women and children being attacked and bitten by vicious police dogs, brutally beaten by police clubs, and washed down the sewers by high-pressure water hoses that would rip the clothes from our bodies and the flesh from our limbs.

And all of these inhuman atrocities have been inflicted upon us by the American governmental authorities, the police themselves, for no reason other than we seek the recognition and respect granted other human beings in America.

Your Excellencies:

The American government is either unable or unwilling to protect the lives and property of your 22 million African-American brothers and sisters. We stand defenseless, at the mercy of American racists who murder us at will for no reason other than we are black and of African descent.

Two black bodies were found in the Mississippi River this week; last week an unarmed African-American educator was murdered in cold blood in Georgia; a few days before that three civil-rights workers disappeared completely, perhaps murdered also, only because they were teaching our people in Mississippi how to vote and how to secure their political rights.

Our problems are your problems. We have lived for over 300 years in that American den of racist wolves in constant fear of losing life and limb. Recently, three students from Kenya were mistaken for American Negroes and were brutally beaten by New York police. Shortly after that, two diplomats from Uganda were also beaten by the New York City police, who mistook them for American Negroes.

If Africans are brutally beaten while only visiting in America, imagine the physical and psychological suffering received by your brothers and sisters who have lived there for over 300 years.

Our problem is your problem. No matter how much independence Africans get here on the mother continent, unless you wear your national dress at all times, when you visit America, you may be mistaken for one of us and suffer the same psychological humiliation and physical mutilation that is an everyday occurrence in our lives.

Your problems will never be fully solved until and unless ours are solved. You will never be fully respected until and unless we are also respected. You will never be recognized as free human beings until and unless we are also recognized and treated as human beings.

Our problem is your problem. It is not a Negro problem, nor an American problem. This is a world problem; a problem for humanity. It is not a problem of civil rights but a problem of human rights.

If the United States Supreme Court justice, Arthur Goldberg, a few weeks ago, could find legal grounds to threaten to bring Russia before the United Nations and charge her with violating the human rights of less than three million Russian Jews, what makes our African brothers hesitate to bring the United States government before the United Nations and charge her with violating the human rights of 22 million African-Americans?

We pray that our African brothers have not freed themselves of European colonialism only to be overcome and held in check now by American *dollarism*. Don't let American racism be "legalized" by American dollarism.

America is worse than South Africa, because not only is America racist, but she also is deceitful and hypocritical. South Africa preaches segregation and practices segregation. She, at least, practices what she preaches. America preaches integration and practices segregation. She preaches one thing while deceitfully practicing another.

South Africa is like a vicious wolf, openly hostile towards black humanity. But America is cunning like a fox, friendly and smiling, but even more vicious and deadly than the wolf.

The wolf and the fox are both enemies of humanity; both are canine; both humiliate and mutilate their victims. Both have the same objectives, but differ only in methods.

If South Africa is guilty of violating the human rights

of Africans here on the mother continent, then America is guilty of worse violations of the 22 million Africans on the American continent. And if South African racism is not a domestic issue, then American racism also is not a *domestic* issue. Many of you have been led to believe that the much publicized, recently passed civil-rights bill is a sign that America is making a sincere effort to correct the injustices we have suffered there. This propaganda maneuver is part of her deceit and trickery to keep the African nations from condemning her racist practices before the United Nations, as you are now doing as regards the same practices of South Africa.

The United States Supreme Court passed a law ten years ago making America's segregated school system illegal. But the federal government has yet to enforce this law even in the North. If the federal government cannot enforce the law of the highest court in the land when it comes to nothing but equal rights to education for African-Americans, how can anyone be so naive as to think all the additional laws brought into being by the civil-rights bill will be enforced?

These are nothing but tricks of the century's leading neo-colonialist power. Surely, our intellectually mature African brothers will not fall for this trickery.

The Organization of Afro-American Unity, in cooperation with a coalition of other Negro leaders and organizations, has decided to elevate our freedom struggle above the domestic level of civil rights. We intend to "internationalize" it by placing it at the level of human rights. Our freedom struggle for human dignity is no longer confined to the domestic jurisdiction of the United States government.

We beseech the independent African states to help us bring our problem before the United Nations, on the grounds that the United States government is morally incapable of protecting the lives and the property of 22 million African-Americans. And on the grounds that our deteriorating plight is definitely becoming a threat to world peace.

Out of frustration and hopelessness our young people have reached the point of no return. We no longer endorse patience and turning-the-other-cheek. We assert the right of self-defense by whatever means necessary, and reserve the right of maximum retaliation against our racist oppressors, no matter what the odds against us are.

From here on in, if we must die anyway, we will die fighting back and we will not die alone. We intend to see that our racist oppressors also get a taste of death.

We are well aware that our future efforts to defend ourselves by retaliating—by meeting violence with violence, eye for eye and tooth for tooth—could create the type of racial conflict in America that could easily escalate into a violent, world-wide, bloody race war.

In the interests of world peace and security, we beseech the heads of the independent African states to recommend an immediate investigation into our problem by the United Nations Commission on Human Rights.

If this humble plea that I am voicing at this conference is not properly worded, then let our elder brothers, who know the legal language, come to our aid and word our plea in the proper language necessary for it to be heard.

One last word, my beloved brothers at this African summit:

"No one knows the master better than his servant." We have been servants in America for over 300 years. We have a thorough, inside knowledge of this man who calls himself "Uncle Sam." Therefore, you must heed our warning: Don't escape from European colonialism only to become even more enslaved by deceitful, "friendly" American dollarism.

May Allah's blessings of good health and wisdom be upon you all. Salaam Alaikum.

Malcolm X,
Chairman
ORGANIZATION OF
AFRO-AMERICAN UNITY

Shortly after the OAU conference, Malcolm was interviewed in Cairo by Milton Henry, attorney, former city councilman in Pontiac, Michigan, and president of the Afro-American Broadcasting and Recording Company in Detroit. From this interview, which was originally played over the Group On Advanced Leadership (GOAL) radio program in Detroit, the following extracts about the conference have been taken:

MILTON HENRY: Once again the GOAL Show microphones have with us our brother, Malcolm X. This time we are on the other side of the world. We're at Cairo, Egypt, where the independent African states have met in serious confrontation for the last week. One of the significant additions to the confrontation here was the presence of Malcolm X as a black American delegate to the conference of black peoples here in Africa. Malcolm, would you tell us something about the conference? First of all, we'd like to know about your appearance—how did it happen that you as an American were permitted to appear at this conference of African people?

MALCOLM: First, I want to point out that we are sitting here along the banks of the Nile, and the last time I spoke to you we were in Harlem. Here along the banks of the Nile it's not much different from Harlem—same people, same feeling, same pulse.

About my appearing here at the conference: At first it did create a great deal of controversy, and, as you probably know, apprehension on the part of the powers that be in America, because they realize that if any direct contact, communication and understanding and working agreement are ever developed between the 22 million or 30 million Afro-Americans and the Africans here on the continent, there's nothing we couldn't accomplish. When I arrived here, there was a great deal of publicity in all of the press over here concerning my coming. It was historic in a sense because no American Negroes had ever made any effort in the past to try and get their problems placed in the same category as the African problems, nor had they tried to internationalize it. So this was something new, it was unique, and everyone wondered what the reaction of the Africans would be.

It is true that at first there were stumbling blocks placed in my path in regards to being accepted into the conference, or into the meetings. But I'd rather not say what happened in specific details. Thanks to Allah, I was admitted as an observer and I was able to submit a memorandum to each one of the heads of state, which was read and thoroughly analyzed by them. It pointed out the conditions of our people in America and the necessity of something being done and said at this conference toward letting the world know, at least letting the United States know, that our African brothers over here identified themselves with our problems in the States.

HENRY: Now, Malcolm, I have read the speech [memorandum] which was presented. . . . Basically, as you say, it did deal with the abuses that the American Negroes have suffered in America and it asked the consideration of the African states of this problem. Now, will you tell us, was this actually passed upon, and did any action come out of the Cairo conference with reference to the American Negro?

MALCOLM: Yes, a resolution came out, acknowledging the fact that America has passed a civil-rights bill, but at the same time pointing out that, despite the passage of the civil-rights bill, continued abuses of the human rights of the black people in America still existed. And it called upon—I forget the wording; when I read the resolution it was 2:30 in the morning, under very adverse conditions; but I was so happy to read it. In essence, I remember that it outright condemned the racism that existed in America and the continued abuses that our people suffered despite the passage of the civil-rights bill. It was a very good resolution.

HENRY: In other words, this type of resolution coming out of a conference of thirty-four African states should certainly make the United States take a new look at the American Negro?

MALCOLM: Well, I have to say this, that the United States has been looking at the American Negro. When I arrived here I did a great deal of lobbying. I had to do a great deal of lobbying between the lobby of the Hotel Hilton, the lobby of the Shepheard and even the lobby of the "Isis," the ship where the African liberation movement was housed. Lobbying was necessary because the various agencies that the United States has abroad had successfully convinced most Africans that the American Negro in no way identified with Africa, and that the African would be foolish to involve himself in the problems of the American Negroes. And some African leaders were saying this.

So in the memorandum I submitted to them at the conference I pointed out to them that as independent heads of states we looked upon them as the shepherds not only of the African people on the continent, but all people of

African descent abroad; and that a good shepherd is more concerned with the sheep that have gone astray and fallen into the hands of the imperialist wolf than the sheep that are still at home. That the 22 million or 30 million, whatever the case may be, Afro-Americans in the United States were still Africans, and that we felt that the African heads of state were as much responsible for us as they were responsible for the people right here on the continent. This was a sort of a challenge to them and I think that most of them realize it today, more so than they did prior to the conference.

HENRY: Malcolm, I think you are to be greatly applauded because actually you were the only American recognized as a participant of the conference, and of course you had the badge which permitted you access to all of the rooms and so forth. The Americans here, including myself, did not have that privilege, but you had the privilege of actually being with the other black brothers. I had the feeling that there will be a great change in emphasis because you have been here, and because you presented our position—the position of the black man in America—so well, in a way that no one but an American could.

MALCOLM: One thing that made most Africans see the necessity of their intervening on our behalf was [their learning] a bit of the historic steps since 1939 in the so-called rise of the black American. . . . It was the world pressure, brought about by Hitler, that enabled the Negro to rise above where he was [in 1939]. After Hitler was destroyed, there was the threat of Stalin, but it was always the world pressure that was upon America that enabled black people to go forward. It was not the initiative internally that the Negro put forth in America, nor was it a change of moral heart on the part of Uncle Sam—it was world pressure. Once this is realized as a basic fact, then the present

American Negro leaders will be more aware that any gain, even in token form, that they get, isn't coming from any goodness out of Washington, D.C., or from their own initiative—it is coming because of the international situation. And when they see it like this, in cold facts, then they will see the necessity of placing their problem at the world level, internationalizing the Negro struggle and calling upon our brothers and sisters in Africa and Asia and Latin America, and even in some of the European countries, to bring pressure upon the United States government in order to get our problems solved. And this was only the first of a series of steps that the OAAU has in mind to internationalize the black man's problem, and make it not a Negro problem or an American problem, but a world problem, a problem for humanity.

HENRY: I think of another real benefit from this conference, Malcolm. You are living in a very advantageous spot, because it so happens, as you intimated just a minute ago, that you are living with all of the freedom fighters from all of the liberated and unliberated parts of the world down there on the "Isis"—is that the name of the boat?

MALCOLM: Well, I don't know if I should say this, but it is true. The "Isis," a beautiful yacht that floats on the Nile River, was set aside for all the liberation movements that exist on the African continent. The leaders of these movements from places like Angola, the Angola freedom fighters; freedom fighters from Mozambique; freedom fighters from Zambia, known as Northern Rhodesia, which is just on its way toward independence; freedom fighters from Zimbabwe, known in America as Southern Rhodesia; freedom fighters from Southwest Africa; from Swaziland; Basutoland; and South Africa itself—all of the representatives of these different groups of freedom fighters were housed on this yacht called the "Isis."

I was very honored to be permitted to be housed right along with them. Spending so much time with them gave me a real feeling of the pulse of a true revolutionary, and it gave me an opportunity also to listen to them tell of the real brutal atmosphere in which they live in these colonized areas. It also gave me somewhat of a better idea of our problem in America, and what is going to be necessary to bring an end to the brutality and the suffering that we undergo every day.

HENRY: I think that this is one of the advantages of a conference like the one we have just experienced. The fact is that it is important for people to get together to exchange ideas. Even apart from the speeches and the organizational activities which go on with the formal organization, it would seem that, as you indicated, the opportunity for the leaders of each of these parts of the world to get together becomes an invaluable asset to the total freedom struggle. Because without this, leaders very often feel they work by themselves; and with it, they can see the whole picture.

MALCOLM: Yes, this is one thing that I have learned since being out of the Black Muslim movement. It's difficult to look at a thing through the narrow scope of an organizational eye ofttimes and see it in its proper perspective. If the various groups in America had been less selfish and had permitted different representatives from the groups to travel into foreign countries, and broaden their own scope, and come back and educate the movements they represented, not only would this have made the groups to which they belonged more enlightened and more worldly in the international sense, but it also would have given the independent African states abroad a better understanding of the groups in the United States, and what they stand for, what they represent.

In my opinion, a very narrow, backward, almost childish approach has been made by the groups in the United States, and especially the religious groups; very narrow minded. Whenever you belong to a group that just can't work with another group, then that group itself is selfish. Any group, any group that can't work with all other groups, if they are genuinely interested in solving the problems of the Negro collectively—why, I don't think that that group is really sincerely motivated toward reaching a solution. This Organization of African Unity, this summit conference, is the best example of what can be accomplished when people come together and their motives aren't selfish.

HENRY: Yes, it doesn't seem that it should be so difficult for Negroes, if they are sincere, to get together.

MALCOLM: If they are sincere, it is easy for them to get together.

HENRY: Perhaps those leaders will be passed by now, in the events as they move forward. I am enthused about the OAAU, and I expect that there will be some very concrete things happening with respect to that organization that will make the so-called civil-rights movement just a thing of the past almost.

MALCOLM: Well, one of the main objectives of the OAAU is to join the civil-rights struggle and lift it above civil rights to the level of human rights. As long as our people wage a struggle for freedom and label it civil rights, it means that we are under the domestic jurisdiction of Uncle Sam continually, and no outside nation can make any effort whatsoever to help us. As soon as we lift it above civil rights to the level of human rights, the problem becomes internationalized; all of those who belong to the United Nations automatically can take sides with us and help us in condemning, at least charging, Uncle Sam with violation of our human rights.

HENRY: Yes, Malcolm, there is one other thing before we leave. What do you think of this city of Cairo?

MALCOLM: Cairo is probably one of the best examples for the American Negro. More so than any other city on the African continent, the people of Cairo look like the American Negroes—in the sense that we have all complexions, we range in America from the darkest black to the lightest light, and here in Cairo it is the same thing; throughout Egypt, it is the same thing. All of the complexions are blended together here in a truly harmonious society. You know, if ever there was a people who should know how to practice brotherhood, it is the American Negro and it is the people of Egypt. Negroes just can't judge each other according to color, because we are all colors, all complexions. And as Mrs. W.E.B. DuBois pointed out, the problems today are too vast. Just as on the African continent, you have this wide range of complexions—so much so that you can't call it a brown struggle, a red struggle, or a black struggle. . . .

HENRY: By the way, Brother Malcolm, before we close, did you receive any promises of assistance or help from any of the African nations?

MALCOLM: Oh, yes, several of them promised officially that, come the next session of the UN, any effort on our part to bring our problem before the UN—I think it is the Commission on Human Rights—will get support and help from them. They will assist us in showing us how to bring it up legally. So I am very, very happy over the whole result of my trip here.

HENRY: So this conference has been an unqualified success from all standpoints?

MALCOLM: From all standpoints it has been an unqualified success, and one which should change the whole direction of our struggle in America for human dignity as well as human rights.

HENRY: Thank you very much, Brother Malcolm.

In the preceding interview, Malcolm expressed satisfaction with the OAU's resolution on "Racial Discrimination in the United States of America." This may have meant it was better than he had expected, or better than it would have been without his intervention. The actual wording of the resolution was moderate. It noted "with satisfaction the recent enactment of the Civil Rights Act designed to secure for American Negroes their basic human rights," while declaring that the OAU conference was "deeply disturbed, however, by continuing manifestations of racial bigotry and racial oppression against Negro citizens of the United States of America." The resolution concluded by reaffirming the OAU's "belief that the existence of discriminatory practices is a matter of deep concern to member states of the Organization of African Unity," and by urging "the government authorities in the United States of America to intensify their efforts to ensure the total elimination of all forms of discrimination based on race, color, or ethnic origin."

Malcolm's effect on Africa should not be judged merely by the OAU resolution. Following the conference, he made a second, longer and more intensive tour of the continent, continuing his own education but contributing in no small degree to the education of many Africans, in and out of government.

Independent testimony to Malcolm's impact on Africa was provided by John Lewis and Donald Harris, who visited several African countries as representatives of the Student Nonviolent Coordinating Committee in the fall of 1964, when Malcolm was

nearing the end of his tour of fourteen countries. The following is taken from a written report by Lewis and Harris to SNCC,
dated December 14, 1964:

"Among the first days we were in Accra, someone said, 'Look,
you guys might really be doing something—I don't know, but
if you are to the right of Malcolm, you might as well start pack-
ing right now 'cause no one'll listen to you.' Among the first
questions we were continually asked was, 'What's your organization's relationship with Malcolm's?' We ultimately found that
this situation was not peculiar to Ghana; the pattern repeated
itself in every country. After a day of this we found that we must,
immediately on meeting people, state our own position in regard to where we stood on certain issues—Cuba, Vietnam, the
Congo, Red China and the UN, and what SNCC's role, guide-
lines, and involvement in the rights struggle was. Malcolm's
impact on Africa was just fantastic. In every country he was
known and served as the main criteria for categorizing other
Afro-Americans and their political views."

Malcolm's activities in Africa also had impact on high officials
in Washington, D.C. On August 13, 1964, the *New York Times*
printed a dispatch by M.S. Handler from Washington, which
said in part:

"The State Department and the Justice Department have
begun to take an interest in Malcolm's campaign to convince
African states to raise the question of persecution of American
Negroes at the United Nations. . . .

"Malcolm's eight-page memorandum to the heads of state at
the Cairo conference requesting their support became available
here only recently. After studying it, officials said that if Malcolm
succeeded in convincing just one African government to bring
up the charge at the United Nations, the United States government would be faced with a touchy problem.

"The United States, officials here believe, would find itself in
the same category as South Africa, Hungary and other coun-

tries whose domestic policies have become debating issues at the United Nations. The issue, officials say, would be of service to critics of the United States, Communist and non-Communist, and contribute to the undermining of the position the United States has asserted for itself as the leader of the West in the advocacy of human rights.

"In a letter from Cairo to a friend, Malcolm wrote:

"'I have gotten several promises of support in bringing our plight before the UN this year.'

"According to one diplomatic report, Malcolm had not met with success, but the report was not documented and officials here today conceded the possibility that Malcolm might have succeeded. . . .

"Although the State Department's interest in Malcolm's activities in Africa is obvious, that of the Justice Department is shrouded in discretion. Malcolm is regarded as an implacable leader with deep roots in the Negro submerged classes. At one point in the Harlem riots, the same people who booed Bayard Rustin and James Farmer of CORE shouted, 'We want Malcolm.'

"Malcolm's identification with the 'streets in Harlem' and his big following among Negro writers, actors, musicians and entertainers is well known. He has confided in friends that he has been under constant surveillance in New York by the Federal Bureau of Investigation and by the intelligence section of the New York Police Department. . . ."

Malcolm's proposal was not acted on at the United Nations session that began in the fall of 1964, partly because of the deadlock (over the "dues" question) that developed at that session and partly because of the lack of support for Malcolm's proposal by the major American civil-rights organizations.

But Malcolm's influence at the United Nations was seen in the sharp denunciations of American racial policy at home and abroad that were voiced by several African delegations in the

UN debate over the Congo in December, 1964. M.S. Handler in the *New York Times* of January 2, 1965, noted that Malcolm had been urging the Africans to employ "the racial situation in the United States as an instrument of attack in discussing international problems," because "such a strategy would give the African states more leverage in dealing with the United States and would in turn give American Negroes more leverage in American society." Handler continued:

"The spokesmen of some African states acted precisely within the framework of these recommendations last month in the Congo debate at the United Nations. They accused the United States of being indifferent to the fate of the blacks and cited as evidence the attitude of the United States government toward the civil-rights struggle in Mississippi.

"The African move profoundly disturbed the American authorities, who gave the impression that they had been caught off guard.

"However, early last August the State Department and Justice Department began to take an interest in Malcolm's activities in North Africa. . . ."

8

At the Audubon

When Malcolm X returned to the United States on November 24, 1964, he had spent a total of twenty-five weeks abroad during the year. This amounted to a little over half of the less than fifty weeks between his break with the Black Muslims and his death.

His return, a few weeks after the presidential election, coincided with the U.S. government's intervention in the Congolese civil war. This was the main subject of his first public meeting, a rally held on November 29 by the Organization of Afro-American Unity at the Audubon Ballroom in Harlem.

Altogether, in the period after the split with Muhammad, Malcolm spoke at approximately seventeen public Harlem rallies sponsored by the OAAU or the Muslim Mosque, Inc.; he was about to speak at another when he was murdered. For this book we were able to obtain the texts of two Audubon speeches (December 13 and December 20).

In Malcolm's December 13 speech, which this chapter contains, there is a reference to an exchange that had taken place at the November 29 meeting. Denouncing the government for financing the white mercenaries sent to the Congo, he had speculated on what would happen if the people of Harlem sent black mercenaries to fight the white mercenaries in the Congo: "In the paper tomorrow you're going to read that a whole lot of frantic, you know, statements were made. As long as there are white people going over there shooting black people, nothing is said—they glorify them. But when you and I start talking like we want to do the same thing to some of them, then we're 'fanatics,' we're 'bloodthirsty.'"

Soon after this, Malcolm called Harlem rent-strike leader Jesse Gray to the platform and introduced him in laudatory terms. Gray, speaking only two minutes, suggested that the place to send black mercenaries was Mississippi, and concluded: "It's always very easy for us to be ready to move and ready to talk and ready to act, but unless we truly get down into the heart of the ghetto and begin to deal with the problem of jobs, schools and the other basic questions, we are going to be unable to deal with any revolutionary perspective, or with any revolution for that matter."

Malcolm's response was: "Very good. That was our brother, Jesse Gray, the leader of the Harlem rent strike, and what he said is true. When I speak of some action for the Congo, that action also includes Congo, Mississippi. But the point and thing that I would like to impress upon every Afro-American leader is that there is no kind of action in this country ever going to bear fruit unless that action is tied in with the over-all international struggle. You waste your time when you talk to this man, just you and him. So when you talk to him, let him know your brother is behind you, and you've got some brothers behind that brother. That's the only way to talk to him, that's the only language he knows."

The December 13 rally began late because the featured speaker, Abdul Rahman Muhammad Babu, a member of the

Tanzanian government, was detained elsewhere. Malcolm opened the meeting only after getting a telephone message that Babu was on his way and would arrive in ten minutes. But Babu did not arrive for another hour or more, and Malcolm had to speak extemporaneously during that time, with the help provided by a newspaper clipping and by the entertainer, Dick Gregory.

Brothers and sisters: We're very happy to see so many of you out on such a foggy night. We hope that we haven't kept you too long, but a very good friend of mine, and a very good friend of yours, is on his way here and I didn't want to have too much to say in front of him. He's a person whose actions in the past have actually spoken for themselves. He's a master of revolution. We're living in a revolutionary world and in a revolutionary age, but you and I have never met a real dyed-in-the-wool black revolutionary before. So tonight we want to unveil one.

Also, I should explain that one of the reasons that the meeting started late was that we had a movie (right now I'm wrestling with this American mike), we had a movie that we wanted to show on the Congo, which I believe you would have enjoyed and would also have set the tone for what our guest will have to say when he arrives. Due to technical difficulties, which are to be expected in a highly technical society that's kind of running out of gas, we couldn't show the movie. But we will show it at a later date. (Either this microphone is 'way off or I'm getting weak.)

The purpose of our meeting tonight, as was announced, was to show the relationship between the struggle that is going on on the African continent and the struggle that's going on among the Afro-Americans here in this country. I, for one, would like to impress, especially upon those who call themselves leaders, the importance of realizing the direct connection between the struggle of the Afro-American in this country and the struggle of our people all over the world. As long as we think—as one of my good brothers mentioned out of the side of his mouth here a couple of Sundays ago—that we should get Mississippi straightened out before we worry about the Congo, you'll never get Mississippi straightened out. Not until you start realizing your connection with the Congo.

We have to realize what part our struggle has in the overall world struggle. Secondly, we need allies; and as long as you and I think that we can only get allies from the Bronx, or allies, you know, from up on the Grand Concourse, I mean where you don't live; as long as you and I think that's the only source or area from which we can get allies, our source of allies is limited. But when we realize how large this earth is and how many different people there are on it, and how closely they resemble us, then when we turn to them for some sort of help or aid or to form alliances, then we'll make a little faster progress.

Before our visitor gets here, I think it's important to show the importance of keeping an open mind. You'll be surprised how fast, how easy it is for someone to steal your and my mind. You don't think so? We never like to think in terms of being dumb enough to let someone put something over on us in a very deceitful and tricky way. But you and I are living in a very deceitful and tricky society, in a very deceitful and tricky country, which has a very deceitful and tricky government. *All* of them in it aren't tricky and deceitful, but *most* of them are. And any time you have a government in which *most* of them are deceitful and tricky, you have to be on guard at all times. You have to know how they work this deceit and how they work these tricks. Otherwise you'll find yourself in a bind.

One of the best ways to safeguard yourself from being deceived is always to form the habit of looking at things for yourself, listening to things for yourself, thinking for yourself, before you try and come to any judgment. Never base your impression of someone on what someone else has said. Or upon what someone else has written. Or upon what you read about someone that somebody else wrote. Never base your judgment on things like that. Especially in this kind of country and in this kind of society which has mastered the art of very deceitfully painting people whom they don't like in an image that they know you won't like. So you end up hating your friends and loving their enemies.

An example: I was flying from Algiers to Geneva about three or four weeks ago, and seated beside me on the airplane were a couple of Americans, both white, one a male and the other a female. One was an interpreter who worked in Geneva for the United Nations, the other was a girl who worked in one of the embassies in some part of Algeria. We conversed for about forty or forty-five minutes and then the lady, who had been looking at my briefcase, said, "May I ask you a personal question?" And I said, "Yes." Because they always do anyway. She said, "What kind of last name do you have that begins with X?" I said, "That's it, X." So she said, "X?" "Yes." "Well, what is your first name?" I said, "Malcolm." So she waited for about ten minutes and then she said, "You're not *Malcolm* X." And I said, "Yes, I'm Malcolm X. Why, what's the matter?" And she said, "Well, you're not what I was looking for."

What she was looking for was what the newspapers, the press, had created. She was looking for the image that the press had created. Somebody with some horns, you know, about to kill all the white people—as if he could kill all of them, or as if he shouldn't. She was looking for someone who was a rabble-rouser, who couldn't even converse with people with blue eyes, you know, someone who was irrational, and things of that sort. I take time to point this out, because it shows how skilfully someone can take a newspaper and build an image of someone so that before you even meet them, you'll run. You don't even want to hear what they have to say, you don't even know them, all you know is what the *press* has had to say, and the press is white. And when I say the press is white, I mean it is *white*. And it's dangerous.

The FBI can feed information to the press to make your neighbor think you're something subversive. The FBI—they do it very skilfully, they maneuver the press on a national scale; and the CIA maneuvers the press on an international scale. They do all their dirt with the press. They take the newspapers and make the newspapers blow you and me up as if all of us are criminals, all of us are racists, all of us are drug addicts, or all of us are rioting. This is how they do it. When you explode legitimately against the injustices that have been heaped upon you, they use the press to make it look like you're a vandal. If you were a vandal, you have a right to be a vandal.

They master this imagery, this image-making. They give you the image of an extremist, and from then on anything you do is extreme. You can pull a baby out of the water and save it from drowning—you're still an extremist, because they projected this image of you. They can create an image of you as a subversive and you can go out and die fighting for the United States—you're still subversive, because the press has made you a subversive. They can paint the image of you as someone irresponsible, and you can come up with the best program that will save the black man from the oppression of the white man and—When I say oppression, that's where oppression comes from, the white man. There are some oppressive black people, but they're only doing what the white man has taught them.

When I say that, I'm not blanketly condemning all whites. All of them don't oppress. All of them aren't in a position to. But most of them are, and most of them do. The press is so powerful in its image-making role, it can make a criminal look like he's the victim and make the victim look like he's the criminal. This is the press, an irresponsible press. It will make the criminal look like he's the victim and make the victim look like he's the criminal. If you aren't careful, the newspapers will have you hating the people who are being oppressed and loving the people who are doing the oppressing.

If you aren't careful, because I've seen some of you get caught in that bag, you run away hating yourself and loving the man—while you are catching hell from the man. You let the man maneuver you into thinking that it's wrong to fight him when he's fighting you. He's fighting you in the morning, fighting you in the noon, fighting you at night and fighting you all in between, and you still think it's wrong to fight him back. Why? The press. The newspapers make you look wrong. As long as you take a beating, you're all right. As long as you get your head busted, you're all right. As long as you let his dogs fight you, you're all right. Because that's the press. That's the image-making press. That thing is dangerous if you don't guard yourself against it. It'll make you love the criminal, as I say, and make you hate the one who's the victim of the criminal.

A good example of what the press can do with its images is the Congo, the area of Africa that our guest, that's on his way, is going to talk to us about tonight. Right now, in the Congo, defenseless villages are being bombed, black women and children and babies are being blown to bits by airplanes. Where do these airplanes come from? The United States, the U-n-i-t-e-d S-t-a-t-e-s. Yes, and you won't write that. You won't write that American planes are blowing the flesh from the bodies of black women and black babies and black men. No. Why? Because they're American planes. As long as they're American planes, that's humanitarian. As long as they're being piloted by anti-Castro Cubans, that makes it all right. Because Castro's a villain, and anybody who's against him, whatever they do, that's humanitarian. You see how tricky they are? American planes, anti-Castro Cuban pilots, dropping bombs on African villages that have no defense against bombs, and blowing black women to bits. When you drop a bomb, you don't look to see where it explodes.

They're doing the same thing as when they dropped it on the Japanese at Hiroshima. They don't even *think* about dropping it on Congolese. And you, running around here getting all upset because a few white hostages die, you're out of your minds, out of your minds. They take the press with their ability to control you with image-making, and they make mass murder, cold-blooded murder, look like a humanitarian project. All these thousands of black people dying, butchered, and you have no compassion in your hearts whatsoever for them, because the victim has been made to look like he's the criminal and the criminal has been made to look like he's the victim. Why, you and I should go on a rampage. I mean on a rampage—intelligently.

Let's just take it one step farther before our guest arrives, to show you how they use this image-making through the press. I'm not condemning the whole press, because some of them are all right; but most of them aren't. Take Tshombe, there's a man that you should never let set foot in America. That man is the worst African that was ever born. He's a cold-blooded murderer. He murdered Patrice Lumumba, the rightful prime minister of the Congo. And what happened there at the time? They used their press to give Tshombe a good image. Yes, the American press. They take this man who's a murderer, a cold-blooded murderer—didn't murder just somebody, murdered the prime minister—and they go and use their press to make this man acceptable to the world.

He'll never be acceptable to the world. The world is not that dumb, not that easily fooled. Now, some of us in this country may be dumb, but not all of us, just some of us. And those that haven't been fooled will do whatever is necessary to keep that man from setting foot on this continent. He should be afraid to come here. He should think a long time before he comes here. Why? Because they told you and me we came from the Congo. Isn't that what they told you? I mean, isn't that what they taught us in school? So we came from the Congo. We're savages and cannibals and all that kind of stuff from the Congo; they've been teaching me all my life I'm from the Congo. I love the Congo. That's my country. And that's my people that your airplanes are killing over there.

They take Tshombe and they prop him up with American dollars. They glorify his image with the American press. What's the first thing he does? Now, Tshombe's a murderer, he has been hired by the United States to rule the Congo. Yes, that's all it boils down to. You can put it in a whole lot of pretty language, but we don't want pretty language for a nasty situation. He's a murderer, who has been hired by the United States government and is being paid with your tax dollars by the United States government.

And to show you what his thinking is—a hired killer—what's the first thing he did? He hired more killers. He went out and got the mercenaries from South Africa. And what is a mercenary? A hired killer. That's all a mercenary is. The anti-Castro Cuban pilots, what are they? Mercenaries, hired killers. Who hired them? The United States. Who hired the killers from South Africa? The United States; they just used Tshombe to do it. Just like they do with us in this country. They get a Negro and hire him and make him a big shot—so he's a voice of the community—and then he tells all of them to come on in and join the organization with us, and they take it over. Then they give him peace prizes and medals and things. They will probably give Tshombe the peace prize next year for the work that he's doing. I expect them to, he'll be the Nobel Peace Prize winner next year. Because he's doing a good job. But for who? For the man.

So these mercenaries come in, and again, what makes these mercenaries acceptable? The press. The press doesn't refer to them as hired killers. The press doesn't refer to them as murderers. The press refers to the brothers in Stanleyville, who are defending their country, as rebels, savages, cannibals. You know, brothers, the press has a grave responsibility, and it also has the responsibility sometimes as an accessory. Because if it allows itself to be used to make criminals look like victims and victims look like criminals, then the press is an accessory to the same crime. They are permitting themselves to be used as a weapon in the hands of those that are actually guilty.

I cite this tonight, before our guest comes—and I was told ten minutes ago that he should be here in ten minutes—I cite this to show you that, just as they do it on an international level, they also do it with us. Anytime black people in this country are not able to be controlled by the man, the press immediately begins to label those black people as irresponsible or as extremists. They put all these old negative labels up there, and you and I do the same thing—we draw back from it. Not because we know anything about them. But we draw back because of the image of them that the man has created. And if you notice everyone who takes a firm, uncompromising stand against the man—

When I say the man, you know what I'm talking about. I'm talking about the man that lynches, the man that segregates, the man that discriminates, the man that oppresses and exploits, the man that won't let you and me have quality education facilities here in Harlem. That man, whoever he is, that's who I'm talking about. I have to talk about him like this, because if I talk about him any closer, they'll call me a racist. And I'm not a racist. I'm not against somebody because of their race, but I'm sure against them because of what they're doing; and if they're doing wrong, we should stop them, and by any means necessary.

If you'll notice, as long as the blacks in the Congo were being slaughtered on a mass scale, there was no outcry. But as soon as the lives of a few whites were involved, the whole world became in an uproar. What caused the world to become involved in an uproar? The press. The press made it appear that 2,000 white people are being held hostage. And they started crying in big headlines if any of them were killed. Now the Africans didn't kill any of them, the brothers there in Stanleyville didn't kill any of them until the paratroopers landed. If the paratroopers hadn't invaded their property, nobody would have been killed. They hadn't killed them up to that point. And many people say it wasn't the brothers in Stanleyville that killed them; the paratroopers and mercenaries started shooting at everybody.

You think I'm spoofing? I was in London last Sunday, and in the [December 3] *Daily Express* a white writer—I must say white, because if I don't specify that it is a white man writing this, you'd think that I wrote it, or some black man wrote it. Look what he says here in the *Daily Express,* which is a far from left newspaper, far from liberal. It's written by Walter Partington from Stanleyville. Just after the paratroopers had dropped, he says, there was "a dusk strike by cannon-firing T-28s flown by Cuban mercenaries"—these are airplanes, flown by Cuban mercenaries; think of it, hired killers from Cuba. Hired by whom? The Americans. All of you living in our country are going to pay for the sins that it has committed.

They "blew up the rebels' warehouse headquarters and killed the mortar crew . . . yet more Chinese-made mortar shells are still arriving." See, they throw this Chinese thing in there to make you prejudiced. They don't know whether they're Chinese mortars, but this is how the press does it. It always has words to justify their destruction of the people they're destroying. "At 7 a.m. troops with Belgian mercenary armor and the Congo Army's 'Diablos' (Black Devils) paratroops roared into the gunpowder-keg native city of Belge. The troops spotted rebels preparing to open fire from a house"—now, pick up on this—"and smashed their way in, battering down doors and dragging out men, women and children." Now, there weren't rebels in the house, these were just black Congolese in the house. And to justify going in and dragging them out and murdering them on the spot, they've got to call them rebels.

This is the kind of operation that's going on in the Congo, and you don't hear these Negro leaders saying anything about it. I know you don't like me to use the word *Negro,* but when I use it, that's what I'm talking about, knee-grow leaders—because that's what they are. These aren't Afro-American leaders, these are Negro leaders. N-E-G-R, capital O.

"A Belgian colonel snatched the camera from *Express*

photographer Reginald Lancaster and said: 'You are both under house arrest and we will deport you on the next plane.'" Why didn't they want pictures taken? They didn't want pictures taken of what they were doing. "The column moved on and by noon 10,000 men, women and children were crushed neck to neck under a blazing sun and ringed by Congo Army troops armed with tommy guns. To protect them from the trigger-happy Congo Army there were white bandages around 10,000 heads. For this is a black and white city." Think about this: "Anyone without the bandage is usually shot." The bandage distinguishes those already screened or about to be given the treatment, and there are mounds of dead bodies everywhere to indicate those found wanting. Meaning, any Congolese without the bandage around his head was shot on sight, indiscriminately. And this is being written by a white reporter who is not pro-Congolese at all—he's just telling the story as it actually is. Mass murder, wholesale murder of black people by the white people who are using some black mercenaries. . . .

"I saw one mercenary . . . gun down four Congolese who burst out of the bush near the airport as I landed. They may or may not have been Simbas. All died. Yet men like Lieutenant John Peters from Wightman Road, Harringay, London, are capable of strong compassion. Today two starving dogs seized No. 7 Commandos' pet Nigger, a little black kid goat."

This white mercenary had a little black goat that he named "Nigger." That's what they do, anything black they name it nigger. They named you nigger, didn't they? I see one coming right now. Here comes my nigger, Dick Gregory. Say, Dick, come on up here. We're going to get Dick investigated. I heard Dick on the Les Crane Show the other night talking about niggers. Say, Dick, look what it says here, here's my name, just look at it [holding up a copy of Gregory's book, *Nigger*]. Come on, I'm going to get him investigated. Get him, brother, don't let him get away. He's going to lose all his jobs now. You won't get another booking—you'll have to work in Harlem the rest of your life.

Look what it says: "Today, two starving dogs seized No. 7 Commandos' pet Nigger, a little black kid goat. When we got there, Nigger was dying and John Peters shot him. He turned away and covered his eyes." Here's a white mercenary that has been killing so many Congolese they had to stop him up; with no compassion at all, he shot them down. But as soon as his little black goat was bitten by some dogs, he cried. He had more feeling—this is a white man, an Englishman—had more feeling in his heart for a dead goat that was black than he had for all those stacks and stacks and stacks of Congolese who looked just like you and me and Dick Gregory.

So I say, brothers and sisters, it's not a case of worrying about what's going on in Africa before we get things straight over here. It's a case of realizing that the Afro-American problem is not a Negro problem, or an American problem, but a human problem, a problem for humanity. When you realize that, when you look at your and my problem in the context of the entire world and see that it is a world problem, and that there are other people on this earth who look just like you do who also have the same problem, then you and I become allies and we can put forth our efforts in a way to get the best results.

As I announced earlier, Dick, I told them that a friend of mine from Africa who is a real dyed-in-the-wool human revolutionary was on his way here. Then you walked in; they thought I was talking about you. Well, Dick wasn't the one I was talking about, but Dick is a revolutionary.

And Dick is a dyed-in-the-wool African; he doesn't want to be, but he is. I don't mean dyed-in-the-wool, I mean African. Dick is one of the foremost freedom fighters in this country. I say that in all sincerity. Dick has been on the battlefront and has made great sacrifices by taking the stand that he has. I'm quite certain that it has alienated many of the people who weren't alienated from him before he began to take this stand. Whenever you see a person, a celebrity, who is as widely known and as skilled in his profession as Dick, and at the same time has access to almost unlimited bookings which provide unlimited income, and he will jeopardize all of that in order to jump into the frontlines of the battle, then you and I will have to stand behind him. I want Dick also to hear our brother who's coming, but before he gets here, I think Dick had better talk to us. Come on, Dick. Dick Gregory—without the cigarette.

[*Dick Gregory speaks.*]

I'm very thankful that Dick has been able to come out with us tonight. As I said, he is a freedom fighter, you see him on the forefront of the battlelines. And in this country, wherever a black man is, there is a battleline. Whether it's in the North, South, East or West, you and I are living in a country that is a battleline for all of us. And tonight, I'm more than honored with the presence of a person who has been credited with being responsible for correcting the governmental system in an area of this earth where the system wasn't so good prior to the efforts put forth by him.

Many of you have heard of the island called Zanzibar. Zanzibar was famous for its headquarters as a slave-trading post; in fact, many of us probably passed through there on our way to America 400 years ago. And it was on this island some time last year, I think it was, that the government was overturned when the African element on the island got fed up with the situation that existed. Overnight they did what was necessary to bring about a change. So today Zanzibar is free. And as soon as it got its freedom, it got together with Tanganyika, where President Nyerere is. And the combination of Zanzibar and Tanganyika recently became known as the Republic of Tanzania: two countries that united and are one of the most militant and uncompromising when it comes to the struggle for freedom for our people on the African continent, as well as over here and anywhere else on this earth.

Most of you know that my purpose for going to Cairo for the summit conference was to try and get the heads of the African states to realize that they had 22 million brothers and sisters here in America who were catching hell; and that they could put forth a great effort and give us a boost, if they would let the world know that they were on our side and with us in our struggle against this racism that we've been victimized by in this country for so long. The press tried to make it appear that the African countries, the African heads of state, were in no way concerned with the plight of the Afro-American. But at that conference, toward the end of it, all of the African heads of state got together, and they did pass a resolution thoroughly condemning the continued practice of racism against the Afro-Americans in this country and thoroughly supporting the struggle of the 22 million Afro-Americans in this country for human rights.

And I'm proud to state that the one who was responsible for bringing that resolution forth and getting it agreed upon by the other African heads of state was probably the last one that you and I would expect to do it, because of the image that he's been given in this country. But the one who came forth and suggested that the African summit conference pass a resolution thoroughly condemning the mistreatment of Afro-Americans in America and also thoroughly supporting the freedom struggle for human rights of our people in this country was President Julius Nyerere.

I was honored to spend three hours with him, when I was in Dar es Salaam and Tanganyika, shortly before it became known as Tanzania, for about seven days. The one who made it possible for me to see him is with us here tonight.

When the revolution took place on Zanzibar, you and I read about it in this country. They tried to make it appear that it was something that was Chinese or Soviet, or anything but what it was. They tried again to build that image that would make you and me react to it negatively. And the one the Western press said was the guiding hand behind that successful revolution is with us on the platform tonight. I have the greatest honor to introduce to you at this time the minister of cooperatives and commerce from Tanzania, a man who is very closely associated with President Julius Nyerere, the one who was responsible for bringing freedom to the people on the island of Zanzibar and linking themselves up with Tanganyika and developing it into the Republic of Tanzania. He's known as Sheik Abdul Rahman Muhammad Babu.

And before he comes forth: He's just left a dinner with another very good friend of ours, and I say a very good friend of ours. I want to point this out to you, I don't let anybody choose my friends. And you shouldn't let anybody choose your friends. You and I should practice the habit of weighing people and weighing situations and weighing groups and weighing governments for ourselves. And don't let somebody else tell us who our enemies should be and who our friends should be.

I love a revolutionary. And one of the most revolutionary men in this country right now was going to come out here along with our friend, Sheik Babu, but he thought better of it. But he did send this message. It says:

"Dear brothers and sisters of Harlem, I would have liked to have been with you and Brother Babu, but the actual conditions are not good for this meeting. Receive the warm salutations of the Cuban people and especially those of Fidel, who remembers enthusiastically his visit to Harlem a few years ago. United we will win." This is from Che Guevara.

I'm happy to hear your warm round of applause in return, because it lets the man know that he's just not in a position today to tell us who we should applaud for and who we shouldn't applaud for. And you don't see any anti-Castro Cubans around here—we eat them up.

Let them go and fight the Ku Klux Klan, or the White Citizens Council. Let them spend some of that energy getting their own house in order. Don't come up to Harlem and tell us who we should applaud for and shouldn't applaud for. Or there will be some ex-anti-Castro Cubans.

So, brothers and sisters, again at this time, a very good friend of mine. I'm honored to call him my friend. He treated me as a brother when I was in Dar es Salaam. I met his family, I met his children—he's a family man. Most people don't think of revolutionaries as family men. All you see him in is his image on the battleline. But when you see him with his children and with his wife and that atmosphere at home, you realize that revolutionaries are human beings too. So here is a man who's not only a revolutionary, but he's a husband—he could be yours; he's a father—he could be yours; he's a brother—he could be yours. And I say he is ours. Sheik Babu.

[*Babu speaks.*]

Brothers and sisters, we're going to dismiss in five

minutes. We want to thank His Excellency, Abdul Rahman Muhammad Babu, for taking the time to come up this evening to give us a good clear picture of how our people back home feel about us. It is very important, as he pointed out—please give us five minutes before you go, we'll let you go in five minutes—it's very important for you and me to realize that our people on the African continent are genuinely interested and concerned with the troubles of our people on this continent. It is important that we know that, and then our battle strategy, our plan of battle, will be much different. As long as we think we're over here in America isolated and all by ourselves and underdogs, then we'll always have that hat-in-hand begging attitude that the man loves to see us display. But when we know that all of our people are behind us—as he said, almost 500 million of us—we don't need to beg anybody. All we need to do is remind them what they did to us; that it's time for them to stop; that if they don't stop, we will stop them. Yes, we will stop them.

You may say, "Well, how in the hell are we going to stop them? A great big man like this?" Brothers and sisters, always remember this. When you're inside another man's house, and the furniture is his, curtains, all those fine decorations, there isn't too much action he can put down in there without messing up his furniture and his windows and his house. And you let him know that when he puts his hands on you, it's not only you he puts his hands on, it's his whole house, you'll burn it down. You're in a position to—you have nothing to lose. Then the man will act right. He won't act right because he loves you or because he thinks you will, you know, not act right. He will only act right when you let him know that you know he has more to lose than you have. You haven't anything to lose but discrimination and segregation.

[*Malcolm announced the time and place of two meetings where Babu would speak, and invited him to return to the next OAAU rally; introduced "my spiritual father," Sheik Ahmud Hassoum; announced a dance celebrating African independence; announced a rally supporting the Mississippi Freedom Democratic Party's campaign to unseat racist congressmen; asked "two brothers from Tanzania" to stand and take a bow; promised soon to show movies he had taken in Africa; and concluded:*]

Next Sunday night, and we will start on time next Sunday night and end on time and we want all of you to be sure and be out, we're going deeper into the Congo question. The Organization of Afro-American Unity intends to spell out its own program in regards to how we feel we can best take advantage of the political potential of the black man in this country and also how we can work with other groups to make sure that quality education is returned to Harlem.

Also, I believe, brothers and sisters, and I say with all my heart, we should start a defense fund in Harlem. We should start a fund in Harlem so that we can offer a reward for whoever gets the head of that sheriff in Mississippi who murdered those civil-rights workers in cold blood. You may think I'm out of my mind. Anytime you have a government that will allow the sheriff, not only one sheriff but some sheriffs and their deputies, to kill in cold blood men who are doing nothing other than trying to ascertain the rights for people who have been denied their rights, and these workers are murdered, and the FBI comes up with all of that pretty-sounding language, like they're going to arrest them and then do nothing but turn them loose—why, then it's time for you and me to let them know that if the federal government can't deal with the Klan, then you and I can deal with the Klan. This is the only way you are going to stop it.

The only way you're going to stop the Ku Klux Klan is stop it yourself. As Dick Gregory said, the government can't stop it because the government has infiltrated the Klan and it has infiltrated the government. You and I have got to stop it ourselves. So let's put a reward on the head of that sheriff, a reward, a dollar, for whoever gets to him first. I know what they're going to do—if something happens, they're going to blame me for it. I'll take the blame.

9

With Mrs. Fannie Lou Hamer

In December, 1964, representatives of the Mississippi Freedom Democratic Party toured Northern cities seeking moral, political and financial support for their campaign to block the seating of Mississippi's five segregationist U.S. representatives when Congress convened on January 4, 1965.

In Harlem, an ad hoc committee supporting the Freedom Democratic Party campaign organized a rally on December 20, 1964. The chief speaker was Mrs. Fannie Lou Hamer, MFDP candidate for Congress, whose personal testimony about racist brutality had attracted wide attention at the Democratic Party national convention in August, 1964. The meeting was held at the Williams Institutional CME Church in Harlem, with the audience about one-third white.

Malcolm X spoke too, after Mrs. Hamer's moving address and after the Student Nonviolent Coordinating Committee's Freedom Singers had presented various songs, including "Oginga Odinga of Kenya."

Rev. [Joseph] Coles [Jr.], Mrs. Hamer, honored guests, brothers and sisters, friends and enemies; also ABC and CBS and FBI and CIA:

I couldn't help but be very impressed at the outstart when the Freedom Singers were singing the song "Oginga Odinga" because Oginga Odinga is one of the foremost freedom fighters on the African continent. At the time he visited in Atlanta, Georgia, I think he was then the minister of home affairs in Kenya. But since Kenya became a republic last week, and Jomo Kenyatta ceased being the prime minister and became the president, the same person you are singing about, Oginga Odinga, is now Kenyatta's vice president. He's the number-two man in the Kenya government.

The fact that you would be singing about him, to me is quite significant. Two or three years ago, this wouldn't have been done. Two or three years ago, most of our people would choose to sing about someone who was, you know, passive and meek and humble and forgiving. Oginga Odinga is not passive. He's not meek. He's not humble. He's not nonviolent. But he's free.

Oginga Odinga is vice president under Jomo Kenyatta, and Jomo Kenyatta was considered to be the organizer of the Mau Mau; I think you mentioned the Mau Mau in that song. And if you analyze closely those words, I think you'll have the key to how to straighten the situation out in Mississippi. When the nations of Africa are truly independent—and they *will* be truly independent because they're going about it in the right way—the historians will give Prime Minister, or rather, President Kenyatta and the Mau Mau their rightful role in African history. They'll go down as the greatest African patriots and freedom fighters that that continent ever knew, and they will be given credit for bringing about the independence of many of the existing independent states on that continent right now. There was a time when their image was negative, but today they're looked upon with respect and their chief is the president and their next chief is the vice president.

I have to take time to mention that because, in my opinion, not only in Mississippi and Alabama, but right here in New York City, you and I can best learn how to get real freedom by studying how Kenyatta brought it to his people in Kenya, and how Odinga helped him, and the excellent job that was done by the Mau Mau freedom fighters. In fact, that's what we need in Mississippi. In Mississippi we need a Mau Mau. In Alabama we need a Mau Mau. In Georgia we need a Mau Mau. Right here in Harlem, in New York City, we need a Mau Mau.

I say it with no anger; I say it with very careful forethought. The language that you and I have been speaking to this man in the past hasn't reached him. And you can never really get your point across to a person until you learn how to communicate with him. If he speaks French, you can't speak German. You have to know what language he speaks and then speak to him in that language.

When I listen to Mrs. Hamer, a black woman—could be my mother, my sister, my daughter—describe what they had done to her in Mississippi, I ask myself how in the world can we ever expect to be respected as *men* when we will allow something like that to be done to our women, and we do nothing about it? How can you and I be looked upon as men with black women being beaten and nothing being done about it, black children and black babies being beaten and nothing being done about it? No, we don't deserve to be recognized and respected as men as long as our women can be brutalized in the manner that this woman described, and nothing being done about it, but we sit around singing "We Shall Overcome."

We *need* a Mau Mau. If they don't want to deal with the Mississippi Freedom Democratic Party, then we'll give them something else to deal with. If they don't want to deal with the Student Nonviolent Committee, then we have to give them an alternative. Never stick someone out there without an alternative. [Or] we waste our time. Give them this or give them that. Give them the choice between this or that.

When I was in Africa, I noticed some of the Africans got their freedom faster than others. Some areas of the African continent became independent faster than other areas. I noticed that in the areas where independence had been gotten, someone got angry. And in the areas where independence had not been achieved yet, no one was angry. They were sad—they'd sit around and talk about their plight, but they weren't mad. And usually, when people are sad, they don't do anything. They just cry over their condition.

But when they get angry, they bring about a change. When they get angry, they aren't interested in logic, they aren't interested in odds, they aren't interested in consequences. When they get angry, they realize the condition that they're in—that their suffering is unjust, immoral, illegal, and that anything they do to correct it or eliminate it, they're justified. When you and I develop that type of anger and speak in that voice, then we'll get some kind of respect and recognition, and some changes from these people who have been promising us falsely already for far too long.

So you have to speak their language. The language that they were speaking to Mrs. Hamer was the language of brutality. Beasts, they were, beating her—The two Negroes, they weren't at fault. They were just puppets. You don't blame the puppet, you blame the puppeteer. They were just carrying out someone else's orders. They were under someone else's jurisdiction. They weren't at fault; in a way they were, but I *still* won't blame them. I put the blame on that man who gave the orders. And when you and I begin to look at him and see the language he speaks, the language of a brute, the language of someone who has no sense of morality, who absolutely ignores law—when you and I learn how to speak his language, then we can communicate. But we will never communicate talking one language while he's talking another language. He's talking the language of violence while you and I are running around with this little chicken-picking type of language— and think that he's going to understand.

Let's learn his language. If his language is with a shotgun, get a shotgun. Yes, I said if he only understands the language of a rifle, get a rifle. If he only understands the language of a rope, get a rope. But don't waste time talking the wrong language to a man if you want to really communicate with him. Speak his language—there's nothing wrong with that. If something was wrong with that language, the federal government would have stopped the cracker from speaking it to you and me.

I might say, secondly, some people wonder, well, what has Mississippi got to do with Harlem? It isn't actually Mississippi; it's America. America is Mississippi. There's no such thing as a Mason-Dixon Line—it's America. There's no such thing as the South—it's America. If one room in your house is dirty, you've got a dirty house. If the closet is dirty, you've got a dirty house. Don't say that that room is dirty but the rest of my house is clean. You're over the whole house. You have authority over the whole house; the entire house is under your jurisdiction. And the mistake that you and I make is letting these *Northern* crackers shift the weight to the Southern crackers.

The senator from Mississippi is over the Judiciary Committee. He's in Washington, D.C., as Mrs. Hamer has pointed out, illegally. Every senator from a state where our people are deprived of the right to vote—they're in Washington, D.C., illegally. This country is a country whose governmental system is run by committees—House committees and Senate committees. The committee chairman occupies that position by dint of his seniority. Eastland is over the Judiciary Committee because he has more seniority than any other senator after the same post or on that committee; he's the chairman. Fulbright, another cracker, from Arkansas, is over the Foreign Relations Committee. Ellender, of Louisiana, is over the Agriculture and Forestry Committee. Russell, of Georgia, is over the Armed Services Committee.

And it goes right on down the line. Out of sixteen committees, ten of them are in the hands of Southern racists. Out of twenty congressional committees, thirteen are in the hands, or at least they were before the recent elections, in the hands of Southern racists. Out of forty-six committees that govern the foreign and domestic direction of this country, twenty-three are in the hands of Southern racists. And the reason they're in the hands of Southern racists is because in the areas from which they come, the black man is deprived of his right to vote. If we had the ballot in that area, those racists would not be in Washington, D.C. There'd be some black faces there, there'd be some brown and some yellow and some red faces there. There'd be some faces other than those cracker faces that are there right now.

So, what happens in Mississippi and the South has a direct bearing on what happens to you and me here in Harlem. Likewise, the Democratic Party, which black people supported recently, I think, something like 97 per cent.

All of these crackers—and that's what they are, crackers—they belong to the Democratic Party. That's the party they belong to—the same one you belong to, the same one you support, the same one you say is going to get you this and get you that. Why, the base of the Democratic Party is in the South. The *foundation* of its authority is in the South. The head of the Democratic Party is sitting in the White House. He could have gotten Mrs. Hamer into Atlantic City. He could have opened up his mouth and had her seated. Hubert Humphrey could have opened his mouth and had her seated. Wagner, the mayor right here, could have opened up his mouth and used his weight and had her seated. Don't be talking about some crackers down in Mississippi and Alabama and Georgia—all of them are playing the same game. Lyndon B. Johnson is the head of the Cracker Party.

Now, I don't want to be stepping on toes or saying things that you didn't think I was going to say, but don't ever, ever, ever call me up here to talk about Mississippi. It's controlled right up here from the North. Mississippi is controlled from the North. Alabama is controlled from the North. These Northern crackers are in cahoots with the Southern crackers, only these Northern crackers smile in your face and show you their teeth and they stick the knife in your back when you turn around. You at least know what that man down there is doing and you know how to deal with him.

So all I say is this, this is all I say: when you start talking about one, talk about the others. When you start worrying about the part or the piece, worry about the whole. And if this piece is no good, the entire pie is no good, because it all comes out of the same plate. It's made up out of the same ingredients. Wagner is a Democrat. He belongs to the same party as Eastland. Johnson is a Democrat. He belongs to the same party as Eastland. Wagner was in Atlantic City, Ray Jones was in Atlantic City, Lyndon B. Johnson was in Atlantic City, Hubert Humphrey was in Atlantic City—the crackers that you voted for were in Atlantic City. What did they do for you when you wanted to sit down? They were quiet. They were silent. They said, "Don't rock the boat, you might get Goldwater elected. . . ."

I have this bit of suggestion. Find out what Wagner is going to do in behalf of this resolution, that you're trying to get through, before January 4. Find out in advance where does he stand on these Mississippi congressmen who are illegally coming up from the South to represent Democrats. Find out where the mayor of this city stands and make him come out on the record without dilly-dallying and without compromise. Find out where his friends stand on seating the Mississippians who are coming forth illegally. Find out where Ray Jones, who is one of the most powerful black Democrats in this city—find out where he stands. Before January 4. You can't talk about Rockefeller because he's a Republican. Although he's in the same boat right along with the rest of them.

So I say, in my conclusion, as Mrs. Hamer pointed out, the brothers and sisters in Mississippi are being beaten and killed for no reason other than they want to be treated as first-class citizens. There's only one way to be a first-class citizen. There's only one way to be independent. There's only one way to be free. It's not something that someone gives to you. It's something that you take. Nobody can give you independence. Nobody can give you freedom. Nobody can give you equality or justice or anything. If you're a man, you take it. If you can't take it, you don't deserve it. Nobody can give it to you. So if you and I want freedom, if we want independence, if we want respect, if we want recognition, we obey the law, we are peaceful—but at the same time, at any moment that you and I are involved in any kind of action that is legal, that is in accord with our civil rights, in accord with the courts of this land, in accord with the Constitution—when all of these things are on our side, and we still can't get it, it's because we aren't on our own side.

We don't yet realize the real price necessary to pay to see that these things are enforced where we're concerned. And until we realize this, they won't be enforced where we're concerned. We have to let the people in Mississippi as well as in Mississippi, New York, and elsewhere know that freedom comes to us either by ballots or by bullets. That's the only way freedom is gotten. Freedom is gotten by ballots or bullets. These are the only two avenues, the only two roads, the only two methods, the only two means— either ballots or bullets. And when you know that, then you are careful how you use the word *freedom*. As long as you think we are going to sing up on some, you come in and sing. I watch you, those of you who are singing—are you also willing to do some swinging?

They've always said that I'm anti-white. I'm for anybody who's for freedom. I'm for anybody who's for justice. I'm for anybody who's for equality. I'm not for anybody who tells me to sit around and wait for mine. I'm not for anybody who tells me to turn the other cheek when a cracker is busting up my jaw. I'm not for anybody who tells black people to be nonviolent while nobody is telling white people to be nonviolent. I know I'm in the church, I probably shouldn't be talking like this—but Jesus himself was ready to turn the synagogue inside out and upside down when things weren't going right. In fact, in the Book of Revelations, they've got Jesus sitting on a horse with a sword in his hand, getting ready to go into action. But they don't tell you or me about that Jesus. They only tell you and me about that peaceful Jesus. They never let you get down to the end of the book. They keep you up there where everything is, you know, nonviolent. No, go and read the whole book, and when you get to Revelations, you'll find that even Jesus' patience ran out. And when his patience ran out, he got the whole situation straightened out. He picked up the sword.

I believe that there are some white people who might be sincere. But I think they should prove it. And you can't prove it to me by singing with me. You can't prove it to me by being nonviolent. No, you can prove it by recognizing the law of justice. And the law of justice is "as ye sow, so shall ye reap." The law of justice is "he who kills by the sword shall be killed by the sword." This is justice. Now if you are with us, all I say is, make the same kind of contribution with us in our struggle for freedom that all white people have always made when they were struggling for their own freedom. You were struggling for your freedom in the Revolutionary War. Your own Patrick Henry said "liberty or death," and George Washington got the cannons out, and all the rest of them that you taught me to worship as my heroes, they were fighters, they were warriors.

But now when the time comes for our freedom, you want to reach back in the bag and grab somebody who's nonviolent and peaceful and forgiving and long-suffering. I don't go for that—no. I say that a black man's freedom is as valuable as a white man's freedom. And I say that a black man has the right to do whatever is necessary to get his freedom that other human beings have done to get their freedom. I say that you and I will never get our freedom nonviolently and patiently and lovingly. We will never get it until we let the world know that as other human beings have laid down their lives for freedom—and also taken life for freedom—that you and I are ready and willing and equipped and qualified to do the same thing.

It's a shame that Mrs. Hamer came out here this afternoon where there are so few people. It's a shame. All of our people in Harlem should have heard her describe what they did to her down there. Because I think the people in Harlem are more capable of evening the score than people are anywhere else in this country. Yes, they are, and they need to hear her story. They need to know more, first hand, about what's happening down there, especially to our women. And then they need some lessons in tactics and strategy on how to get even. I, for one, will make the first contribution to any fund that's raised for the purpose of evening the score. Whenever someone commits murder, what do you do? You put out a "reward, wanted—dead or alive" for the murderer. Yes, learn how to do it. We've had three people murdered. No reward has been put on the head of the murderer. Don't just put a reward—put "dead or alive, dead or alive." And let that Klan know that we can do it tit for tat, tit for tat. What's good for the goose is good for the gander.

And if you all don't want to do it, we'll do it. We'll do it. We have brothers who are equipped, and who are qualified, and who are willing to—As Jesus said, "Little children, go thee where I send thee." We have brothers who can do that, and who will do that, and who are ready to do that. And I say that if the government of the United States cannot bring to justice people who murder Negroes, or people who murder those who are at the forefront fighting in behalf of Negroes, then it's time for you and me to retire quietly to our closets and devise means and methods of seeing that justice is executed against murderers where justice has not been forthcoming in the past.

I say in my conclusion that if you and I here in Harlem,

who form the habit ofttimes of fighting each other, who sneak around trying to wait for an opportunity to throw some acid or some lye on each other, or sprinkle dust on each other's doorsteps—if you and I were really and truly for the freedom of our people, we wouldn't waste all of that energy thinking how to do harm to each other. Since you have that ingenuity, if you know how to do it, let me know; I'll give you some money and show you where to go, and show you who to do it to. And then you'll go down in history as having done an honorable thing.

So, Mrs. Hamer, we have another rally up at the Audubon tonight, at eight o'clock, where there'll be a lot of black people. I myself would like to have you tell them what you told us here this afternoon, so you are welcome to be my guest tonight if you will, at the Audubon. And those singers who sing about Oginga Odinga, if you haven't got anything else to do, you need to come up in Harlem and let some people hear you singing about Oginga Odinga and Kenyatta and Lumumba, and the next time you come to Harlem, you'll have a crowd out here. Thank you.

10

At the Audubon

Malcolm X had invited Fannie Lou Hamer and the Freedom Singers to appear at the Organization of Afro-American Unity meeting held at the Audubon Ballroom on the evening of December 20, 1964. Before they took the floor, Malcolm carried out what was one of his major assignments in the organization—teaching, educating, patiently explaining things to his people in language and style they understood.

Salaam Alaikum. I suppose I should take time to explain what I mean when I say "Salaam Alaikum." Actually, it's an expression that means "peace," and it's one that is always given to one's brother or to one's sister. It only means "peace be unto you." So, when I say "A Salaam Alaikum" or "Salaam Alaikum" and others reply, "Alaikum Salaam," why, they're just returning the peace. It means we're all at peace with one another, as brothers and sisters.

Now, brothers and sisters, first I want to thank those of you who have taken the time to come through that snow, which almost turned me back myself, and come out where we can try and put our heads together and get a better understanding of what is going on, what we've been through and what we're all concerned about. As Sister Sharon has already pointed out, and I think she did so beautifully, during recent years our people have been struggling for some kind of relief from the conditions we're confronted by.

When you go back over the period of struggle, I think it would be agreed that we've gone through different patterns of struggle, that we've struggled in different ways. Each way that we tried never produced what we were looking for. If it had been productive, we would have continued along that same way. We've tried probably more different methods than any people. But at the same time, I think we've tried more wrong methods than any other people, because most others have gotten more freedom than we have. Everywhere you look, people get their freedom faster than we do. They get more respect and recognition faster than we do. We get promises, but we never get the real thing. And primarily because we have yet to learn the proper tactic or strategy or method to bring freedom into existence.

I think that one of the things that has caused our people in this country to try so many methods is that times have changed so rapidly. What would be proper ten years ago would not have been proper seven years ago, or five years ago, or three years ago. Times change so quickly that if you and I don't keep up with the times, we'll find ourselves with an umbrella in our hand, over our head, when the sun is out. Or we'll find ourselves standing in the rain, with the umbrella inside the door. If we don't keep up with what's going on, we will not be able to display the type of intelligence that will show the world we know what time it is and that we know what is happening around us. . . .

Several persons have asked me recently, since I've been back, "What is your program?" I purposely, to this day, have not in any way mentioned what our program is, because there will come a time when we will unveil it so that everybody will understand it. Policies change, and programs change, according to time. But objective never changes. You might change your method of achieving the objective, but the objective never changes. Our objective is complete freedom, complete justice, complete equality, by any means necessary. That never changes. Complete and immediate recognition and respect as human beings, that doesn't change, that's what all of us want. I don't care what you belong to—you still want that, recognition and respect as a human being. But you have changed your methods from time to time on how you go about getting it. The reason you change your method is that you have to change your method according to time and conditions that prevail. And one of the conditions that prevails on this earth right now, that we know too little about, is our relationship with the freedom struggle of people all over the world.

Here in America, we have always thought that we were struggling by ourselves, and most Afro-Americans will tell you just that—that we're a minority. By thinking we're a minority, we struggle like a minority. We struggle like we're an underdog. We struggle like all of the odds are against us. This type of struggle takes place only because we don't yet know where we fit in the scheme of things. We've been maneuvered out of a position where we could rightly know and understand where we fit into the scheme of things. It's impossible for you and me to know where we stand until we look around on this entire earth. Not just look around in Harlem or New York, or Mississippi, or America—we have got to look all around this earth. We don't know where we stand until we know where America stands. You don't know where you stand in America until you know where America stands in the world. We don't know where you and I stand in this context, known to us as America, until we know where America stands in the world context.

When you and I are inside of America and look at America, she looks big and bad and invincible. Oh, yes, and when we approach her in that context, we approach her as beggars, with our hat in our hands. As Toms, actually, only in the twentieth-century sense, but still as Toms. While if we understand what's going on on this earth and what's going on in the world today, and fit America into that context, we find out she's not so bad, after all; she's not very invincible. And when you find out she's not invincible, you don't approach her like you're dealing with someone who's invincible.

As a rule, up to now, the strategy of America has been to tuck all of our leaders up into her dress, and besiege them with money, with prestige, with praise, and make them jump, and tell them what to tell us. And they always tell us we're the underdog, and that we don't have a chance, and that we should do it nonviolently and carefully; otherwise, we'll get hurt or we'll get wasted. We don't buy that.

Number one, we want to know what are we? How did we get to be what we are? Where did we come from? How did we come from there? Who did we leave behind? Where was it that we left them behind, and what are they doing over there where we used to be? This is something that we have not been told. We have been brought over here and isolated—you know the funniest thing about that: they accuse *us* of introducing "separation" and "isolation." No one is more isolated than you and I. There's no system on earth more capable of thoroughly separating and isolating a people than this system that they call the democratic system; and you and I are the best proof of it, the best example of it. We were separated from our people, and have been isolated here for a long time.

So thoroughly has this been done to us that now we don't even know that there is somebody else that looks like we do. When we see them, we look at them like they're strangers. And when we see somebody that doesn't look anything like us, we call them our friends. That's a shame. It shows you what has been done to us. Yes, I mean our own people—we see our people come here who look exactly like we do, our twins, can't tell them apart, and we say, "Those are foreigners." Yet we're getting our heads busted trying to snuggle up to somebody who not only doesn't look like us, but doesn't even smell like us.

So you can see the importance of these meetings on Sunday nights during the past two or three weeks, and for a couple more weeks. It is not so much to spell out any program; you can't give a people a program until they realize they need one, and until they realize that all existing programs aren't programs that are going to produce productive results. So what we would like to do on Sunday nights is to go into our problem, and just analyze and analyze and analyze; and question things that you don't understand, so we can at least try and get a better picture of what faces us.

I, for one, believe that if you give people a thorough understanding of what it is that confronts them, and the basic causes that produce it, they'll create their own program; and when the people create a program, you get action. When these "leaders" create programs, you get no action. The only time you see them is when the people are exploding. Then the leaders are shot into the situation and told to control things. You can't show me a leader that has set off an explosion. No, they come and contain the explosion. They say, "Don't get rough, you know, do the smart thing." This is their role—they're there just to restrain you and me, to restrain the struggle, to keep it in a certain groove, and not let it get out of control. Whereas you and I don't want anybody to keep us from getting out of control. We want to get out of control. We want to smash anything that gets in our way that doesn't belong there.

Listen to the last part of what I said: I didn't just say we want to smash anything that gets in our way. I said we want to smash anything that gets in our way that doesn't belong there. You see, I had to give you the whole thing, because when you read it, you'll hear we're going to smash up everybody. No, I didn't say that. I said we'll smash up anything that gets in the way that doesn't belong there. I mean that. If it doesn't belong there, it's worthy to be smashed. This country practices that—power. This country smashes anything that gets in its way. It crushes anything that gets in its way. And since we're Americans, they tell us, well, we'll do it the American way. We'll smash anything that gets in our way.

This is the type of philosophy that we want to express among our people. We don't need to give them a program, not yet. First, give them something to think about. If we give them something to think about, and start them thinking in a way that they should think, they'll see through all this camouflage that's going on right now. It's just a show—the result of a script written by somebody else. The people will take that script and tear it up and write one for themselves. And you can bet that when you write the script for yourself, you're always doing something differ-ent than you'd be doing if you followed somebody else's script.

So, brothers and sisters, the thing that you and I must have an understanding of is the role that's being played in world affairs today, number one, by the continent of Africa; number two, by the people on that continent; num-ber three, by those of us who are related to the people on that continent, but who, by some quirk in our own his-tory, find ourselves today here in the Western hemisphere. Always bear that in mind that our being in the Western hemisphere differs from anyone else, because everyone else here came voluntarily. Everyone that you see in this part of the world got on a boat and came here voluntarily; whether they were immigrants or what have you, they came here voluntarily. So they don't have any real squawk, because they got what they were looking for. But you and I can squawk because we didn't come here voluntarily. We didn't ask to be brought here. We were brought here forc-ibly, against our will, and in chains. And at no time since we have been here, have they even acted like they wanted us here. At no time. At no time have they even tried to pre-tend that we were brought here to be citizens. Why, they don't even *pretend*. So why should we pretend?

Look at the continent of Africa today and see what po-sition it occupies on this earth, and you realize that there's a tussle going on between East and West. It used to be be-tween America and the West and Russia, but they're not tussling with each other any more. Kennedy made a satel-lite out of Russia. He put Khrushchev in his pocket; yes, he did—lost him his job. The tussle now is between America and China. In the camp of the West, America is foremost. Most other Western nations are satellites to America. En-gland is an American satellite. All of them are satellites, perhaps with the exception of France. France wants America to be her satellite. You never can tell what the future might bring. Better nations than this have fallen, if you read history. Most of the European Communist nations are still satelliting around Russia. But in Asia, China is the center of power.

Among Asian countries, whether they are communist, socialist—you don't find any capitalist countries over there too much nowadays. Almost every one of the countries that has gotten independence has devised some kind of socialistic system, and this is no accident. This is another reason why I say that you and I here in America—who are looking for a job, who are looking for better housing, looking for a better education—before you start trying to be incorporated, or integrated, or disintegrated, into this capitalistic system, should look over there and find out what are the people who have gotten their freedom adopting to provide themselves with better housing and better education and better food and better clothing.

None of them are adopting the capitalistic system because they realize they can't. You can't operate a capitalistic system unless you are vulturistic; you have to have someone else's blood to suck to be a capitalist. You show me a capitalist, I'll show you a bloodsucker. He cannot be anything but a bloodsucker if he's going to be a capitalist. He's got to get it from somewhere other than himself, and that's where he gets it—from somewhere or someone other than himself. So, when we look at the African continent, when we look at the trouble that's going on between East and West, we find that the nations in Africa are developing socialistic systems to solve their problems.

There's one thing that Martin Luther King mentioned at the Armory the other night, which I thought was most significant. I hope he really understood what he was saying. He mentioned that while he was in some of those Scandinavian countries he saw no poverty. There was no unemployment, no poverty. Everyone was getting education, everyone had decent housing, decent whatever-they-needed to exist. But why did he mention those countries on his list as different?

This is the richest country on earth and there's poverty, there's bad housing, there's slums, there's inferior education. And this is the richest country on earth. Now, you know, if those countries that are poor can come up with a solution to their problems so that there's no unemployment, then instead of you running downtown picketing city hall, you should stop and find out what they do over there to solve their problems. This is why the man doesn't want you and me to look beyond Harlem or beyond the shores of America. As long as you don't know what's happening on the outside, you'll be all messed up dealing with this man on the inside. I mean what they use to solve the problem is not capitalism. What they are using to solve their problem in Africa and Asia is not capitalism. So what you and I should do is find out what they are using to get rid of poverty and all the other negative characteristics of a rundown society.

Africa is strategically located, geographically between East and West; it's the most valuable piece of property involved in the struggle between East and West. You can't get to the East without going past it, and can't get from the East to West without going past it. It sits right there between all of them. It sits snuggled into a nest between Asia and Europe; it can reach either one. None of the natural resources that are needed in Europe that they get from Asia can get to Europe without coming either around Africa, over Africa, or in between the Suez Canal which is sitting at the tip of Africa. She can cut off Europe's bread. She can put Europe to sleep overnight, just like that. Because she's in a position to; the African continent is in a position to do this. But they want you and me to think Africa is a jungle, of no value, of no consequence. Because they also know that if you knew how valuable it was, you'd realize why they're over there killing our people. And you'd realize that it's not for some kind of humanitarian purpose or reason.

Also, Africa as a continent is important because of its tropical climate. It's so heavily vegetated you can take any section of Africa and use modern agricultural methods and turn that section alone into the breadbasket for the world. Almost any country over there can feed the whole continent, if it only had access to people who had the technical know-how to bring into that area modern methods of agriculture. It's rich. A jungle is only a place that's heavily vegetated—the soil is so rich and the climate is so good that everything grows, and it doesn't grow in season—it grows all the time. All the time is the season. That means it can grow anything, produce anything.

Added to its richness and its strategic position geographically is the fact of the existence of the Suez Canal and the Strait of Gibraltar. Those two narrow straits can cut off from Europe anything and everything Europe needs. All of the oil that runs Europe goes through the Suez Canal, up the Mediterranean Sea to places like Greece and Italy and Southern Spain and France and along through there; or through the Strait of Gibraltar and around on into England. And they need it. They need access through the Suez. When Nasser took over the Suez, they almost died in Europe. It scared them to death—why? Because Egypt is in Africa, in fact, Egypt is in both Africa and Asia. . . .

Before the Suez Canal was built, it was all one, you couldn't really make a distinction between Africa and Asia.

It was all one. When President Nasser took the Suez Canal, that meant that for the first time the Suez Canal was under the complete jurisdiction of an African nation, and it meant that other nations had to cater to this African nation if they wanted to survive, if they didn't want their oil and other sources of supply cut off. Immediately this had an effect on European attitudes and European economic measures. They began to try and devise new means, new routes, to get the things that they needed.

Another reason the continent is so important is because of its gold. It has some of the largest deposits of gold on earth, and diamonds. Not only the diamonds you put on your finger and in your ear, but industrial diamonds, diamonds that are needed to make machines—machines that can't function or can't run unless they have these diamonds. These industrial diamonds play a major role in the entire industrialization of the European nations, and without these diamonds their industry would fall.

You and I usually know of diamonds for rings—because those are the only diamonds we get close to, or the only diamonds within our line of thinking. We don't think in terms of diamonds for other uses. Or baseball diamonds—some of us only get that far.

Not only diamonds, but also cobalt. Cobalt is one of the most valuable minerals on this earth today, and I think Africa is one of the only places where it is found. They use it in cancer treatment, plus they use it in this nuclear field that you've heard so much about. Cobalt and uranium—the largest deposits are right there on the African continent. And this is what the man is after. The man is after keeping you over here worrying about a cup of coffee, while he's over there in your motherland taking control over minerals that have so much value they make the world go around. While you and I are still walking around over here, yes, trying to drink some coffee—with a cracker.

It's one of the largest sources of iron and bauxite and lumber and even oil, and Western industry needs all of these minerals in order to survive. All of these natural minerals are needed by the Western industrialists in order for their industry to keep running at the clip that it's been used to. Can we prove it? Yes. You know that France lost her French West African possessions, Belgium lost the Congo, England lost Nigeria and Ghana and some of the other English-speaking areas; France also lost Algeria, or the Algerians took Algeria.

As soon as these European powers lost their African possessions, Belgium had an economic crisis—the same year she turned the Congo loose. She had to rearrange her entire economy and her economic methods had to be revised, because she had lost possession of the source of most of her raw materials—raw materials that she got almost free, almost with no price or output whatsoever. When she got into a position where she didn't have access to these free raw materials anymore, it affected her economy. It affected the French economy. It affected the British economy. It drove all of these European countries to the point where they had to come together and form what's known as the European Common Market. Prior to that, you wouldn't hear anything about a European Common Market.

Being the gateway to Southwest Africa, Southern Rhodesia, Basutoland, Swaziland, and South Africa, the Congo is a country on the African continent which is so strategically located geographically that if it were to fall into the hands of a real dyed-in-the-wool African nationalist, he could then make it possible for African soldiers to train in the Congo for the purpose of invading Angola. When they invade Angola, that means Angola must fall, because there are more Africans than there are Portuguese, and they just couldn't control Angola any longer. And if the Congo fell into good hands, other than Tshombe, then it would mean that Angola would fall, Southern Rhodesia would fall, Southwest Africa would fall and South Africa would fall. And that's the only way they would fall.

When these countries fall, it would mean that the source of raw material, natural resources, some of the richest mineral deposits on earth, would then be taken away from the European economy. And without free access to this, the economy of Europe wouldn't be worth two cents. All of your European countries would be of no more importance than a country like Norway, which is all right for Norwegians, but has no influence beyond that. It's just another country stuck up some place in the northern part, like Sweden and some of those places. Every European country would be just as insignificant as the smallest insignificant country in Europe right now—if they lost the rest of Africa. Because the rest of Africa that's still colonized is the part of the African continent that's still backing up the European economy. And if the economy of Europe was to sink any farther, it would really wash away the American economy. American economy can never be any stronger than the European economy because both of them are one. It's one and the same economy. They are brothers.

I say this because it is necessary for you and me to understand what is at stake. You can't understand what is going on in Mississippi if you don't understand what is going on in the Congo. And you can't really be interested in what's going on in Mississippi if you're not also interested in what's going on in the Congo. They're both the same. The same interests are at stake. The same sides are drawn up, the same schemes are at work in the Congo that are at work in Mississippi. The same stake—no difference whatsoever.

Another frightening thing for this continent and the European continent is the fact that the Africans are trying to industrialize. One of the most highly industrialized African nations is Egypt. They have had a limited source of power up to now, but they are building a dam in upper Egypt, where the black Egyptians live. I was there, I took some pictures—I'm going to show you some movies, probably on the first Sunday in January, a week from next Sunday. The Aswan Dam is something that everybody should see. The Aswan is being built on the Nile in the heart of the desert, surrounded by mountains. One of the most outstanding things about this dam isn't so much its miraculous technical aspects, but the human aspects.

When you build a dam in an area where there's already vegetation, that's one thing. But this dam is being built in an area where there's no vegetation. Once this river is dammed, it will create a lake in the middle of the desert which will set up a water cycle—rain, you know, clouds, and all of that stuff—and it will turn the desert into a civilization, into a very fertile valley. In order for this artificial lake to be built in that way, from that dam, it washed away the homes of the Nubians—people who look just like you and I do, who have been living there for thousands of years. They had to replace them, they had to transplant them from where they were living for thousands of years to another area.

This in itself was an operation that would hold you spellbound if you could see all the aspects of it. It meant taking a people from one place and putting them in another place. The place where they had been was antiquated. Their methods, their customs, their homes were thousands of years old. But overnight these people, who lived that far in the past, were taken to new cities that had been built by the government. Modern cities, where they had modern schools, modern rooms in which to live, and modern hospitals. When you go into these new cities that are Nubian villages, the first thing you always see is a mosque. Their religion is Islam, they're Muslims.

The Egyptian government, the revolutionary government, differs from most revolutions in that it's one of the few revolutions that have taken place where religion has not been minimized. In most revolutions, religion is immediately de-emphasized. Eventually that revolution loses something. Always. But the thing about the Egyptian revolution was that it never de-emphasized the importance of religion. In these new cities, the first thing they build is a mosque, so people can practice their religion. Then they build schools so the people can be educated free; and then they build hospitals. They believe that the religious aspect keeps the people spiritually and morally balanced, and then everyone should have the best education and free hospitalization.

These new villages actually reflect the whole motive behind the Egyptian revolution. I found this quite interesting. I was there and could study it for two months. It's a balanced revolution. I go for revolution, but revolution should always do something for the people and it should always keep them balanced. You don't find anybody that's more revolutionary than those people over there in Egypt; they're revolutionary, they're involved in every revolution that's going on on the African continent right now.

So the Aswan Dam creates enough additional power to make it possible to step up or speed up the industrialization of that particular African nation. And as their industrialization is stepped up, it means that they can produce their own cars, their own tractors, their own tools, their own machinery, plus a lot of other things. Not only Egypt, but Ghana too. Ghana is building a dam, they're damming the Volta River. There's the Volta High Dam, and it's being built for the purpose of increasing the power potential of Ghana, so that Ghana also can increase its industrial output.

As these African nations get in a position to increase their own power and to industrialize, what does it mean? It means that where they now are a market for American goods and America's finished products, and a market for European finished products, when they're able to finish their own products, they will be able to get their products cheaper because they're putting their own raw materials into the finished products. Now the raw materials are taken from Africa, shipped all the way to Europe, used to feed the machines of the Europeans, and make jobs for them, and then turned around and sold back to the Africans as finished products. But when the African nations become industrialized, they can take their own products and stick them in the machines and finish them into whatever they want. Then they can live cheaper. The whole system will be a system with a high standard of living but a cheaper standard of living.

This standard of living automatically will threaten the standard of living in Europe because it will cut off the European market. European factories can't produce unless they have some place to market the products. American factories can't produce unless she has some place to market her products. It is for this reason that the European nations in the past have kept the nations in Latin America and in Africa and in Asia from becoming industrial powers. They keep the machinery and the ability to produce and manufacture limited to Europe and limited to America. Then this puts America and the Europeans in a position to control the economy of all other nations and keep them living at a low standard.

These people are beginning to see that. The Africans see it, the Latin Americans see it, the Asians see it. So when you hear them talking about freedom, they're not talking about a cup of coffee with a cracker. No, they're talking about getting in a position to feed themselves and clothe themselves and make these other things that, when you have them, make life worth living. So this is the way you and I have to understand the world revolution that's taking place right now.

When you understand the motive behind the world revolution, the drive behind the African and the drive behind the Asian, then you get some of that drive yourself. You'll be driving for real. The man downtown knows the difference between when you're driving for real and when you're driving not for real. As long as you keep asking about coffee, he doesn't have to worry about you; he can send you to Brazil. So these dams being set up over there in different parts of the continent are putting African nations in a position to have more power, to become more industrial and also to be self-sustained and self-sufficient.

In line with that: In the past it was the World Bank, controlled again by Europeans and from Europe, that subsidized most of the effort that was being made by African nations and Asian nations to develop underdeveloped areas. But the African nations are now getting together and forming their own bank, the African bank. The details of it aren't as much in my mind as I would like them to be, but when I was in Lagos, Nigeria, they were having a meeting there. It was among African bankers and African nations, and the Organization of African Unity, which is the best thing that has ever happened on the African continent, had taken up as part of its program the task of getting all of the African nations to pool their efforts in creating an African bank, so that there would be an internal bank in the internal African structure to which underdeveloped African nations can turn for financial assistance in projects that they're trying to undertake that would be beneficial to the whole continent. . . .

Politically, Africa as a continent, and the African people as a people, have the largest representation of any continent in the United Nations. Politically, the Africans are in a more strategic position and in a stronger position whenever a conference is taking place at the international level. Today, power is international, real power is international; today, real power is not local. The only kind of power that can help you and me is international power, not local power. Any power that's local, if it's real power, is only a reflection or a part of that international power. If you think you've got some power, and it isn't in some way tied into that international thing, brother, don't get too far out on a limb.

If your power base is only here, you can forget it. You can't build a power base here. You have to have a power base among brothers and sisters. You have to have your power base among people who have something in common with you. They have to have some kind of cultural identity, or there has to be some relationship between you and your power base. When you build a power base in this country, you're building it where you aren't in any way related to what you build it on. No, you have to have that base somewhere else. You can work here, but you'd better put your base somewhere else. Don't put it in this man's hand. Any kind of organization that is based here can't be an effective organization. Anything you've got going for you, if the base is here, is not going to be effective. Your and my base must be at home, and this is not at home.

When you see that the African nations at the international level comprise the largest representative body and the largest force of any continent, why, you and I would be out of our minds not to identify with that power bloc. We would be out of our minds, we would actually be traitors to ourselves, to be reluctant or fearful to identify with people with whom we have so much in common. If it was a people who had nothing to offer, nothing to contribute to our well-being, you might be justified, even though they looked like we do; if there was no contribution to be made, you might be justified. But when you have people who look exactly like you, and you are catching hell, to boot, and you still are reluctant or hesitant or slow to identify with them, then you need to catch hell, yes. You deserve all the hell you get.

The African representatives, coupled with the Asians and Arabs, form a bloc that's almost impossible for anybody to contend with. The African-Asian-Arab bloc was the bloc that started the real independence movement among the oppressed peoples of the world. The first coming together of that bloc was at the Bandung conference. . . .

To show you the power of that bloc and the results that they've gotten and how well the Europeans know it: On the African continent, when I was there, one thing I noticed was the twenty-four-hour-a-day effort being made in East Africa to turn the African against the Asian; and in West Africa to turn the African against the Arab; and in parts of Africa where there are no Asians or Arabs, to turn the Muslim African against the Christian African. When you go over there and study this thing, you can see that it is not something that's indigenous, it's not a divisive situation that's indigenous to the African himself. But someone realizes that the power of the oppressed black, brown, red and yellow people began at the Bandung conference, which was a coalition between the Arab and the Asian and the African, and how much pressure they've been able to put on the oppressor since then.

So, very shrewdly they have moved in. Now when you travel on the continent, you see the African in East Africa is being sicked on the Asian—there's a division taking place. And in West Africa he's being sicked on the Arab—there's a division taking place. And where the oppressor, this ingenious oppressor, diabolically ingenious—where he hasn't found an Asian to sic the African on, or an Arab to sic the African on, he uses the Muslim African against the Christian African. Or the one that believes in religion against the one that doesn't believe in religion. But the main thing he's doing is causing this division, division, division to in some way keep the African, the Arab and the Asian from beating up on him.

He's doing the same thing in British Guiana. He's got the black Guianians down there fighting against the so-called Indians. He's got them fighting each other. They didn't fight each other when the British were there in full control. If you notice, as long as the place was an old-style colony, no fight. But as soon as the British are supposed to be moving away, the black one starts fighting the red one. Why? This is no accident. If they didn't fight before, they don't need to fight now. There's no reason for it. But their fighting each other keeps the man on top. The fact that he can turn one against the other keeps the man on top.

He does the same thing with you and me right here in Harlem. All day long. I turned on the radio last night. I heard them say, every hour on the hour, that James Farmer, the head of CORE, was going to Africa, Egypt and Israel. And they said the reason he was going was because he wanted to correct false statements made by black nationalist leader Malcolm X when he was over there. If I hadn't had this experience before, immediately I would have started blasting Farmer. But I called him up today. He said he didn't know what they were talking about. But why do they do it? They do it to make us fight each other. As long as we're fighting each other, we can't get at the man who should be fought against from the start. Do you understand? Once we see the strategy that they use at the international level, then we can better understand the strategy that they use at the national and at the local level.

Lastly, I would like to point out my understanding of what I think is the position taken in African policy. Their policy, in a nutshell, is positive neutrality, non-alignment. They don't line up either way. Africa is for the Africans. And the Africans are for the Africans. The policy of the independent African states, by and large, is positive neutrality, non-alignment. Egypt is a good example. They take from East and West and don't take sides with either one. Nasser took everything Russia could give him, and then put all the communists in jail. Not that I mean the communists should necessarily have been put in jail. For the communist is a man, a capitalist is a man, and a socialist is a man. Well, if all of them are men, why should they be put in jail, unless one of them is committing a crime? And if being a communist or being a capitalist or being a socialist is a crime, first you have to study which of those systems is the most criminal. And then you'll be slow to say which one should be in jail.

I cite that as an example just to show what this positive neutrality means: If you want to help us, help us; we're still not with you. If you have a contribution to make to our development, do it. But that doesn't mean we're with you or against you. We're neutral. We're for ourselves. Whatever is good for us, that's what we're interested in. That doesn't mean we're against you. But it does mean we're for ourselves.

This is what you and I need to learn. You and I need to

learn how to be positively neutral. You and I need to learn how to be non-aligned. And if you and I ever study the science of non-alignment, then you'll find out that there's more power in non-alignment than there is alignment. In this country, it's impossible for you to be aligned—with either party. Either party that you align yourself with is suicide. Because both parties are criminal. Both parties are responsible for the criminal condition that exists. So you can't align yourself with a party.

What you can do is get registered so that you have power—political potential. When you register your political potential, that means your gun is loaded. But just because it's loaded, you don't have to shoot until you see a target that will be beneficial to you. If you want a duck, don't shoot when you see a bear; wait till you see a duck. And if you want a bear, don't shoot when see a duck; wait till you see a bear. Wait till you see what you want—then take aim and shoot!

What they do with you and me is tell us, "Register and vote." Don't register and vote—register! That's intelligent. Don't register and vote—you can vote for a dummy, you can vote for a crook, you can vote for another who'd want to exploit you. "Register" means being in a position to take political action any time, any place and in any manner that would be beneficial to you and me; being in a position to take advantage of our position. Then we'll be in a position to be respected and recognized. But as soon as you get registered, and you want to be a Democrat or a Republican, you are aligning. And once you are aligning, you have no bargaining power—none whatsoever. We've got a program we are going to launch, which will involve the absolute maximum registering of as many of our people as we can. But they will be registered as independents. And by being registered as independents, it means we can do whatever is necessary, wherever it's necessary, and whenever the time comes. Do you understand?

So, I say in my conclusion, we have a lady that I want to introduce you to, who I think is one of the best freedom fighters in America today. She's from Mississippi, and you've got to be a freedom fighter to even live in Mississippi. You've got to be a freedom fighter to live anywhere in this country, but especially Mississippi. This woman has been in the forefront of the struggle in Mississippi. I was on a program with her this afternoon. . . .

As I mentioned today—and you'll probably read about it tomorrow; they'll blow it up, and out of context—what we need in this country (and I believe it with all my heart, and with all my mind, and with all my soul) is the same type of Mau Mau here that they had over there in Kenya. Don't you ever be ashamed of the Mau Mau. They're not to be ashamed of. They are to be proud of. Those brothers were freedom fighters. Not only brothers, there were sisters over there. I met a lot of them. They're brave. They hug you and kiss you—glad to see you. In fact, if they were over here, they'd get this problem straightened up just like that.

I read a little story once, and Mau Mau proved it. I read a story once where someone asked some group of people how many of them wanted freedom. They all put up their hand. Think there were about 300 of them. Then the person says, "Well, how many of you are ready to kill anybody who gets in your way for freedom?" About fifty put up their hands. And he told those fifty, "You stand over here." That left 250 sitting who wanted freedom, but weren't ready to kill for it. So he told this fifty, "Now you wanted freedom and you said you'd kill anybody who'd get in your way. You see those 250? You get them first. Some of them are your own brothers and sisters and mothers and fathers. But they're the ones who stand in the way of your freedom. They're afraid to do whatever is necessary to get it and they'll stop you from doing it. Get rid of them and freedom will come naturally."

I go for that. That's what the Mau Mau learned. The Mau Mau realized that the only thing that was standing in the way of the independence of the African in Kenya was another African. So they started getting them one by one, all those Toms. One after another, they'd find another Uncle Tom African by the roadside. Today they're free. The white man didn't even get involved—he got out of the way. That's the same thing that will happen here. We've got too many of our own people who stand in the way. They're too squeamish. They want to be looked upon as respectable Uncle Toms. They want to be looked upon by the white man as responsible. They don't want to be classified by him as extremist, or violent, or, you know, irresponsible. They want that good image. And nobody who's looking for a good image will ever be free. No, that kind of image doesn't get you free. You've got to take something in your hand and say, "Look, it's you or me." And I guarantee you he'll give you freedom then. He'll say, "This man is ready for it." I said something in your hand—I won't define what I mean by "something in your hand." I don't mean bananas.

So, we are honored to have with us tonight not only a freedom fighter, but some singers on that program today—I think they're all here; I asked them to come out tonight because they sang one song that just knocked me out. I'm not one who goes for "We Shall Overcome." I just don't believe we're going to overcome, singing. If you're going to get yourself a .45 and start singing "We Shall Overcome," I'm with you. But I'm not for singing that doesn't at the same time tell you how to get something to use after you get through singing. I realize I'm saying some things that you think can get me in trouble, but, brothers, I was born in trouble. I don't even care about trouble. I'm interested in one thing alone, and that's freedom—by any means necessary. So I'll bring you now the country's number one freedom-fighting woman. . . .

[*Mrs. Hamer speaks.*]

Now you see why Mississippi is in trouble. And I hope that our brothers, especially our brothers here in Harlem, listened very well, very closely, to what I call one of this country's foremost freedom fighters. You don't have to be a man to fight for freedom. All you have to do is be an intelligent human being. And automatically, your intelligence makes you want freedom so badly that you'll do anything, by any means necessary, to get that freedom. And I want Mrs. Hamer to know that anything we can do to help them in Mississippi, we're at their disposal. One of the things that we will definitely provide you with, because I think it's the only real help that you can get down there: You can let those hooded people know that, from here on in, when they start taking the lives of innocent black people, we believe in tit for tat.

If I were to go home and find some blood on the leg of one of my little girls, and my wife told me that a snake bit the child, I'd go looking for the snake. And if I found the snake, I wouldn't necessarily take time to see if it had blood on its jaws. As far as I'm concerned the snake is the snake. So if snakes don't want someone hunting snakes indiscriminately, I say that snakes should get together and clean out their snakey house. If snakes don't want people running around indiscriminately chopping off the heads of snakes, my advice to snakes would be to keep their house in order. I think you well understand what I'm saying. Now those were twenty-one snakes that killed those three brothers down there. Twenty-one—those are snakes. And there is no law in any society on earth that would hold it against anyone for taking the heads of those snakes. Believe it, the whole world would honor you or honor anyone who did what the federal government refused to do. . . .

We should let them know that we believe in giving them what they deserve. There are brothers around the country right now, a lot of them, who feel like I do, a lot of them who feel like I do. I've even met white students who feel that way. When they tell me that they're liberal, I tell them, "Great, go get me one of those snake heads." I'm sincere about this. I think that there are many whites who are sincere, especially at the student level. They just don't know how to show their sincerity. They think that they're showing sincerity by going down there and encouraging our people to be nonviolent. That's not where it's at. Since they're white, they can get closer to whitey than we can. They can put on a sheet and walk right on into camp with the rest of them.

I'm telling you how to do it: You're a liberal; get you a sheet. And get you something up under that sheet that you know how to use, and walk right on in that camp of sheeted people with the rest of them. And show how liberal you are. I'll come back and shake your hand all day long. I'll walk you around Harlem and tell everybody what a good white person you are. Because you've proved it. But I don't accept any nonviolent liberals. This doesn't mean that you've got to be violent; but it does mean that you can't be nonviolent. . . .

[*Introduces Freedom Singers.*]

11

To Mississippi youth

At the end of 1964, a delegation of thirty-seven teenagers from McComb, Mississippi, came to New York for their Christmas vacation. The eight-day trip was sponsored by the Student Nonviolent Coordinating Committee for young people who had been outstanding in the civil-rights struggle in their home town.

The McComb youth attended various meetings and discussions in Harlem. Toward the end of their stay, on January 1, 1965, they visited the Hotel Theresa to learn what Malcolm X stood for. The following is a small portion of what he told them.

One of the first things I think young people, especially nowadays, should learn is how to see for yourself and listen for yourself and think for yourself. Then you can come to an intelligent decision for yourself. If you form the habit of going by what you hear others say about someone, or going by what others think about someone, instead of searching that thing out for yourself and seeing for yourself, you will be walking west when you think you're going east, and you will be walking east when you think you're going west. This generation, especially of our people, has a burden, more so than any other time in history. The most important thing that we can learn to do today is think for ourselves.

It's good to keep wide-open ears and listen to what everybody else has to say, but when you come to make a decision, you have to weigh all of what you've heard on its own, and place it where it belongs, and come to a decision for yourself; you'll never regret it. But if you form the habit of taking what someone else says about a thing without checking it out for yourself, you'll find that other people will have you hating your friends and loving your enemies. This is one of the things that our people are beginning to learn today—that it is very important to think out a situation for yourself. If you don't do it, you'll always be maneuvered into a situation where you are never fighting your actual enemies, where you will find yourself fighting your own self.

I think our people in this country are the best examples of that. Many of us want to be nonviolent and we talk very loudly, you know, about being nonviolent. Here in Harlem, where there are probably more black people concentrated than any place in the world, some talk that nonviolent talk too. But we find that they aren't nonviolent with each other. You can go out to Harlem Hospital, where there are more black patients than any hospital in the world, and see them going in there all cut up and shot up and busted up where they got violent with each other.

My experience has been that in many instances where you find Negroes talking about nonviolence, they are not nonviolent with each other, and they're not loving with each other, or forgiving with each other. Usually when they say they're nonviolent, they mean they're nonviolent with somebody else. I think you understand what I mean. They are nonviolent with the enemy. A person can come to your home, and if he's white and wants to heap some kind of brutality on you, you're nonviolent; or he can come to take your father and put a rope around his neck, and you're nonviolent. But if another Negro just stomps his foot, you'll rumble with him in a minute. Which shows you that there's an inconsistency there.

I myself would go for nonviolence if it was consistent, if everybody was going to be nonviolent all the time. I'd say, okay, let's get with it, we'll all be nonviolent. But I don't go along with any kind of nonviolence unless everybody's going to be nonviolent. If they make the Ku Klux Klan nonviolent, I'll be nonviolent. If they make the White Citizens Council nonviolent, I'll be nonviolent. But as long as you've got somebody else not being nonviolent, I don't want anybody coming to me talking any nonviolent talk. I don't think it is fair to tell our people to be nonviolent unless someone is out there making the Klan and the Citizens Council and these other groups also be nonviolent.

Now, I'm not criticizing those here who are nonviolent. I think everybody should do it the way they feel is best, and I congratulate anybody who can be nonviolent in the face of all that kind of action in that part of the world. I don't think that in 1965 you will find the upcoming generation of our people, especially those who have been doing some thinking, who will go along with any form of nonviolence unless nonviolence is going to be practiced all the way around.

If the leaders of the nonviolent movement can go into the white community and teach nonviolence, good. I'd go along with that. But as long as I see them teaching nonviolence only in the black community, we can't go along with that. We believe in equality, and equality means that you have to put the same thing over here that you put over there. And if black people alone are going to be the ones who are nonviolent, then it's not fair. We throw ourselves off guard. In fact, we disarm ourselves and make ourselves defenseless. . . .

The Organization of Afro-American Unity is a non-religious group of black people who believe that the problems confronting our people in this country need to be re-analyzed and a new approach devised toward trying to get a solution. Studying the problem, we recall that prior to 1939 all of our people, in the North, South, East and West, no matter how much education we had, were segregated. We were segregated in the North just as much as we were segregated in the South. Even now there's as much segregation in the North as there is in the South. There's some worse segregation right here in New York City than there is in McComb, Mississippi; but up here they're subtle and tricky and deceitful, and they make you think you've got it made when you haven't even begun to make it yet.

Prior to 1939, our people were in a very menial position or condition. Most of us were waiters and porters and bellhops and janitors and waitresses and things of that sort. It was not until war was declared with Germany, and America became involved in a manpower shortage in regards to her factories plus her army, that the black man in this country was permitted to make a few strides forward. It was never out of some kind of moral enlightenment or moral awareness on the part of Uncle Sam. Uncle Sam only let the black man take a step forward when he himself had his back to the wall.

In Michigan, where I was brought up at that time, I recall that the best jobs in the city for blacks were waiters out at the country club. In those days if you had a job waiting table in the country club, you had it made. Or if you had a job at the State House. Having a job at the State House didn't mean that you were a clerk or something of that sort; you had a shoeshine stand at the State House. Just by being there you could be around all those big-shot politicians—that made you a big-shot Negro. You were shining shoes, but you were a big-shot Negro because you were around big-shot white people and you could bend their ear and get up next to them. And ofttimes you were chosen by them to be the voice of the Negro community.

Around that time, 1939 or '40 or '41, they weren't drafting Negroes in the army or the navy. A Negro couldn't join the navy in 1940 or '41. They wouldn't take a black man in the navy except to make him a cook. He couldn't just go and join the navy, and I don't think he could just go and join the army. They weren't drafting him when the war first started. This is what they thought of you and me in those days. For one thing, they didn't trust us; they feared that if they put us in the army and trained us in how to use rifles and other things, we might shoot at some targets that they hadn't picked out. And we would have. Any thinking man knows what target to shoot at. If a man has to have someone else to choose his target, then he isn't thinking for himself—they're doing the thinking for him.

The Negro leaders in those days were the same type we have today. When the Negro leaders saw all the white fellows being drafted and taken into the army and dying on the battlefield, and no Negroes were dying because they weren't being drafted, the Negro leaders came up and said, "We've got to die too. We want to be drafted too, and we demand that you take us in there and let us die for our country too." That was what the Negro leaders did back in

1940, I remember. A. Philip Randolph was one of the leading Negroes in those days who said it, and he's one of the Big Six right now; and this is why he's one of the Big Six.

So they started drafting Negro soldiers then, and started letting Negroes get into the navy. But not until Hitler and Tojo and the foreign powers were strong enough to put pressure on this country, so that it had its back to the wall and needed us, [did] they let us work in factories. Up until that time we couldn't work in the factories; I'm talking about the North as well as the South. And when they let us work in the factories, at first they let us in only as janitors. After a year or so passed by, they let us work on machines. We became machinists, got a little more skill. If we got a little more skill, we made a little more money, which enabled us to live in a little better neighborhood. When we lived in a little better neighborhood, we went to a little better school, got a little better education and could come out and get a little better job. So the cycle was broken somewhat.

But the cycle was not broken out of some kind of sense of moral responsibility on the part of the government. No, the only time that cycle was broken even to a degree was when world pressure was brought to bear on the United States government. They didn't look at us as human beings—they just put us into their system and let us advance a little bit farther because it served their interests. They never let us advance a little bit farther because they were interested in us as human beings. Any of you who have a knowledge of history, sociology, or political science, or the economic development of this country and its race relations—go back and do some research on it and you'll have to admit that this is true.

It was during the time that Hitler and Tojo made war with this country and put pressure on it [that] Negroes in this country advanced a little bit. At the end of the war with Germany and Japan, then Joe Stalin and Communist Russia were a threat. During that period we made a little more headway. Now the point that I'm making is this: Never at any time in the history of our people in this country have we made advances or progress in any way based upon the internal good will of this country. We have made advancement in this country only when this country was under pressure from forces above and beyond its control. The internal moral consciousness of this country is bankrupt. It hasn't existed since they first brought us over here and made slaves out of us. They make it appear they have our good interests at heart, but when you study it, every time, no matter how many steps they take us forward, it's like we're standing on a—what do you call that thing?—a treadmill. The treadmill is moving backwards faster than we're able to go forward in this direction. We're not even standing still—we're going backwards.

In studying the process of this so-called progress during the past twenty years, we of the Organization of Afro-American Unity realized that the only time the black man in this country is given any kind of recognition, or even listened to, is when America is afraid of outside pressure, or when she's afraid of her image abroad. So we saw that it was necessary to expand the problem and the struggle of the black man in this country until it went above and beyond the jurisdiction of the United States. . . .

I was fortunate enough to be able to take a tour of the African continent during the summer. I went to Egypt, then to Arabia, Kuwait, Lebanon, Sudan, Ethiopia, Kenya, Tanganyika, Zanzibar, Nigeria, Ghana, Guinea, Liberia and Algeria. I found, while I was traveling on the African continent, I had already detected it in May, that someone had very shrewdly planted the seed of division on this continent to make the Africans not show genuine concern with our problem, just as they plant seeds in your and my minds so that we won't show concern with the African problem. . . .

I also found that in many of these African countries the head of state is genuinely concerned with the problem of the black man in this country; but many of them thought if they opened their mouths and voiced their concern that they would be insulted by the American Negro leaders. Because one head of state in Asia voiced his support of the civil-rights struggle [in 1963] and a couple of the Big Six had the audacity to slap his face and say they weren't interested in that kind of help—which in my opinion is asinine. So the African leaders only had to be convinced that if they took an open stand at the governmental level and showed interest in the problem of black people in this country, they wouldn't be rebuffed.

And today you'll find in the United Nations, and it's not an accident, that every time the Congo question or anything on the African continent is being debated, they couple it with what is going on, or what is happening to you and me, in Mississippi and Alabama and these other places. In my opinion, the greatest accomplishment that was made in the struggle of the black man in America in 1964 toward some kind of real progress was the successful linking together of our problem with the African problem, or making our problem a world problem. Because now, whenever anything happens to you in Mississippi, it's not just a case of somebody in Alabama getting indignant, or somebody in New York getting indignant. The same repercussions that you see all over the world when an imperialist or foreign power interferes in some section of Africa—you see repercussions, you see the embassies being bombed and burned and overturned—nowadays, when something happens to black people in Mississippi, you'll see the same repercussions all over the world.

I wanted to point this out to you because it is important for you to know that when you're in Mississippi, you're not alone. As long as you think you're alone, then you take a stand as if you're a minority or as if you're outnumbered, and that kind of stand will never enable you to win a battle. You've got to know that you've got as much power on your side as that Ku Klux Klan has on its side. And when you know that you've got as much power on your side as the Klan has on its side, you'll talk the same kind of language with that Klan as the Klan is talking with you. . . .

I think in 1965, whether you like it, or I like it, or they like it, or not, you will see that there is a generation of black people becoming mature to the point where they feel that they have no more business being asked to take a peaceful approach than anybody else takes, unless everybody's going to take a peaceful approach.

So we here in the Organization of Afro-American Unity are with the struggle in Mississippi one thousand per cent. We're with the efforts to register our people in Mississippi to vote one thousand per cent. But we do not go along with anybody telling us to help nonviolently. We think that if the government says that Negroes have a right to vote, and then some Negroes come out to vote, and some kind of Ku Klux Klan is going to put them in the river, and the government doesn't do anything about it, it's time for us to organize and band together and equip ourselves and qualify ourselves to protect ourselves. And once you can protect yourself, you don't have to worry about being hurt. . . .

If you don't have enough people down there to do it, we'll come down there and help you do it. Because we're tired of this old runaround that our people have been given in this country. For a long time they accused me of not getting involved in politics. They should've been glad I didn't get involved in politics, because anything I get in, I'm in it all the way. If they say we don't take part in the Mississippi struggle, we will organize brothers here in New York who know how to handle these kind of affairs, and they'll slip into Mississippi like Jesus slipped into Jerusalem.

That doesn't mean we're against white people, but we sure are against the Ku Klux Klan and the White Citizens Councils; and anything that looks like it's against us, we're against it. Excuse me for raising my voice, but this thing, you know, gets me upset. Imagine that—a country that's supposed to be a democracy, supposed to be for freedom and all of that kind of stuff when they want to draft you and put you in the army and send you to Saigon to fight for them—and then you've got to turn around and all night long discuss how you're going to just get a right to register and vote without being murdered. Why, that's the most hypocritical government since the world began! . . .

I hope you don't think I'm trying to incite you. Just look here: Look at yourselves. Some of you are teen-agers, students. How do you think I feel—and I belong to a generation ahead of you—how do you think I feel to have to tell you, "We, my generation, sat around like a knot on a wall while the whole world was fighting for its human rights—and you've got to be born into a society where you still have that same fight." What did we do, who preceded you? I'll tell you what we did: Nothing. And don't you make the same mistake we made. . . .

You get freedom by letting your enemy know that you'll do anything to get your freedom; then you'll get it. It's the only way you'll get it. When you get that kind of attitude, they'll label you as a "crazy Negro," or they'll call you a "crazy nigger"—they don't say Negro. Or they'll call you an extremist or a subversive, or seditious, or a red or a radical. But when you stay radical long enough, and get enough people to be like you, you'll get your freedom. . . .

So don't you run around here trying to make friends with somebody who's depriving you of your rights. They're not your friends, no, they're your enemies. Treat them like that and fight them, and you'll get your freedom; and after you get your freedom, your enemy will respect you. And we'll respect you. And I say that with no hate. I don't have hate in me. I have no hate at all. I don't have any hate. I've got some sense. I'm not going to let somebody who hates me tell me to love him. I'm not that way-out. And you, young as you are, and because you start thinking, you're not going to do it either. The only time you're going to get in that bag is if somebody puts you there. Somebody else, who doesn't have your welfare at heart. . . .

I want to thank all of you for taking the time to come to Harlem and especially here. I hope that you've gotten a better understanding about me. I put it to you just as plain as I know how to put it; there's no interpretation necessary. And I want you to know we're not in any way trying to advocate any kind of indiscriminate, unintelligent action. Any kind of action that you are ever involved in that's designed to protect the lives and property of our mistreated people in this country, we're with you one thousand per cent. And if you don't feel you're qualified to do it, we have some brothers who will slip in, as I said earlier, and help train you and show you how to equip yourself and let you know how to deal with the man who deals with you. . . .

12

Prospects for freedom in 1965

To a mixed but predominantly white audience on January 7, 1965, Malcolm X gave a talk, "Prospects for Freedom in 1965," sponsored by the Militant Labor Forum and held at Palm Gardens in New York. Excerpts from the lengthy question-and-answer period that followed the speech are printed in the final chapter of this book.

Mr. Chairman (who's one of my brothers), ladies and gentlemen, brothers and sisters: It is an honor to me to come back to the Militant Labor Forum again this evening. It's my third time here. I was just telling my brother up here that probably tomorrow morning the press will try to make it appear that this little chat that we're having here this evening took place in Peking or someplace else. They have a tendency to discolor things in that way, to try and make people not place the proper importance upon what they hear, especially when they're hearing it from persons they can't control, or, as my brother just pointed out, persons whom they consider "irresponsible."

It's the third time that I've had the opportunity to be a guest of the Militant Labor Forum. I always feel that it is an honor and every time that they open the door for me to do so, I will be right here. The *Militant* newspaper is one of the best in New York City. In fact, it is one of the best anywhere you go today because everywhere I go I see it. I saw it even in Paris about a month ago; they were reading it over there. And I saw it in some parts of Africa where I was during the summer. I don't know how it gets there. But if you put the right things in it, what you put in it will see that it gets around.

Tonight, during the few moments that we have, we're going to have a little chat, like brothers and sisters and friends, and probably enemies too, about the prospects for peace—or the prospects for freedom in 1965. As you notice, I almost slipped and said peace. Actually you can't separate peace from freedom because no one can be at peace unless he has his freedom. You can't separate the two—and this is the thing that makes 1965 so explosive and so dangerous.

The people in this country who in the past have been at peace and have been peaceful were that way only because they didn't know what freedom was. They let somebody else define it for them, but today, 1965, you find those who have not had freedom, and were not in a position to define freedom, are beginning to define it for themselves. And as they get in a position intellectually to define freedom for themselves, they see that they don't have it, and it makes them less peaceful, or less inclined towards peace. . . .

In 1964, oppressed people all over the world, in Africa, in Asia and Latin America, in the Caribbean, made some progress. Northern Rhodesia threw off the yoke of colonialism and became Zambia, and was accepted into the

United Nations, the society of independent governments. Nyasaland became Malawi and also was accepted into the UN, into the family of independent governments. Zanzibar had a revolution, threw out the colonialists and their lackeys and then united with Tanganyika into what is now known as the Republic of Tanzania—which is progress, indeed. . . .

Also in 1964, the oppressed people of South Vietnam, and in that entire Southeast Asia area, were successful in fighting off the agents of imperialism. All the king's horses and all the king's men haven't enabled them to put North and South Vietnam together again. Little rice farmers, peasants, with a rifle—up against all the highly-mechanized weapons of warfare—jets, napalm, battleships, everything else, and they can't put those rice farmers back where they want them. Somebody's waking up.

In the Congo, the People's Republic of the Congo, headquartered at Stanleyville, fought a war for freedom against Tshombe, who is an agent for Western imperialism—and by Western imperialism I mean that which is headquartered in the United States, in the State Department.

In 1964 this government, subsidizing Tshombe, the murderer of Lumumba, and Tshombe's mercenaries, hired killers from South Africa, along with the former colonial power, Belgium, dropped paratroopers on the people of the Congo, used Cubans, that they had trained, to drop bombs on the people of the Congo with American-made planes—to no avail. The struggle is still going on, and America's man, Tshombe, is still losing.

All of this in 1964. Now, in speaking like this, it doesn't mean that I am anti-American. I am not. I'm not anti-American, or un-American. And I'm not saying that to defend myself. Because if I was that, I'd have a right to be that—after what America has done to us.

This government should feel lucky that our people aren't anti-American. They should get down on their hands and knees every morning and thank God that 22 million black people have not become anti-American. You've given us every right to. The whole world would side with us, if we became anti-American. You know, that's something to think about.

But we are not anti-American. We are anti or against what America is doing wrong in other parts of the world as well as here. And what she did in the Congo in 1964 is wrong. It's criminal, criminal. And what she did to the American public, to get the American public to go along with it, is criminal. What she's doing in South Vietnam is criminal. She's causing American soldiers to be murdered every day, killed every day, die every day, for no reason at all. That's wrong. Now, you're not supposed to be so blind with patriotism that you can't face reality. Wrong is wrong, no matter who does it or who says it. . . .

Also in 1964, China exploded her bomb, which was a scientific breakthrough for the oppressed people in China, who suffered for a long time. I, for one, was very happy to hear that the great people of China were able to display their scientific advancement, their advanced knowledge of science, to the point where a country which is as backward as *this* country keeps saying China is, and so behind everybody, and so poor, could come up with an atomic bomb. Why, I had to marvel at that. It made me realize that poor people can do it as well as rich people.

So all these little advances were made by oppressed people in other parts of the world during 1964. These were tangible gains, and the reason that they were able to make these gains was they realized that power was the magic word—power against power. Power in defense of freedom is greater than power in behalf of tyranny and oppression, because power, real power, comes from conviction which produces action, uncompromising action. It also produces insurrection against oppression. This is the only way you end oppression—with power. Power never takes a back step—only in the face of more power. Power doesn't back up in the face of a smile, or in the face of a threat, or in the face of some kind of nonviolent loving action. It's not the nature of power to back up in the face of anything but some more power. And this is what the people have realized in Southeast Asia, in the Congo, in Cuba, in other parts of the world. Power recognizes only power, and all of them who realize this have made gains.

Now here in America it's different. When you compare our strides in 1964 with strides that have been made forward by people elsewhere all over the world, only then can you appreciate the great doublecross experienced by black people here in America in 1964. The power structure started out the new year the same way they started it out in Washington the other day. Only now they call it— what's that?—"The Great Society?" Last year, 1964, was supposed to be the "Year of Promise." They opened up the new year in Washington, D.C., and in the city hall and in Albany talking about the Year of Promise. . . .

But by the end of 1964, we had to agree that instead of the Year of Promise, instead of those promises materializing, they substituted devices to create the illusion of progress; 1964 was the Year of Illusion and Delusion. We received nothing but a promise. . . . In 1963, one of their devices to let off the steam of frustration was the march on Washington. They used that to make us think we were making progress. Imagine, marching to Washington and getting nothing for it whatsoever. . . .

In '63, it was the march on Washington. In '64, what

was it? The civil-rights bill. Right after they passed the civil-rights bill, they murdered a Negro in Georgia and did nothing about it; murdered two whites and a Negro in Mississippi and did nothing about it. So that the civil-rights bill has produced nothing where we're concerned. It was only a valve, a vent, that was designed to enable us to let off our frustrations. But the bill itself was not designed to solve our problems.

Since we see what they did in 1963, and we saw what they did in 1964, what will they do now, in 1965? If the march on Washington was supposed to lessen the explosion, and the civil-rights bill was designed to lessen the explosion—That's all it was designed to do; it wasn't designed to solve the problems; it was designed to lessen the explosion. Everyone in his right mind knows there should have been an explosion. You can't have all those ingredients, those explosive ingredients that exist in Harlem and elsewhere where our people suffer, and not have an explosion. So these are devices to lessen the danger of the explosion, but not designed to remove the material that's going to explode.

What will they give us in 1965? I just read where they planned to make a black cabinet member. Yes, they have a new gimmick every year. They're going to take one of their boys, black boys, and put him in the cabinet, so he can walk around Washington with a cigar—fire on one end and fool on the other.

And because his immediate personal problem will have been solved, he will be the one to tell our people, "Look how much progress we're making: I'm in Washington, D.C. I can have tea in the White House. I'm your spokesman, I'm your, you know, your leader." . . . But will it work? Can that one, whom they are going to put down there, step into the fire and put it out when the flames begin to leap up?

When people take to the streets in their explosive mood, will that one, that they're going to put in the cabinet, be able to go among those people? Why, they'll burn him faster than they burn the ones who sent him.

At the international level in 1964, they used the device of sending well-chosen black representatives to the African continent, whose mission it was to make the people on that continent think all our problems had been solved. They went over there as apologists. I saw some of them, trailed some of them and saw the results that some of them had left there. Their prime mission was to go into Africa, which is most vital to the United States' interests. These Toms—you're not supposed to call them Toms nowadays; they'll sue you—so these Uncles were sent over there— [*commotion*] Don't bother the man. He's doing his job. He's going to put you on TV, so you can get investigated.

These Toms don't go to Africa because they want to explore, learn something for themselves, broaden their scope, or communicate between their people and our people over there. They go primarily to represent the United States government. And when they go, they gloss things over, they tell how well we are doing here, how the civil-rights bill has settled everything, and how the Nobel Peace Prize was handed down. Oh, yes, that's how they tell it. Actually they succeed in widening the gap between Afro-Americans and the Africans. The image that they leave there of the Afro-American is so obnoxious that the African ends up not wanting to identify with us or be related to us.

It is only when the nationalist-minded or black-minded Afro-American goes abroad to the African continent and establishes direct lines of communication and lets the African brothers know what is happening over here, and know that our people are not so dumb that we are blind to our true condition and position in this structure, that the Africans begin to understand us and identify with us and sympathize with our problems, to the point where they are willing to make whatever sacrifices are necessary to see that their long-lost brothers get a better break than we have been getting up to now.

On the national scale during 1964, as I just mentioned, politically, the Mississippi Freedom Democratic Party had its face slapped at Atlantic City, at a convention over which Lyndon B. Johnson was the boss, and Hubert Humphrey was the next boss, and Mayor Wagner had a lot of influence himself. Still none of that influence was shown in any way whatsoever when the hopes and aspirations of the people, the black people of Mississippi, were at stake.

Though at the beginning of '64 we were told that our political rights would be broadened, it was in 1964 that the two white civil-rights workers, working with the black civil-rights worker, were murdered. . . . They were trying to show our people in Mississippi how to become registered voters. This was their crime. This was the reason for which they were murdered.

And the most pitiful part about them being murdered was the civil-rights organizations themselves being so chicken when it comes to reacting in the way that they should have reacted to the murder of these three civil-rights workers. The civil-rights groups sold those three brothers out—sold them out—sold them right down the river. Because they died and what has been done about it? And what voice is being raised every day today in regards to the murder of those three civil-rights workers? . . .

So this is why I say if *we* get involved in the civil-rights movement and go to Mississippi, or anyplace else, to help our people get registered to vote, *we intend to go prepared.* We don't intend to break the law, but when you're trying to register to vote you're upholding the law. It's the one who tries to prevent you from registering to vote who's breaking the law, and you've got a right to protect yourself by any means necessary. And if the government doesn't want civil-rights groups going equipped, the government should do its job.

Concerning the Harlem incident that took place during the summer when the citizens of Harlem were attacked in a pogrom. (I can't pronounce it, because it's not my word.) We had heard long before it took place that it was going to take place. We had gotten the word that there were elements in the power structure that were going to incite something in Harlem that they could call a riot—in order that they could step in and be justified in using whatever measures necessary to crush the militant groups which were still considered in the embryonic stage.

And realizing that there was a plan afoot to instigate something in Harlem, so they could step in and crush it, there were elements in Harlem, who were prepared and qualified and equipped to retaliate in situations like that, who purposely did not get involved. And the real miracle of the Harlem explosion was the restraint exercised by the people of Harlem. The miracle of 1964, I'll tell it to you straight, the miracle of 1964, during the incidents that took place in Harlem, was the restraint exercised by the people in Harlem who are qualified and equipped, and whatever else there is, to protect themselves when they are being illegally and immorally and unjustly attacked.

An illegal attack, an unjust attack and an immoral attack can be made against you by anyone. Just because a person has on a uniform does not give him the right to come and shoot up your neighborhood. No, this is not right, and my suggestion would be that as long as the police department doesn't use those methods in white neighborhoods, they shouldn't come to Harlem and use them in our neighborhood.

I wasn't here. I'm glad I wasn't here. Because I'd be dead, they'd have to kill me. I'd rather be dead than let someone walk around my house or in my neighborhood shooting it up, where my children are in the line of fire. Either they'd die or I'd die.

It's not intelligent—and it all started when a little boy was shot by a policeman, and he was turned loose the same as the sheriff was turned loose in Mississippi when he killed the three civil-rights workers. . . .

I'm almost finished. I'm taking my time tonight because I'm overworked. I'm taking my time by not hurrying up, I mean. . . . In 1964 we had still with us the slumlords, people who own the houses but don't live there themselves; usually they live up around the Grand Concourse or somewhere. They contribute to the NAACP and CORE and all the civil-rights organizations; give you money to go out and picket, and they own the house that you're picketing.

These bad housing conditions that continue to exist up there keep our people victims of health problems—high infant and adult mortality rates, higher in Harlem than any other part of the city. They promised us jobs and gave us welfare checks instead; we're still jobless, still unemployed; the welfare is taking care of us, making us beggars, robbing us of our dignity, of our manhood.

So I point out that 1964 was not a pie-in-the-sky Year of Promise, as was promised in January of that year. Blood did flow in the streets of Harlem, Philadelphia, Rochester, some places over in New Jersey and elsewhere. In 1965 even more blood will flow. More than you ever dreamed. It'll flow downtown as well as uptown. Why? Why will it flow? Have the causes that forced it to flow in '64 been removed? Have the causes that made it flow in '63 been removed? The causes are still there. . . .

In 1964, 97 per cent of the black American voters supported Lyndon B. Johnson, Hubert Humphrey and the Democratic Party. Ninety-seven per cent! No one minority group in the history of the world has ever given so much of its uncompromising support to one candidate and one party. No one people, no one group, has ever gone all the way to support a party and its candidate as did the black people in America in 1964. . . .

And the first act of the Democratic Party, Lyndon B. included, in 1965, when the representatives from the state of Mississippi who *refused* to support Johnson came to Washington, D.C., and the black people of Mississippi sent representatives there to challenge the legality of these people being seated—what did Johnson say? Nothing! What did Humphrey say? Nothing! What did Robert Pretty-Boy Kennedy say? Nothing! Nothing! Not one thing! These are the people that black people have supported. This is the party that they have supported. Where were they when the black man needed them a couple days ago in Washington, D.C.? They were where they always are—twiddling their thumbs someplace in the poolroom, or in the gallery.

Black people in 1965 will not be controlled by these Uncle Tom leaders, believe me; they won't be held in check, they won't be held on the plantation by these overseers, they won't be held on the corral, they won't be held back at all.

The frustration of these black representatives from Mississippi, when they arrived in Washington, D.C., the other day, thinking, you know, that the Great Society was going to include them—only to see the door closed in their face like that—that's what makes them think. That's what makes them realize what they're up against. It is this type of frustration that produced the Mau Mau. They reached the point where they saw that it takes power to talk to power. It takes power to make power respect you. It takes madness almost to deal with a power structure that's so corrupt, so corrupt.

So in 1965 we should see a lot of action. Since the old methods haven't worked, they'll be forced to try new methods. . . .

13

After the bombing

On February 13, 1965, Malcolm X returned home from a trip to the European continent where, among other things, the French government had, without explanation, barred him from entry. A few hours later, at 2:30 a.m. on February 14, Molotov cocktails were hurled into the home in East Elmhurst, Queens, where Malcolm, his wife and four young children were asleep. The house was seriously damaged, but the family managed to escape without injury. In the following week Malcolm actually had to defend himself against hints and charges, spread by the police, the press and the Black Muslims, that he had arranged the arson-bombing himself.

Malcolm was scheduled to speak on the day of the bombing at a meeting in Detroit sponsored by the Afro-American Broadcasting Company. Although he was fatigued and distraught, he felt it necessary to appear at this meeting, which the local press had refused to publicize in any way.

Attorney Milton Henry, distinguished guests, brothers and sisters, ladies and gentlemen, friends and enemies: I want to point out first that I am very happy to be here this evening and I am thankful to the Afro-American Broadcasting Company for the invitation to come here this evening. As Attorney Milton Henry has stated—I should say Brother Milton Henry because that's what he is, our brother—I was in a house last night that was bombed, my own. It didn't destroy all my clothes but you know what fire and smoke do to things. The only thing I could get my hands on before leaving was what I have on now.

It isn't something that made me lose confidence in what I am doing, because my wife understands and I have children from this size on down, and even in their young age they understand. I think they would rather have a father or brother or whatever the situation may be who will take a stand in the face of reaction from any narrow-minded people rather than to compromise and later on have to grow up in shame and disgrace.

So I ask you to excuse my appearance. I don't normally come out in front of people without a shirt and tie. I guess that's somewhat a holdover from the Black Muslim movement which I was in. That's one of the good aspects of that movement. It teaches you to be very careful and conscious of how you look, which is a positive contribution on their part. But that positive contribution on their part is greatly offset by too many liabilities.

Also, last night, when the temperature was about 20 above and when this explosion took place, I was caught in what I had on—some pajamas. In trying to get my family out of the house, none of us stopped for any clothes at that point, so we were out in the 20 degree cold. I got them into the house of the neighbor next door. I thought perhaps being in that condition for so long I would get pneumonia or a cold or something like that, so a doctor came today, a nice doctor, and shot something in my arm that naturally put me to sleep. I've been back there asleep ever since the program started in order to get back in shape. So if I have a tendency to stutter or slow down, it's still the effect of that drug. I don't know what kind it was, but it was good; it makes you sleep, and there's nothing like sleeping through a whole lot of excitement.

Tonight one of the things that has to be stressed, which has not only the United States very much worried but also has France, Great Britain and most of the powers who formerly were known as colonial powers worried, and that is the African revolution. They are more concerned with the revolution that is taking place on the African continent than they are with the revolution in Asia and in Latin America. And this is because there are so many people of African ancestry within the domestic confines or jurisdictions of these various governments. . . . There is an increasing number of dark-skinned people in England and also in France.

When I was in Africa in May, I noticed a tendency on the part of the Afro-Americans to—what I call lollygag. Everybody else who was over there had something on the ball, something they were doing, something constructive. Let's take Ghana as an example. There would be many refugees in Ghana from South Africa. . . . Some were being trained in how to be soldiers but others were involved as a pressure group or lobby group to let the people of Ghana never forget what happened to the brother in South Africa. Also you had brothers there from Angola and Mozambique. All of the Africans who were exiles from their particular country and would be in a place like Ghana or Tanganyika, now Tanzania—they would be training. Their every move would be designed to offset what was happening to their people back home where they had left. . . . When they escaped from their respective countries that were still colonized, they didn't try and run away from the family; as soon as they got where they were going, they began to organize into pressure groups to get support at the international level against the injustices they were experiencing back home.

But the American Negroes or the Afro-Americans, who were in these various countries, some working for this government, some working for that government, some in business—they were just socializing, they had turned their back on the cause over here, they were partying, you know. When I went through one country in particular, I heard a lot of their complaints and I didn't make any move. But when I got to another country, I found the Afro-Americans there were making the same complaints. So we sat down and talked and we organized a branch in this particular country of the Organization of Afro-American Unity. That one was the only one in existence at that time. Then during the summer when I went back to Africa, I was able in each country that I visited to get the Afro-American community together and organize them and make them aware of their responsibility to those of us who are still here in the lion's den.

They began to do this quite well, and when I got to Paris and London—there are many Afro-Americans in Paris, and many in London—in November, we organized a group in Paris and within a very short time they had grown into a well-organized unit. In conjunction with the African community, they invited me to Paris Tuesday to address a large gathering of Parisians and Afro-Americans and people from the Caribbean and also from Africa who were interested in our struggle in this country and the rate of progress that we have been making. But the French government and the British government and this government here, the United States, know that I have been almost fanatically stressing the importance of the Afro-Americans uniting with the Africans and working as a coalition, especially in areas which are of mutual benefit to all of us. And the governments in these different places were frightened. . . .

I might point out here that colonialism or imperialism, as the slave system of the West is called, is not something that is just confined to England or France or the United States. The interests in this country are in cahoots with the interests in France and the interests in Britain. It's one huge complex or combine, and it creates what's known not as the American power structure or the French power structure, but an international power structure. This international power structure is used to suppress the masses of dark-skinned people all over the world and exploit them of their natural resources, so that the era in which you and I have been living during the past ten years most specifically has witnessed the upsurge on the part of the black man in Africa against the power structure.

He wants his freedom and now. Mind you, the power structure is international, and its domestic base is in London, in Paris, in Washington, D.C., and so forth. The outside or external phase of the revolution which is manifest in the attitude and action of the Africans today is troublesome enough. The revolution on the outside of the house, or the outside of the structure, is troublesome enough. But now the powers that be are beginning to see that this struggle on the outside by the black man is affecting, infecting the black man who is on the inside of that structure—I hope you understand what I am trying to say. The newly awakened people all over the world pose a problem for what is known as Western interests, which is imperialism, colonialism, racism and all these other negative isms or vulturistic isms. Just as the external forces pose a grave threat, they can now see that the internal forces pose an even greater threat. But the internal forces pose an even greater threat only when they have properly analyzed the situation and know what the stakes really are.

Just advocating a coalition of African, Afro-Americans, Arabs, and Asians who live within the structure automatically has upset France, which is supposed to be one of the most liberal countries on earth, and it made them expose their hand. England is the same way. And I don't have to tell you about this country that we are living in now. When you count the number of dark-skinned people in the Western hemisphere you can see that there are probably over 100 million. When you consider Brazil has two-thirds what we call colored, or non-white, and Venezuela, Honduras and other Central American countries, Cuba and Jamaica, and the United States and even Canada—when you total all these people up, you have probably over 100 million. And this 100 million on the inside of the power structure today is what is causing a great deal of concern for the power structure itself. . . .

We thought that the first thing to do was to unite our people, not only internally, but with our brothers and sisters abroad. It was for that purpose that I spent five months in the Middle East and Africa during the summer. The trip was very enlightening, inspiring, and fruitful. I didn't go into any African country, or any country in the Middle East for that matter, and run into any closed door, closed mind, or closed heart. I found a warm reception and an amazingly deep interest and sympathy for the black man in this country in regards to our struggle for human rights. . . .

I hope you will forgive me for speaking so informally tonight, but I frankly think it is always better to be informal. As far as I am concerned, I can speak to people better in an informal way than I can with all of this stiff formality that ends up meaning nothing. Plus, when people are informal, they are relaxed. When they are relaxed, their mind is more open, and they can weigh things more objectively. Whenever you and I are discussing our problems we need to be very objective, very cool, calm and collected. That doesn't mean we should always be. There is a time to be cool and a time to be hot. See—you got messed up into thinking that there is only one time for everything. There is a time to love and a time to hate. Even Solomon said that, and he was in that book too. You're just taking something out of the book that fits your cowardly nature when you don't want to fight, and you say, "Well, Jesus said don't fight." But I don't even believe Jesus said that. . . .

Before I get involved in anything nowadays, I have to straighten out my own position, which is clear. I am not a racist in any form whatsoever. I don't believe in any form of racism. I don't believe in any form of discrimination or segregation. I believe in Islam. I am a Muslim and there is nothing wrong with being a Muslim, nothing wrong with the religion of Islam. It just teaches us to believe in Allah as the God. Those of you who are Christians probably believe in the same God, because I think you believe in the God who created the universe. That's the one we believe in, the one who created the universe—the only difference being you call him God and we call him Allah. The Jews call him Jehovah. If you could understand Hebrew, you would probably call him Jehovah too. If you could understand Arabic, you would probably call him Allah. But since the white man, your friend, took your language away from you during slavery, the only language you know is his language. You know your friend's language, so when he's putting the rope around your neck, you call for God and he calls for God. And you wonder why the one you call on never answers. . . .

Elijah Muhammad had taught us that the white man could not enter into Mecca in Arabia and all of us who followed him, we believed it. . . . When I got over there and went to Mecca and saw these people who were blond and blue-eyed and pale-skinned and all those things, I said, "Well," but I watched them closely. And I noticed that though they were white, and they would call themselves white, there was a difference between them and the white ones over here. And that basic difference was this: In Asia or the Arab world or in Africa, where the Muslims are, if you find one who says he's white, all he's doing is using an adjective to describe something that's incidental about him, one of his incidental characteristics; there is nothing else to it, he's just white.

But when you get the white man over here in America and he says he's white, he means something else. You can listen to the sound of his voice—when he says he's white, he means he's boss. That's right. That's what white means in this language. You know the expression, "free, white and twenty-one." He made that up. He's letting you know that white means free, boss. He's up there, so that when he says he's white he has a little different sound in his voice. I know you know what I'm talking about. . . .

Despite the fact that I saw that Islam was a religion of brotherhood, I also had to face reality. And when I got back into this American society, I'm not in a society that practices brotherhood. I'm in a society that might preach it on Sunday, but they don't practice it on any day. America is a society where there is no brotherhood. This society is controlled primarily by the racists and segregationists who are in Washington, D.C., in positions of power. And from Washington, D.C., they exercise the same forms of brutal oppression against dark-skinned people in South and North Vietnam, or in the Congo, or in Cuba or any other place on this earth where they are trying to exploit and oppress. That is a society whose government doesn't hesitate to inflict the most brutal form of punishment and oppression upon dark-skinned people all over the world.

Look right now what's going on in and around Saigon and Hanoi and in the Congo and elsewhere. They are violent when their interests are at stake. But for all that violence they display at the international level, when you and I want just a little bit of freedom, we're supposed to be nonviolent. They're violent in Korea, they're violent in Germany, they're violent in the South Pacific, they're violent in Cuba, they're violent wherever they go. But when it comes time for you and me to protect ourselves against lynchings, they tell us to be nonviolent.

That's a shame. Because we get tricked into being nonviolent, and when somebody stands up and talks like I just did, they say, "Why, he's advocating violence." Isn't that what they say? Every time you pick up your newspaper, you see where one of these things has written into it that I am advocating violence. I have never advocated any violence. I have only said that black people who are the victims of organized violence perpetrated upon us by the Klan, the Citizens Councils, and many other forms, should defend ourselves. And when I say we should defend ourselves against the violence of others, they use their press skilfully to make the world think that I am calling for violence, period. I wouldn't call on anybody to be violent without a cause. But I think the black man in this country, above and beyond people all over the world, will be more justified when he stands up and starts to protect himself, no matter how many necks he has to break and heads he has to crack. . . .

The Klan is a cowardly outfit. They have perfected the

art of making Negroes be afraid. As long as the Negro is afraid, the Klan is safe. But the Klan itself is cowardly. One of them never come after one of you. They all come together. They're scared of you. And you sit there when they're putting the rope around your neck saying, "Forgive them, Lord, they know not what they do." As long as they've been doing it, they're experts at it, they know what they're doing. No, since the federal government has shown that it isn't going to do anything about it but *talk,* then it is a duty, it's your and my duty as men, as human beings, it is our duty to our people, to organize ourselves and let the government know that if they don't stop that Klan, we'll stop it ourselves. *Then* you'll see the government start doing something about it. But don't ever think that they're going to do it just on some kind of morality basis. No. So I don't believe in violence—that's why I want to stop it. And you can't stop it with love, not love of those things down there. No! So, we only mean vigorous action in self-defense, and that vigorous action we feel we're justified in initiating by any means necessary.

Now, for saying something like that, the press calls us racist and people who are "violent in reverse." This is how they psycho you. They make you think that if you try to stop the Klan from lynching you, you're practicing violence in reverse. Pick up on this, I hear a lot of you parrot what the man says. You say, "I don't want to be a Ku Klux Klan in reverse." Well, if a criminal comes around your house with his gun, brother, just because he's got a gun and he's robbing your house, and he's a robber, it doesn't make you a robber because you grab your gun and run him out. No, the man is using some tricky logic on you. I say it is time for black people to put together the type of action, the unity, that is necessary to pull the sheet off of them so they won't be frightening black people any longer.

That's all. And when we say this, the press calls us "racist in reverse." "Don't struggle except within the ground rules that the people you're struggling against have laid down." Why, this is insane, but it shows how they can do it. With skilful manipulating of the press they're able to make the victim look like the criminal and the criminal look like the victim.

Right now in New York we have a couple of cases where the police grabbed a brother and beat him unmercifully—and charged him with assaulting them. They used the press to make it look like he is the criminal and they are the victims. This is how they do it, and if you study how they do it here then you'll know how they do it over there. It's the same game going all the time, and if you and I don't awaken and see what this man is doing to us, then it will be too late. They may have the gas ovens built before you realize that they're already hot.

One of the shrewd ways that they project us in the image of a criminal is that they take statistics and with the press feed these statistics to the public, primarily the white public. Because there are some well-meaning persons in the white public as well as bad-meaning persons in the white public. And whatever the government is going to do, it always wants the public on its side—whether it is the local government, state government or federal government. At the local level, they will create an image by feeding statistics to the public through the press showing the high crime rate in the Negro community. As soon as this high crime rate is emphasized through the press, then people begin to look upon the Negro community as a community of criminals.

And then any Negro in the community can be stopped in the street. "Put your hands up," and they pat you down. Might be a doctor, a lawyer, a preacher or some other kind of Uncle Tom, but despite your professional standing, you'll find that you're the same victim as the man who's in the alley. Just because you're black and you live in a black community which has been projected as a community of criminals. And once the public accepts this image, it also paves the way for police-state type of activity in the Negro community—they can use any kind of brutal methods to suppress blacks because they're criminals anyway. And what has given us this image? The press again, by letting the power structure or the racist element in the power structure use them in that way.

A very good example was the riots that took place during the summer. I was in Africa, I read about them over there. If you noticed, they referred to the rioters as vandals, hoodlums, thieves, and they skilfully took the burden off the society for its failure to correct these negative conditions in the black community. They took the burden completely off the society and put it right on the community by using the press to make it appear that the looting and all of this was proof that the whole act was nothing but vandals and robbers and thieves, who weren't really interested in anything other than that which was negative. And I hear many dumb, brainwashed Negroes who parrot the same old party line that the man handed down in his paper.

It was not the case that they were just knocking out store windows ignorantly. In Harlem, for instance, all of the stores are owned by white people, all of the buildings are owned by white people. The black people are just there—paying rent, buying the groceries; but they don't own the stores, clothing stores, food stores, any kind of stores; don't even own the homes that they live in. These are all owned by outsiders, and for these run-down apartment dwellings, the black man in Harlem pays more money than the man down in the rich Park Avenue section. It costs us more money to live in the slums than it costs them to live down on Park Avenue. Black people in Harlem know this, and that the white merchants charge us more money for food in Harlem—and it's the cheap food, the worst food; we have to pay more money for it than the man has to pay for it downtown. So black people know that they're being exploited and that their blood is being sucked and they see no way out.

When the thing is finally sparked, the white man is not there—he's gone. The merchant is not there, the landlord is not there, the one they consider to be the enemy isn't there. So, they knock at his property. This is what makes them knock down the store windows and set fire to things, and things of that sort. It's not that they're thieves. But they [the newspapers] are trying to project the image to the public that this is being done by thieves, and thieves alone. And they ignore the fact that it is not thievery alone. It's a corrupt, vicious, hypocritical system that has castrated the black man, and the only way the black man can get back at it is to strike it in the only way he knows how.

[When I say] they use the press, that doesn't mean that all reporters are bad. Some of them are good, I suppose. But you can take their collective approach to any problem and see that they can always agree when it gets to you and me. They knew that the Afro-American Broadcasting Company was giving this affair—which is designed to honor outstanding black Americans, is it not? But you find nothing in the newspapers that gives the slightest hint that this affair was going to take place—not one hint, though there are supposed to be many sources of news. If you don't think that they're in cahoots, watch. They're all interested, or none of them are interested. It's not a staggering thing. They're not going to say anything in advance about an affair that's being given by any black people who believe in functioning beyond the scope of the ground rules that are laid down by the liberal elements of the power structure.

When you start thinking for yourselves, you frighten them, and they try and block your getting to the public, for the fear that if the public listens to you then the public won't listen to them anymore. And they've got certain Negroes whom they have to keep blowing up in the papers to make them look like leaders. So that the people will keep on following them, no matter how many knocks they get on their heads following them. This is how the man does it, and if you don't wake up and find out how he does it, I tell you, they'll be building gas chambers and gas ovens pretty soon—I don't mean those kind you've got at home in your kitchen—[and] . . . you'll be in one of them, just like the Jews ended up in gas ovens over there in Germany. You're in a society that's just as capable of building gas ovens for black people as Hitler's society was. . . .

Now what effect does [the struggle over Africa] have on us? Why should the black man in America concern himself since he's been away from the African continent for three or four hundred years? Why should we concern ourselves? What impact does what happens to them have upon us? Number one, you have to realize that up until 1959 Africa was dominated by the colonial powers. Having complete control over Africa, the colonial powers of Europe projected the image of Africa negatively. They always project Africa in a negative light: jungle savages, cannibals, nothing civilized. Why then naturally it was so negative that it was negative to you and me, and you and I began to hate it. We didn't want anybody telling us anything about Africa, much less calling us Africans. In hating Africa and in hating the Africans, we ended up hating ourselves, without even realizing it. Because you can't hate the roots of a tree, and not hate the tree. You can't hate your origin and not end up hating yourself. You can't hate Africa and not hate yourself.

You show me one of these people over here who has been thoroughly brainwashed and has a negative attitude toward Africa, and I'll show you one who has a negative attitude toward himself. You can't have a positive attitude toward yourself and a negative attitude toward Africa at the same time. To the same degree that your understanding of and attitude toward Africa become positive, you'll find that your understanding of and your attitude toward yourself will also become positive. And this is what the white man knows. So they very skilfully make you and me hate our African identity, our African characteristics.

You know yourself that we have been a people who hated our African characteristics. We hated our hair, we hated the shape of our nose, we wanted one of those long dog-like noses, you know; we hated the color of our skin, hated the blood of Africa that was in our veins. And in hating our features and our skin and our blood, why, we had to end up hating ourselves. And we hated ourselves. Our color became to us a chain—we felt that it was holding us back; our color became to us like a prison which we felt was keeping us confined, not letting us go this way or that way. We felt that all of these restrictions were based solely upon our color, and the psychological reaction to that would have to be that as long as we felt imprisoned or chained or trapped by black skin, black features and black blood, that skin and those features and that blood holding us back automatically had to become hateful to us. And it became hateful to us.

It made us feel inferior; it made us feel inadequate; made us feel helpless. And when we fell victims to this feeling of inadequacy or inferiority or helplessness, we turned to somebody else to show us the way. We didn't have confidence in another black man to show us the way, or black people to show us the way. In those days we didn't. We didn't think a black man could do anything except play some horns—you know, make some sound and make you happy with some songs and in that way. But in serious things, where our food, clothing, shelter and education were concerned, we turned to the man. We never thought in terms of bringing these things into existence for ourselves, we never thought in terms of doing things for ourselves. Because we felt helpless. What made us feel helpless was our hatred for ourselves. And our hatred for ourselves stemmed from our hatred for things African. . . .

After 1959 the spirit of African nationalism was fanned to a high flame and we then began to witness the complete collapse of colonialism. France began to get out of French West Africa, Belgium began to make moves to get out of the Congo, Britain began to make moves to get out of Kenya, Tanganyika, Uganda, Nigeria and some of these other places. And although it looked like they were getting out, they pulled a trick that was colossal.

When you're playing ball and they've got you trapped, you don't throw the ball away—you throw it to one of your teammates who's in the clear. And this is what the European powers did. They were trapped on the African continent, they couldn't stay there—they were looked upon as colonial and imperialist. They had to pass the ball to someone whose image was different, and they passed the ball to Uncle Sam. And he picked it up and has been running it for a touchdown ever since. He was in the clear, he was not looked upon as one who had colonized the African continent. At that time, the Africans couldn't see that though the United States hadn't colonized the African continent, it had colonized 22 million blacks here on this continent. Because we're just as thoroughly colonized as anybody else.

When the ball was passed to the United States, it was passed at the time when John Kennedy came into power. He picked it up and helped to run it. He was one of the shrewdest backfield runners that history has ever recorded. He surrounded himself with intellectuals—highly educated, learned and well-informed people. And their analysis told him that the government of America was confronted with a new problem. And this new problem stemmed from the fact that Africans were now awakened, they were enlightened, they were fearless, they would fight. This meant that the Western powers couldn't stay there by force. Since their own economy, the European economy and the American economy, was based upon their continued influence over the African continent, they had to find some means of staying there. So they used the friendly approach.

They switched from the old openly colonial imperialistic approach to the benevolent approach. They came up with some benevolent colonialism, philanthropic colonialism, humanitarianism, or dollarism. Immediately everything was Peace Corps, [Operation] Crossroads, "We've got to help our African brothers." Pick up on that: Can't help us in Mississippi. Can't help us in Alabama, or Detroit, or out here in Dearborn where some real Ku Klux Klan lives. They're going to send all the way to Africa to help. I know Dearborn; you know, I'm from Detroit, I used to live out here in Inkster. And you had to go through Dearborn to get to Inkster. Just like driving through Mississippi when you got to Dearborn. Is it still that way? Well, you should straighten it out.

So, realizing that it was necessary to come up with these new approaches, Kennedy did it. He created an image of himself that was skilfully designed to make the people on the African continent think that he was Jesus, the great white father, come to make things right. I'm telling you, some of these Negroes cried harder when he died than they cried for Jesus when he was crucified. From 1954 to 1964 was the era in which we witnessed the emerging of Africa. The impact that this had on the civil-rights struggle in America has never been fully told.

For one thing, one of the primary ingredients in the complete civil-rights struggle was the Black Muslim movement. The Black Muslim movement took no part in things political, civic—it didn't take too much part in anything other than stopping people from doing this drinking, smoking, and so on. Moral reform it had, but beyond that it did nothing. But it talked such a strong talk that it put the other Negro organizations on the spot. Before the Black Muslim movement came along, the NAACP was looked upon as radical; they were getting ready to investigate it. And then along came the Muslim movement and frightened the white man so hard that he began to say, "Thank God for old Uncle Roy, and Uncle Whitney and Uncle A. Philip and Uncle"—you've got a whole lot of uncles in there; I can't remember their names, they're all older than I so I call them "uncle." Plus, if you use the word "Uncle Tom" nowadays, I hear they can sue you for libel, you know. So I don't call any of them Uncle Tom anymore. I call them Uncle Roy.

One of the things that made the Black Muslim movement grow was its emphasis upon things African. This was the secret to the growth of the Black Muslim movement. African blood, African origin, African culture, African ties. And you'd be surprised—we discovered that deep within the subconscious of the black man in this country, he is still more African than he is American. He *thinks* that he's more American than African, because the man is jiving him, the man is brainwashing him every day. He's telling him, "You're an American, you're an American." Man, how could you think you're an American when you haven't ever had any kind of an American treat over here? You have never, never. Ten men can be sitting at a table eating, you know, dining, and I can come and sit down where they're dining. They're dining; I've got a plate in front of me, but nothing is on it. Because all of us are sitting at the same table, are all of us diners? I'm not a diner until you let me dine. Just being at the table with others who are dining doesn't make me a diner, and this is what you've got to get in your head here in this country.

Just because you're in this country doesn't make you an American. No, you've got to go farther than that before you can become an American. You've got to enjoy the fruits of Americanism. You haven't enjoyed those fruits. You've enjoyed the thorns. You've enjoyed the thistles. But you have not enjoyed the fruits, no sir. You have fought harder for the fruits than the white man has, you have worked harder for the fruits than the white man has, but you've enjoyed less. When the man put the uniform on you and sent you abroad, you fought harder than they did. Yes, I know you—when you're fighting for them, you can fight.

The Black Muslim movement did make that contribution. They made the whole civil-rights movement become more militant, and more acceptable to the white power structure. He would rather have them than us. In fact, I think we forced many of the civil-rights leaders to be even more militant than they intended. I know some of them who get out there and "boom, boom, boom" and don't mean it. Because they're right on back in their corner as soon as the action comes.

John F. Kennedy also saw that it was necessary for a new approach among the American Negroes. And during his entire term in office, he specialized in how to psycho the American Negro. Now, a lot of you all don't like my saying that—but I wouldn't ever take a stand on that if I didn't know what I was talking about. By living in this kind of society, pretty much around them, and you know what I mean when I say "them," I learned to study them. You can think that they mean you some good ofttimes, but if you look at it a little closer you'll see that they don't mean you any good. That doesn't mean there aren't some of them who mean good. But it does mean that most of them don't mean good.

Kennedy's new approach was pretending to go along with us in our struggle for civil rights and different other forms of rights. But I remember the exposé that *Look* magazine did on the Meredith situation in Mississippi. *Look* magazine did an exposé showing that Robert Kennedy and Governor Barnett had made a deal, wherein the Attorney General was going to come down and try to force Meredith into school, and Barnett was going to stand at the door, you know, and say, "No, you can't come in." He was going to get in anyway, but it was all arranged in advance and then Barnett was supposed to keep the support of the white racists, because that's who he was upholding, and Kennedy would keep the support of the Negroes, because that's who he'd be upholding. It was a cut-and-dried deal. And it's not a secret; it was written, they write about it. But if that's a deal, how many other deals do you think go down? What you think is on the level is crookeder, brothers and sisters, than a pretzel, which is most crooked.

So in my conclusion I would like to point out that the approach that was used by the administration right up until today was designed skilfully to make it appear they were trying to solve the problem when they actually weren't. They would deal with the conditions, but never the cause. They only gave us tokenism. Tokenism benefits only a few. It never benefits the masses, and the masses are the ones who have the problem, not the few. That one who benefits from tokenism, he doesn't want to be around us anyway—that's why he picks up on the token. . . .

The masses of our people still have bad housing, bad schooling and inferior jobs, jobs that don't compensate with sufficient salaries for them to carry on their life in this world. So that the problem for the masses has gone absolutely unsolved. The only ones for whom it has been solved are people like Whitney Young, who is supposed to be placed in the cabinet, so the rumor says. He'll be the first black cabinet man. And that answers where he's at. And others have been given jobs, like Carl Rowan, who was put over the USIA, and is very skilfully trying to make Africans think that the problem of black men in this country is all solved.

The worst thing the white man can do to himself is to take one of these kinds of Negroes and ask him, "How do your people feel, boy?" He's going to tell that man that we are satisfied. That's what they do, brothers and sisters. They get behind the door and tell the white man we're satisfied. "Just keep on keeping me up here in front of them, boss, and I'll keep them behind you." That's what they talk when they're behind closed doors. Because, you see, the white man doesn't go along with anybody who's not for him. He doesn't care are you for right or wrong, he wants to know are you for him. And if you're for him, he doesn't care what else you're for. As long as you're for him, then he puts you up over the Negro community. You become a spokesman.

In your struggle it's like standing on a revolving wheel;

you're running, but you're not going anywhere. You run faster and faster and the wheel just goes faster and faster. You don't ever leave the spot that you're standing in. So, it is very important for you and me to see that our problem has to have a solution that will benefit the masses, not the upper class—so-called upper class. Actually, there's no such thing as an upper-class Negro, because he catches the same hell as the other class Negro. All of them catch the same hell, which is one of the things that's good about this racist system—it makes us all one. . . .

If you'd tell them right now what is in store for 1965, they'd think you crazy for sure. But 1965 will be the longest and hottest and bloodiest year of them all. It has to be, not because you want it to be, or I want it to be, or we want it to be, but because the conditions that created these explosions in 1963 are still here; the conditions that created explosions in 1964 are still here. You can't say that you're not going to have an explosion when you leave the conditions, the ingredients, still here. As long as those explosive ingredients remain, then you're going to have the potential for explosion on your hands.

And, brothers and sisters, let me tell you, I spend my time out there in the streets with people, all kinds of people, listening to what they have to say. And they're dissatisfied, they're disillusioned, they're fed up, they're getting to the point of frustration where they begin to feel, "What do we have to lose?" When you get to that point, you're the type of person who can create a very dangerously explosive atmosphere. This is what's happening in our neighborhoods, to our people.

I read in a poll taken by *Newsweek* magazine this week, saying that Negroes are satisfied. Oh, yes, *Newsweek*, you know, supposed to be a top magazine with a top pollster, talking about how satisfied Negroes are. Maybe I haven't met the Negroes he met. Because I know he hasn't met the ones that I've met. And this is dangerous. This is where the white man does himself the most harm. He invents statistics to create an image, thinking that that image is going to hold things in check. You know why they always say Negroes are lazy? Because they want Negroes to be lazy. They always say Negroes can't unite because they don't want Negroes to unite. And once they put this thing in the Negro's mind, they feel that he tries to fulfill their image. If they say you can't unite black people, and then you come to them to unite them, they won't unite because it's been said that they're not supposed to unite. It's a psycho that they work, and it's the same way with these statistics.

When they think that an explosive era is coming up, then they grab their press again and begin to shower the Negro public, to make it appear that all Negroes are satisfied. Because if you know you're dissatisfied all by yourself and ten others aren't, you play it cool; but if you know that all ten of you are dissatisfied, you get with it. This is what the man knows. The man knows that if these Negroes find out how dissatisfied they really are—even Uncle Tom is dissatisfied, he's just playing his part for now—this is what makes the man frightened. It frightens them in France and frightens them in England, and it frightens them in the United States.

And it is for this reason that it is so important for you and me to start organizing among ourselves, intelligently, and try to find out: "What are we going to do if this happens, that happens or the next thing happens?" Don't think that you're going to run to the man and say, "Look, boss, this is me." Why, when the deal goes down, you'll look just like me in his eyesight; I'll make it tough for you. Yes, when the deal goes down, he doesn't look at you in any better light than he looks at me. . . .

I point these things out, brothers and sisters, so that you and I will know the importance in 1965 of being in complete unity with each other, in harmony with each other, and not letting the man maneuver us into fighting one another. The situation I have been maneuvered into right now, between me and the Black Muslim movement, is something that I really deeply regret, because I don't think anything is more destructive than two groups of black people fighting each other. But it's something that can't be avoided because it goes deep down beneath the surface, and these things will come up in the very near future.

I might say this before I sit down. If you recall, when I left the Black Muslim movement, I stated clearly that it wasn't my intention to even continue to be aware that they existed; I was going to spend my time working in the non-Muslim community. But they were fearful if they didn't do something that perhaps many of those who were in the [Black Muslim] mosque would leave it and follow a different direction. So they had to start doing a take-off on me, plus, they had to try and silence me because of what they know that I know. I think that they should know me well enough to know that they certainly can't frighten me. But when it does come to the light—excuse me for keeping coughing like that, but I got some of that smoke last night—there are some things involving the Black Muslim movement which, when they come to light, will shock you.

The thing that you have to understand about those of us in the Black Muslim movement was that all of us believed 100 per cent in the divinity of Elijah Muhammad. We believed in him. We actually believed that God, in Detroit by the way, that God had taught him and all of that. I always believed that he believed it himself. And I was shocked when I found out that he himself didn't believe it. And when that shock reached me, then I began to look everywhere else and try and get a better understanding of the things that confront all of us so that we can get together in some kind of way to offset them.

I want to thank you for coming out this evening. I think it's wonderful that as many of you came out, considering the blackout on the meeting that took place. Milton Henry and the brothers who are here in Detroit are very progressive young men, and I would advise all of you to get with them in any way that you can to try and create some kind of united effort toward common goals, common objectives. Don't let the power structure maneuver you into a time-wasting battle with others when you could be involved in something that is constructive and getting a real job done. . . .

I say again that I'm not a racist, I don't believe in any form of segregation or anything like that. I'm for brotherhood for everybody, but I don't believe in forcing brotherhood upon people who don't want it. Let us practice brotherhood among ourselves, and then if others want to practice brotherhood with us, we're for practicing it with them also. But I don't think that we should run around trying to love somebody who doesn't love us. Thank you.

14

Confrontation with an 'expert'

Malcolm X's last appearance on the airwaves took place in New York over Station WINS on the night of February 18, 1965. This was four days after the bombing of his home, nine days after the Selma police had used cattle-prods and clubs to drive 170 students on a brutal and grueling, double-time "march" into the countryside, and the same day that hundreds of Brooklyn students had "rioted" in demonstrations against segregated school conditions.

It was a phone-in panel show, *Contact,* conducted by Stan Bernard. The guests were Aubrey Barnette, ex-Muslim who had just co-authored an article, "The Black Muslims Are a Fraud," in the February 27 *Saturday Evening Post;* Gordon Hall, an "expert on extremist organizations"; and Malcolm. In the first hour of the program, which dealt mainly with the Black Muslims and the bombing of Malcolm's home, Hall's tone toward Malcolm was hostile and contemptuous. Malcolm at first tried to ignore this, but gave up the attempt in the final third of the program, from which the following is transcribed.

STAN BERNARD: Gordon, you're a professional observer of extremist organizations, and you classify the black nationalists, and of course the Muslims, as extremist organizations. How do you appraise this political warfare that's going on in the black nationalist organizations?

GORDON HALL: Well, to be perfectly frank with you, and I do believe in speaking frankly, I think at the moment the Muslims are a dying organization, they're on the way out, they've made no impact in the Negro community nationally at any point, and even less so now. Malcolm has no place to go, which is why he's floundering so badly. For example, he's been breaking bread with the communists downtown—

MALCOLM: What communists, what communists have I been—

HALL: Socialist Workers Party—

MALCOLM: You are absolutely out of your mind, I have never broken bread with—

HALL: You have given several speeches which they have reprinted—

MALCOLM: Well, that's not breaking bread. I speak anywhere, I spoke in London, England, and—

HALL: You were very glad to go back several times, and they are reprinting one of your major addresses in *The Militant*—

MALCOLM: I spoke in a church, I spoke in a church in Rochester a couple of nights ago. Does that make me a Methodist?—

HALL: We're not talking about churches, we're not talking about churches, we're talking about the Socialist Workers Party—

MALCOLM: Just because you speak somewhere doesn't make you that. You speak to the public and you speak on any platform—

HALL: Oh, I don't, Malcolm.

MALCOLM: —and I speak to the public and I speak on any platform.

HALL: I'm afraid that's not the case, Malcolm.

MALCOLM: If speaking on the socialist platform makes me a socialist, then when I speak in a Methodist church—

HALL: It was a communist platform—

MALCOLM: I was in Selma, Alabama, last week, speaking in Martin Luther King's church. Does that make me a follower of Martin Luther King? No, your line of reasoning, sir, doesn't fit me.

HALL: I was just saying that I was asked a question by Stan, and I think that at the moment the nationalist movement has no place to go, they're floundering, and they're putting out lines everywhere. And there is an alliance in the general Harlem area between some of the Peking-based communists, the Progressive Labor Movement, and some of the others, the Bill Epton crowd. Bill Epton is a self-confessed avowed communist—you'd agree to that, wouldn't you, Malcolm?

MALCOLM: I know nothing about what Bill Epton's political philosophy is. Bill Epton, in my opinion, is one of the militant leaders in Harlem. Now, what his political beliefs are, I think that he has a right to them.

HALL: I didn't say he didn't have a right, I'm just saying what he is.

MALCOLM: Well—

HALL: He has stated to me personally—

MALCOLM: Well, whatever they are—

HALL: I have interviewed him, he told me that he was an avowed communist—

MALCOLM: So whatever they are, he has a right to them.

HALL: —and he'd like to see this system of ours completely

junked, as well. All I'm saying is that there's a lot of warfare—

MALCOLM: I think you'll find that a lot of the children that are out there in Brooklyn—

HALL: May I speak, Malcolm, may I speak—

MALCOLM: —on the rampage against the segregated school system here in New York City—

HALL: May I speak?

MALCOLM: —and King and some of his followers in Alabama right now are fighting against the same system.

HALL: You're a great clock-killer, but you don't let other people speak.

MALCOLM: Well, say your words.

HALL: I'm trying to—if you would be kind enough to let me speak—

BERNARD: Go ahead.

MALCOLM: Go right ahead, Mr. Hall. Dr. Hall.

HALL: Well, at any rate, they're floundering now, and there's a lot of internecine warfare going on in the Harlem section, and most of the movements are small and splintered, and are splinters of splinters. And I suppose only the future will tell which one will emerge victorious and perhaps claim the most members. I would make a prediction, and I think we could come back a year from now, Stan, and I think you may find Malcolm preaching a completely separate doctrine, and leading some other kind of movement.

MALCOLM: Well, you know, one of the best compliments that Dr. Hall here can pay me is just the things that he says. When he begins to pat me on the back, I'll be worried—

HALL: I'm not patting you on the back. I told you up in Boston—

MALCOLM: —I said, *when* you begin to pat me on the back—

HALL: —give a little time and you'd be preaching a new line, and you are.

MALCOLM: I said, *when* you begin to pat me on the back, I'll be worried. When *you* begin, people of your profession, who make a profession out of dealing with groups in this country. When *you* begin to pat me on the back, then I'll be worried, sir. Now I would advise you, if you think that nationalism has no influence whatsoever, the nationalists, the Organization of Afro-American Unity are having a rally at the Audubon Ballroom on Broadway—

HALL: I think you mentioned it earlier, you're getting in a couple of plugs.

MALCOLM: I'm going to mention it again. I wouldn't come on the program and not mention it. Because one of the most difficult things for nationalists to do is to let the public know what they're doing. So we're having this rally at the Audubon—

HALL: The public is engaged in a vast conspiracy against you; it's obvious from what you say—

MALCOLM: You're going to make me mention it four or five times. We're having this rally at the Audubon Ballroom this coming Sunday at 2 o'clock and people just like you, who consider themselves experts on nationalists, are given front-seat invitations, and I would advise you, since it's your profession to know what nationalists and other so-called extremists are doing, to come and be our guest. Now, one thing I'd like to point out to you, Dr. Hall, whenever you find black—

HALL: You know perfectly well I'm not a doctor, Malcolm.

MALCOLM: Well, you sound like you're an expert on something, I thought you were a doctor. Whenever you find the condition that black people are confronted by in this country, being permitted by the government to exist so long, the condition in itself is extreme—and any black man, who really feels about this situation that our people are confronted by, his feelings are extreme. You can't take a cough syrup and cure somebody who has pneumonia. And the black people are becoming more extreme every day. I was in Alabama a couple of weeks ago, before I went to England, down there with Dr. King and some of the others, who are trying to just register and vote. Now I'll tell you frankly, with King supposed to be the most moderate, most conservative, most loving, most endorsed, most supported—

HALL: The word is responsible, but go ahead.

MALCOLM: O.K., responsible to the white power structure. To me, when white people talk about responsible—

HALL: He's a responsible American, that's what he is.

MALCOLM: When people like you usually refer to Negroes as responsible, you mean Negroes who are responsible in the context of your type of thinking. So, getting right back to Dr. King, any time you find a person who goes along with the government, to the degree that Dr. King does, and still Dr. King's followers, children, are made to run down the road by brute policemen who are nothing but Klansmen, and the federal government can step in and do nothing about it, I will guarantee you that you are producing extremists by the thousands. Now when I was down there, they wanted me to speak to the press, but didn't want me to speak to the church, or the children or the students. It was the students themselves that insisted that I speak, that gave me the opportunity to speak.

BERNARD: Malcolm, how do you think that's going to be changed?

MALCOLM: Sir, I think that—

BERNARD: How? I mean, I know you're talking about these children being made into extremists, but how, how is the situation going to be changed? Do you think by warfare?

MALCOLM: It's not going to be changed by making believe that it doesn't exist to the intense degree that it exists. And it's not going to be changed by putting out polls, like *Newsweek* magazine did last week, implying that Negroes are satisfied with the rate of progress. This is deluding yourself. And my contention is that white people do themselves a disservice by putting out these kinds of things to make it appear that Negroes are satisfied when the most explosive situation, racially, that has ever existed in this country, exists right now. And all of your so-called responsible leaders, when they speak about the situation, they say everything is in check. Yet every day you find Negro children becoming more explosive than ever—

BERNARD: You're not answering my question, you're avoiding it. I asked you how is it going to change? Is it going to change through extreme behavior, let's call it extreme reaction—in other words, you are going to react extremely to a situation that you don't like? Now, how extreme can your reaction be?

MALCOLM: Well, sir, when Russia put missiles in Cuba, the only thing that made Russia get her missiles out of Cuba was when America pointed missiles right back at Russia.

BERNARD: Are you suggesting revolution?

MALCOLM: No, I'm saying this: that when you respect the intelligence of black people in this country as being equal to that of whites, then you will realize that the reaction of the black man to oppression will be the same as the reaction of the white man to oppression. The white man will not turn the other cheek when he's being oppressed. He will not practice any kind of love of a Klan or a Citizens Council or anyone else. But at the same time the white man is asking the black man to do this. So all I'm saying is, I absolutely believe the situation can be changed. But I don't think it can be changed by white people taking a hypocritical approach, pretending that it is not as bad as it is, and by black leaders, so-called responsible leaders, taking a hypocritical approach, trying to make white people think that black people are patient and long-suffering and are willing to sit around here a long time, or a great deal of time longer, until the problem is made better.

BERNARD: Let's go back to the phone. The WINS *Contact* number: Judson 2-6405. This is *Contact,* you're on the air.

GIRL (phoning in): Hello, Malcolm?

MALCOLM: Yes?

GIRL: The Ku Klux Klan should get you.

MALCOLM: Ha-ha-ha-ha.

BERNARD: Thank you very much.

MALCOLM: Let me point something out to this lady. I'm invited to Mississippi next week. I'll be going to Mississippi next week. The Ku Klux Klan will have all the opportunity it wants to get me. I was in Alabama last week; they had an opportunity then. You don't always have to go down South to find the Ku Klux Klan. Evidently one is your father, or you wouldn't be able to speak as you do.

BERNARD: This is *Contact,* you're on the air.

WOMAN (phoning in): I'd like to ask Mr. Barnette a question. In Louis Lomax's book, *When the Word Is Given . . . ,* he says none of the rumors about the Muslims receiving help from outside, communist or segregationist sources has proved true. Does Mr. Barnette have any information that will verify or refute that statement?

BERNARD: I didn't quite get it, but Mr. Barnette has left the room. He's left the studio during this last part of the debate, and he's not here to answer it.

WOMAN: Could Mr. Hall answer it?

BERNARD: Could Mr. Hall answer it?

HALL: I didn't quite understand your question. Could you quote that again for us?

WOMAN: Yes. Louis Lomax says that none of the rumors about Muslims receiving help from outside, communist or segregationist sources has proved true. And I'd like to know what they think about this.

HALL: I would agree with Mr. Lomax's statement on that. I think that's an actual statement. I'm not so sure that that is applicable to other militant groups in the Negro community, but I think it's applicable to the Muslims.

BERNARD: I'm not sure—

MALCOLM: They don't get any help from outside sources?

HALL: She's talking about outside communist or segregationist sources.

MALCOLM: Do they get any help from *inside* segregationist sources? You're the expert.

HALL: I would doubt that very much. I have no evidence of that, and neither do you; and if you do, then—

MALCOLM: I'm not saying that I do.

HALL: —put up, Malcolm. You're implying; you're a very sly implier.

MALCOLM: Because you give me the impression, all of a sudden, that you're a protector of the Black Muslim movement—

HALL: Not a bit, not a bit.

MALCOLM: —when it comes to rallying them against the black nationalists. Because you know that the Black Muslim movement is in a bag, and has no place to go.

HALL: I'm the one, I'm the one—Just to show how faulty your logic is—let me speak. Just to show you how faulty your logic is, I arranged for the *Saturday Evening Post* story, which you have praised with your own mouth tonight as the best thing ever written on the Black Muslims.

MALCOLM: Not because you arranged it—

HALL: I arranged it.

MALCOLM: It's the best, not because you arranged it. That doesn't make it best. It's best because Aubrey—

BERNARD: Mr. Hall is saying that he arranged for it to be written because he thought it was valid and valuable.

MALCOLM: What he arranged, what he did, is immaterial to me. I'm not commenting on—

HALL: You never want to louse up an argument with facts, Malcolm.

MALCOLM: Sir, I'm not commenting on what you did; it's immaterial to me.

HALL: But you said it was a wonderful piece.

MALCOLM: I'm saying what Aubrey did. Aubrey is the one who did the piece. You can arrange for Rockwell to write a piece.

HALL: Aubrey came to me—

MALCOLM: You can arrange for Rockwell to write a piece.

HALL: —because he knew that I could get this story told in the best fashion.

MALCOLM: You can arrange for Rockwell, you can arrange for the Klan to write a piece.

HALL: No, I could not, I could not.

MALCOLM: So what you can arrange doesn't impress me.

HALL: Malcolm, you know perfectly well that I couldn't. That's just a smear.

MALCOLM: You could, sir. You're a mercenary.

HALL: (to Bernard): You can't see the technique?

MALCOLM: No, you're a professional, you said that yourself; that's why I call you a doctor—

BERNARD: Next call, can we go on to our next call? Now?

HALL: I like it when he talks this way, because he exposes himself.

MALCOLM: No, I'm exposing you as a mercenary, an opportunist.

BERNARD: Here we go, it's the next call time, here we go. This is *Contact,* you're on the air.

MAN (phoning in): I'd like to direct a question to Malcolm X.

BERNARD: Go ahead.

MAN: I heard him on a newsreel say that Charlie's enemies are his enemies, and this was supposed to refer to the white man as Charlie.

MALCOLM: Charlie is the Ku Klux Klan, and the White Citizens Council, and white people who practice discrimination and segregation against black people.

MAN: Right. Then I'd like to ask you, something which you mentioned about aid from Red China.

MALCOLM: I've never mentioned anything about aid from Red China. Ask Dr. Hall here, he's an expert; I think he'll even have to agree to that.

MAN: This man asked you if the aid to fight Charlie came from the Red Chinese, would you accept it? You said from anybody.

MALCOLM: Well, that doesn't specify Red China. I said this, that when you're in the den of a wolf, and a fox comes along and offers to help you, you'll accept help from any source available against that wolf.

BERNARD: Yeah, but they asked you—

MALCOLM: This doesn't mean that you love foxes.

BERNARD: Did they specify when they asked you the question whether they—

MALCOLM: I don't think they said Communist China; if I recall, I could be wrong, but I don't think they specified Communist China. Although let me say this about Communist China: China is a nation of 700 million people. Physically they exist; physically they exist. I don't go along with the American reaction of pretending that 700 million Chinese don't exist. When I was in Africa during the summer, everywhere I looked, I saw Chinese. It's only when I get back to America that I don't see any Chinese. I just don't think it's mature to pretend that 700 million people don't exist.

HALL: That doesn't happen to be U.S. policy, to pretend that they don't exist, Malcolm. You just say things that aren't so.

MALCOLM: No, but I—

HALL: The United States is well aware of Red China.

MALCOLM: She certainly is. They just detonated some nuclear bombs over there. Plus their forces have the United States soldiers tied down in Saigon. She'd have to be well aware. She has half of your forces tied up. You'd be crazy not to be aware of her existence. But at the same time you're trying to give the public, the people over here, the impression that they don't exist.

HALL: You're just saying that; that's not the case at all.

MALCOLM: They're human beings, just the same as you and I are.

BERNARD: You, of course, espouse recognition of Red China and her admission into the United Nations?

MALCOLM: Many of your senators in Washington, D.C., espouse the same thing. I think most intelligent, progressive people, who are up to date in their thinking, have finally reached intellectual and political maturity to the point where they feel that when you've got that many people on this earth, you'd better recognize them and deal with them as human beings, and then they will deal with you as human beings. If you say you shouldn't deal with them because they are communist, then why deal with Russia? Or if you say you shouldn't deal with them because they fought United Nations forces in Korea, then why deal with Tshombe? Tshombe also fought United Nations forces in Katanga. If you use the same yardstick to measure these people all the time, I think you'll end up with better results.

BERNARD: All right, let's go on to our next call. Our WINS *Contact* number—Judson 2-6405. This is Stan Bernard's *Contact,* you're on the air.

MAN (phoning in): Hello? Malcolm, I'd like to ask you whether you feel that the recent action of the Gaullist government in refusing you entry into France is in any way inconsistent with France's general policy towards the Afro-Asian community and Africa in particular.

MALCOLM: Yes, I dispatched a wire to Dean Rusk, the Secretary of State here today, demanding an investigation into the reason why the French government could ban an American citizen and no reaction come from the American Embassy whatsoever. But I might point out, I was in Paris last November and was successful in organizing a good organization—another one that Dr. Hall over here can investigate in his capacity—in the American Negro community in Paris, and they have been working in conjunction with the African community. And it was the African community and the Afro-American community in Paris that invited me there to address a mass rally, and the French government permitted my entry into that country. And I might point out that it was the Communist trade-union workers in Paris that refused to let them have the hall initially, blocked their attempt to get the second hall, and eventually exercised influence in the French government to stop it. The Communist trade-union workers, one of the largest unions in that country. The reason I was in London—I had been invited there to attend the first congress that had been given by the Council of African Organizations, who had a four-day congress, and invited me to make the closing address, because they were interested in the struggle of the black man in this country in his quest for human dignity and human rights.

BERNARD: O.K., we're going to move on to our next call. This is *Contact,* you're on the air.

WOMAN (phoning in): Hello. May I speak to Malcolm X, please?

BERNARD: Yes, go right ahead.

WOMAN: I would like to—I don't have a question for Malcolm X. I would like to tell him that I am 100 per cent with him for whatever he goes along with toward helping the Negro. I think it's an awful shame that anyone should throw a bomb into a house where there's human beings, particularly children. And I don't go along at all with the Muslims, the so-called Muslims, because to me they're only teaching hate.

MALCOLM: Well, I confess that I was one of the leaders in projecting the Muslim movement and causing so many people to believe in the distorted version of Islam that is taught there. But at the same time I have to point out that there are some progressive elements, right-meaning persons, in the Muslim movement. All of them are not wrong. There are many in there that mean well but are just being misled by the hierarchy, many of which do not mean well. But there is a large progressive element within the movement, and usually they are the ones who come in, they stay a year and they get disillusioned, and they go back out. But I was responsible for giving the people the impression that the Black Muslim movement was more than what it is, and I take that responsibility. You can put the complete blame upon me. But at the same time that I take that responsibility, I want to point out that no white man or white group or agency can use me against Elijah Muhammad or against the Black Muslim movement. When you hear me open up my mouth against another black man, no white man can put words in my mouth, nor can any white man sic me on another black group. When I have analyzed the man and the group with my own understanding, and feel that it is detrimental to the interests of the black community, then I'm going to attack it with that same intensity.

BERNARD: Gordon, you were going to say something?

HALL: Well, again, as you know, it's more words. He began by saying that he has to confess that he was responsible for misleading so many people on the Muslim count. There were never very many Muslims. Let's always come back to the fact that not very many people were ever misled. The white press was misled into believing there were a lot of Muslims.

MALCOLM: Dr. Hall—

HALL: There were never more than 15,000 Muslims in America, and there are only now 6,000. And we have 22 million Negroes in the United States. Keep these facts uppermost in one's mind.

MALCOLM: Dr. Hall—

BERNARD: You admitted this at the very beginning, Malcolm. You said the 15,000 figure is correct.

HALL: These are facts, Malcolm.

MALCOLM: Here's another fact you have to keep in mind. There were never many Mau Mau. There never were. There were always more Kikuyu, more Kenyans, than Mau Mau.

HALL: What is this supposed to prove?

MALCOLM: But it was the Mau Mau who brought independence to Kenya. And the man that was regarded as an extremist and a monster, just five years ago, Jomo Kenyatta, is the president of the Republic of Kenya today; and it is this same man, who five years ago—

HALL: The situation in colonial Africa today is not like it is in the United States.

MALCOLM: Well, this is colonial. Any time you have a system, in 1965, that will take children and let them be marched down the road by not the criminal elements but—

BERNARD: But in numbers you have to draw one big analogy. In the United States, the Negro is still a minority. In the United States. And when you are talking about minorities within minorities within minorities, and you start boiling it all down, you can't really draw that analogy with a colony.

MALCOLM: I say this: The Mau Mau was also a minority, a microscopic minority, but it was the Mau Mau who not only brought independence to Kenya, but—

BERNARD: Within a vast Negro majority.

MALCOLM: But it brought it—that wick. The powder keg is always larger than the wick. The smallest thing in the powder keg is the wick. You can touch the powder all day long and nothing happens. It's the wick that you touch that sets the powder off.

BERNARD: I wouldn't want to, I think it'll blow up.

MALCOLM: It's the wick that you touch that sets the powder off. You go here in Harlem, and you take all these moderate Negroes that Dr. Hall here puts the stamp of approval on, and regards them as responsible—they don't explode. It's the wick, it's that small element that you refer to as nationalist and other—

HALL: You're doing all you can to encourage it, Malcolm, with your demagogic language—

MALCOLM: No, no, I don't encourage it—

HALL: Oh, yes you do.

MALCOLM: I don't encourage it; but I'm not going to sit here and pretend that it doesn't exist.

BERNARD: Don't you incite, Malcolm? Don't you incite?

MALCOLM: I don't think so. How are you going to incite people who are living in slums and ghettos? It's the city structure that incites. A city that continues to let people live in rat-nest dens in Harlem and pay higher rent in Harlem than they pay downtown. This is what incites it. Who lets merchants outcharge or overcharge people for their groceries and their clothing and other commodities in Harlem, while you pay less for it downtown. This is what incites it. A city that will not create some kind of employment for people who are barred from having jobs just because their skin is black. That's what incites it. Don't ever accuse a black man for voicing his resentment and dissatisfaction over the criminal condition of his people as being responsible for inciting the situation. You have to indict the society that allows these things to exist. And this is where I differ with Dr. Hall.

BERNARD: Well, in a sense—

HALL: We differ in many places, Malcolm.

MALCOLM: This is another one of the many places where we differ, Dr. Hall.

BERNARD: Well, in a sense, didn't Hitler also talk about different points of view, didn't he say that conditions existed, and didn't he also incite?

MALCOLM: I don't know anything about Hitler, I wasn't in Germany. I'm in America.

BERNARD: Don't—don't, please, Malcolm—

MALCOLM: I say, I wasn't in Germany.

BERNARD: You know about Hitler as well as—

MALCOLM: You can't point to Hitler and Germany behind what's going on here in America! Turn on the television tonight and see what's—

BERNARD: In Harlem—

MALCOLM: No, no, no—turn on the television tonight

and see what they're doing to Dr. King.

HALL: Dr. King's methods are not your methods. You couldn't do in Alabama what he is doing.

MALCOLM: Sir—sir—

HALL: You could not do—

MALCOLM: Sir, you had better pray that I don't go and try to do what he is doing. Any time Dr. King—

HALL: Oh, these are just, these are just words, Malcolm—

MALCOLM: Any time Dr. King goes along with people like you—like you—you should put forth more effort to keep him out of jail. You should put forth more effort to protect him. And you should put forth more effort to protect the people who go along with him and display this love and this patience. If you would do more for those people and spend some of your time trying to help those people instead of trying to attack me, probably this country would be a much better place in which to live. You spend too much of your time, doctor, trying to investigate—

HALL: I rarely ever mention you, Malcolm, you're hardly worth mentioning—

MALCOLM: You spend too much of your time, doctor, running around trying to keep track of dissatisfied black people whom you label as extremists—

HALL: Hardly, hardly—

MALCOLM: —whereas if you would spend some of your time in these places where Dr. King is fighting, then you would make this country a better place to live in.

HALL: Malcolm, I lectured all over the state of Alabama, when you had nothing to do with the Muslims or anybody else.

MALCOLM: Did you have on a white sheet? Did you have on a white sheet?

HALL: See what I mean?

BERNARD: Gentlemen, time. Bell—here we go—bell. O.K.,

that's round 15. We've just had it.

MALCOLM: Dr. Hall, come up to the Audubon Sunday at 2 o'clock, and we'll continue from there.

HALL: I have more important things to do.

BERNARD: Gentlemen, we have to move on. Time has run out. I'd like to thank all of you for showing up tonight. Thank you very much, Gordon—Malcolm—and, of course, Aubrey Barnette. . . .

15

Last answers and interviews

The following is a selection of statements made by Malcolm X during the last three months of his life, taken from various interviews and answers to questions at meetings.

A con man?

MALCOLM: A lot of people have warned me about the *Village Voice*. It's supposed to be a liberal paper, but they say it is very narrow.

MARLENE NADLE: Some people on the staff think you're a con man.

MALCOLM: If I wanted to be just a con man, I wouldn't be fool enough to try it on these streets where people are looking for my life, where I can't walk around after dark. If I wanted power, I could have gone anywhere in the world. They offered me jobs in all the African countries.

Muhammad is the man, with his house in Phoenix, his $200 suits, and his harem. He didn't believe in the

black state or in getting anything for the people. That's
why I got out.

*From Marlene Nadle's
article, "Malcolm X:
The Complexity of a
Man in the Jungle,"*
Village Voice,
FEBRUARY 25, 1965

Not afraid of investigation

Malcolm was asked if he would tell the House Un-American
Activities Committee the same things he had just told a public
meeting in New York.

MALCOLM: I would welcome an opportunity to defend
anything you ever hear me say—to anyone, anywhere,
at any time. I'll go there without being called. The only
thing is: You don't question me behind closed doors. Keep
it public, and I'll take anything you can throw. Keep it
out in public.

Frankly, I don't think there is a committee in Washington, D.C., that can defend itself when it comes to the
race problem in this country. You are taken to Washington when they are trying to connect you with a foreign
power. They treat black people in this country like we're
foreigners. If we get connected with ourselves we're supposed to be subversive.

No, brother, I never worry about any kind of investigation. I think that our cause is just. And I think that our
patience has been sufficient up to now to justify showing
some impatience. We're justified. As I said earlier, both
Johnson and Humphrey, when they wake up every morning, should thank God, whatever God they believe in, that

black people have shown the patience that we've shown, or the ignorance that we've displayed. They should thank God, and they should try to do something about it before the impatience increases.

Answer to question,
Militant Labor Forum,
NEW YORK, JANUARY 7, 1965

On racism

Malcolm was asked the difference between white racism and black racism.

MALCOLM: Usually the black racist has been produced by the white racist. In most cases where you see it, it is the reaction to white racism, and if you analyze it closely, it's not really black racism. I think black people have shown less racist tendencies than any people since the beginning of history. . . .

If we react to white racism with a violent reaction, to me that's not black racism. If you come to put a rope around my neck and I hang you for it, to me that's not racism. Yours is racism, but my reaction has nothing to do with racism. My reaction is the reaction of a human being, reacting to defend himself and protect himself. This is what our people haven't done, and some of them, at least at the high academic level, don't want to. But most of us aren't at that level.

Answer to question,
Harvard Law School
Forum,
DECEMBER 16, 1964

QUESTION: What do you think is responsible for race prejudice in the U.S.?

MALCOLM: Ignorance and greed. And a skilfully designed program of miseducation that goes right along with the American system of exploitation and oppression.

If the entire American population were properly educated—by properly educated, I mean given a true picture of the history and contributions of the black man—I think many whites would be less racist in their feelings. They would have more respect for the black man as a human being. Knowing what the black man's contributions to science and civilization have been in the past, the white man's feelings of superiority would be at least partially negated. Also, the feeling of inferiority that the black man has would be replaced by a balanced knowledge of himself. He'd feel more like a human being. He'd function more like a human being, in a society of human beings.

So it takes education to eliminate it. And just because you have colleges and universities, doesn't mean you have education. The colleges and universities in the American educational system are skilfully used to miseducate.

From interview on
January 18, 1965,
printed in
Young Socialist,
MARCH–APRIL, 1965

Intermarriage and a black state

PIERRE BERTON: Now before you left Elijah Muhammad and went to Mecca and saw the original world of Islam, you believed in complete segregation of the whites and the Negroes. You were opposed both to integration and to intermarriage. Have you changed your views there?

MALCOLM: I believe in recognizing every human being

as a human being—neither white, black, brown or red; and when you are dealing with humanity as a family there's no question of integration or intermarriage. It's just one human being marrying another human being, or one human being living around and with another human being.

I may say, though, that I don't think it should ever be put upon a black man, I don't think the burden to defend any position should ever be put upon the black man, because it is the white man collectively who has shown that he is hostile toward integration and toward intermarriage and toward these other strides toward oneness.

So as a black man and especially as a black American, any stand that I formerly took, I don't think that I would have to defend it, because it's still a reaction to the society, and it's a reaction that was produced by the society; and I think that it is the society that produced this that should be attacked, not the reaction that develops among the people who are the victims of that negative society.

BERTON: But you no longer believe in a black state?

MALCOLM: No.

BERTON: In North America?

MALCOLM: No, I believe in a society in which people can live like human beings on the basis of equality.

From the Pierre Berton Show, taped at Station CFTO-TV in Toronto, JANUARY 19, 1965

The man you think you are

MALCOLM: I'm the man you think you are. And if it doesn't take legislation to make you a man and get your rights recognized, don't even talk that legislative talk to me. No, if we're both human beings we'll both do the same thing. And if you want to know what I'll do, figure out what you'll do I'll do the same thing—only more of it.

Answer to question,
Militant Labor Forum,
JANUARY 7, 1965

How to organize the people

MALCOLM: The only person who can organize the man in the street is the one who is unacceptable to the white community. They don't trust the other kind. They don't know who controls his actions. . . .

Marlene Nadle asked if he planned to use hate to organize the people.

MALCOLM: I won't permit you to call it hate. Let's say I'm going to create an awareness of what has been done to them. This awareness will produce an abundance of energy, both negative and positive, that can then be channeled constructively. . . .

The greatest mistake of the movement has been trying to organize a sleeping people around specific goals. You have to wake the people up first, then you'll get action.

MISS NADLE: Wake them up to their exploitation?

MALCOLM: No, to their humanity, to their own worth, and to their heritage. The biggest difference between the parallel oppression of the Jew and the Negro is that the Jew never lost his pride in being a Jew. He never ceased to be a man. He knew he had made a significant contribution to the world, and his sense of his own value gave him the courage to fight back. It enabled him to act and think independently, unlike our people and our leaders.

From Marlene Nadle's article Village Voice,
FEBRUARY 25, 1965

Dollarism and capitalism

MALCOLM: It is true that most of your South American countries are satellites of the United States. But they don't have to feel bad. This country made a satellite out of Khrushchev, made him lose his job. Everybody becomes a satellite nowadays.

They did—go and study the relations between the United States and Russia during the past four or five years and you'll find this country maneuvered Russia into almost becoming a satellite. They had to get rid of Khrushchev in order to get some of their independence back.

I say that as objectively as I can. I'm not trying to jump into anybody's camp, I don't have any axes to grind. This is just my own opinion from observations that I've made traveling around the world and listening with big ears.

It's easy to become a satellite today without even being aware of it. This country can seduce God. Yes, it has that seductive power—the power of dollarism. You can cuss out colonialism, imperialism and all other kinds of isms, but it's hard for you to cuss that dollarism. When they drop those dollars on you, your soul goes.

*Answer to question,
Militant Labor Forum,*
JANUARY 7, 1965

QUESTION: What is your opinion of the world-wide struggle now going on between capitalism and socialism?

MALCOLM: It is impossible for capitalism to survive, primarily because the system of capitalism needs some blood to suck. Capitalism used to be like an eagle, but now it's more like a vulture. It used to be strong enough to go and suck anybody's blood whether they were strong or not. But now it has become more cowardly, like the vulture, and it can only suck the blood of the helpless. As the nations of the world free themselves, then capitalism has less victims, less to suck, and it becomes weaker and weaker. It's only a matter of time in my opinion before it will collapse completely.

> *From interview,*
> Young Socialist,
> MARCH–APRIL, 1965

The police commissioner

HARRY RING: A week or so ago, Police Commissioner Murphy asserted that the recent warnings of danger of a new outbreak in Harlem could actually provide the fuel for such an outbreak. I know that you were one of those who recently made such a warning. What would you say about this?

MALCOLM: Well, Commissioner Murphy's attitude is one of the things primarily responsible for much of the ill feeling among the races, and especially in the black communities like Harlem, Bedford-Stuyvesant and other places. When he says—when he *warns*—against anyone mentioning that there is a great chance for continued violence this summer, what he is doing is trying to stick his head in the sand.

His attitude is the same as the American attitude toward the existence of China. The general American attitude is that Americans are supposed to pretend that 700 million Chinese don't exist, and that a little island off the coast of China is *China*. Well now, Commissioner Murphy has this same attitude toward the conditions that exist in the black community. These conditions are so explosive that it is impossible for them to continue to exist without there being violent explosions.

Instead of Police Commissioner Murphy involving himself in some kind of work that will eliminate the *causes* of these explosions, he wants to *condemn* the people who are pointing toward the continued existence of these conditions and who at the same time are warning that the continued existence of the causes is going to create the explosions.

So I think that the police commissioner is probably the best example of an imbecile. I hate to use this kind of word on your program, but he actually has a very imbecilic approach to the problems that exist in the black community, and his continued mouthing of this type of thing will do nothing to better the condition; rather, it makes the condition worse.

> *From interview on*
> *Station WBAI-FM*
> NEW YORK, JANUARY 28,
> 1965

Public notice to Rockwell

At a public rally of the Organization of Afro-American Unity in Harlem on January 24, 1965, Malcolm said that on a television news broadcast he had seen Rev. Martin Luther King knocked down by a racist, that "it hurt me," and that if he had been there he would have gone to King's aid. He also read aloud the text of a telegram he had sent to George Lincoln Rockwell, head of the American Nazi Party:

This is to warn you that I am no longer held in check from fighting white supremacists by Elijah Muhammad's separatist Black Muslim movement, and that if your present racist agitation against our people there in Alabama causes physical harm to Reverend King or any other black Americans who are only attempting to enjoy their rights as free human beings, that you and your Ku Klux Klan friends will be met with maximum physical retaliation from those of us who are not handcuffed by the disarming philosophy of nonviolence, and who believe in asserting our right of self-defense—by any means necessary.

On politics

Malcolm was asked about the outcome of the recent presidential election in the United States.

MALCOLM: It isn't a president who can help or hurt; it is the system. And this system is not only ruling us in America, it is ruling the world. Nowadays, when a man is running for president of the United States, he is not running for president of the United States alone; he has to be acceptable to other areas of the world where American influence rules.

If Johnson had been running all by himself, he would not have been acceptable to anyone. The only thing that made him acceptable to the world was that the shrewd capitalists, the shrewd imperialists, knew that the only way people would run toward the fox would be if you showed them a wolf. So they created a ghastly alternative. And it had the whole world—including people who call themselves Marxists—hoping that Johnson would beat Goldwater.

I have to say this: Those who claim to be enemies of the system were on their hands and knees waiting for Johnson to get elected—because he is supposed to be a man of peace. And *at that moment* he had troops invading the Congo and South Vietnam! He even has troops in areas where other imperialists have already withdrawn. Peace Corps to Nigeria, mercenaries to the Congo!

> *Answer to question,*
> *Presence Africaine*
> *meeting, Paris,*
> NOVEMBER 23, 1964

MALCOLM: First, our people have to become registered voters. But they should not become involved actively in politics until we have gotten a much better understanding than we now have of the gains to be made from politics in this country. We go into politics in a sort of gullible way, an emotional way, whereas politics, especially in this country, is cold-blooded and heartless. We have to be given a better understanding of the science of politics as well as becoming registered voters.

And then we shouldn't take sides either way with any of these parties. In my opinion, we should reserve our political action for the situation at hand, in no way identifying with either party or selling ourselves to either party, but taking political action that's for the good of human beings and that will eliminate these injustices. I, for one, do not think that the present man who's in the White House is morally capable of taking the kind of action necessary to eliminate these things.

> *Answer to question,*
> *Harvard Law School*
> *Forum,*
> DECEMBER 16, 1964

MALCOLM: The reluctance of Negroes to vote isn't always because they don't have the right to vote. Political machines in most states and cities select as a rule [as candidates for political office] not black people who are intellectually capable to deal with politics as it is, but puppets that serve as their mouthpieces to control the politics of the community. The black people in Harlem have witnessed this thing year in and year out, and have seen how the politics of Harlem, and other Negro communities have been pretty much controlled from outside.

It's not that they're politically lethargic or dead—they purposely have abstained. When you give them something to point toward, or vote for, you'll find that they'll be just as active as they've been inactive. It's the purpose of the OAAU to work among that element of politically inactive black people. We intend to charge them and get them active out here, so we can get a little action.

Those who haven't been involved in politics actively are the ones who get involved in physical action. They have not seen anything that could be made to materialize in politics in the past, so they didn't resort to politics. They resorted to things physical, to methods physical, if you understand what I mean. What we intend to do is try and harness their energy by giving them an understanding of politics.

Answer to question by
member of delegation
from McComb
Mississippi,
JANUARY 1, 1965

MALCOLM: The gentleman asks me if I believe in political action, number one. And if the leftist groups got together and put me up for mayor, would I run? I believe in political action, yes. Any kind of political action. I believe in action, period. Whatever kind of action is necessary. When you hear me say "by any means necessary," I mean exactly that. I believe in anything that is necessary to correct unjust conditions—political, economic, social, physical, anything that's necessary. I believe in it—as long as it's intelligently directed and designed to get results.

But I don't believe in getting involved in any kind of political action or other kind of action without sitting down and analyzing the possibilities of success or failure. And I also don't believe that groups should refer to themselves as "leftist," "rightist," or "middle-ist." I think that they should just be whatever they are and don't let people put labels on them—and don't ever put them on yourself. Sometimes a label can kill you.

Answer to question,
Militant Labor Forum,
JANUARY 7, 1965

Marlene Nadle, noting that Malcolm wanted to run militant black candidates for office, asked him if he would be a candidate.

MALCOLM: I don't know at this point. I think I am more effective attacking the establishment. You can't do that as well once you're inside it.

Miss Nadle asked if he thought an all-black party like the Freedom Now Party in Michigan was needed.

MALCOLM: Yes, in some cases you have to create new machinery. In others it's better to take over existing machinery. Either way, we're going to be involved in all levels of politics from '65 on.

From Marlene Nadle,
Village Voice,
FEBRUARY 25, 1965

Slumlords and anti-Semitism

In his talk, "Prospects for Freedom in 1965," Malcolm referred to the slumlords who own the houses in Harlem, "but don't live there themselves; usually they live up around the Grand Concourse [Bronx] or somewhere." In the discussion period first a woman, then a man, objected to this remark.

MALCOLM: The lady said that she'd enjoyed herself, but she ceased to feel joyful—I'm paraphrasing the question—when I mentioned the landlords living up on the Grand Concourse. Well, they also live other places besides the Grand Concourse. But many of them live on the Grand Concourse. This is no reflection on anybody on the Grand Concourse—only on those who are guilty, only those who are guilty. I imagine if I said Central Park West or Central Park East, someone over there probably would have felt bad. But I can't think of all those places, you know.

Yes ma'am. [*Woman resumes speaking*] What did you mean? You see there—you're touchy. You say it sounds like an anti-Semitic statement. Why does it sound like an anti-Semitic statement? Are Jews the only ones who live on the Grand Concourse? You know, you might have some Italians up there, or some Irish, or something else. But if Jews are the only ones who live up there, then you should investigate, and find out why. Now you're going to say I really sound anti-Semitic. No, you let yourself in for it.

When you say that some of the black bourgeoisie also live on the Concourse, the implication of what you are saying is that some of our own people also are slum landlords. If you noticed, when I made my reference to the Concourse, I didn't say anything about any particular color. I mentioned slumlords and whoever lives up there. I included everybody. Some of you all are on the defensive. I mean this. It's a dangerous thing, you know, to let yourself get to where everytime someone's talking, you think they're talking about you. It's not so good.

Now, where the black bourgeoisie is concerned, and the bourgeoisie maintaining this particular black establishment— Here's a book, called *The Negro Mood* [by Lerone Bennett, Jr.]—one of the best. If you can't find this book anywhere else, you can get it from the Nationalist Memorial Bookstore, up on Seventh Avenue, between 125th and 126th—Dr. Michaux—*The Negro Mood*. There's a chapter in there called "The Black Establishment," and you ought to read it. It tells you how the white power structure downtown controls the black community through the black establishment.

And you'll see that it's not the black bourgeoisie that supports the black leaders—it's the white power structure downtown. This is what they mean when they say a "responsible" Negro leader—one that they have put in power and use to maintain the status quo. When they refer to "responsible," that's what they're talking about. An "irresponsible" Negro leader is one who is not inside their bag, you know—he's going somewhere else.

So don't try to put it back on us. No, we'll accept whatever guilt we have, that is, the black community will accept our black bourgeoisie, their mistakes, and all else, we'll accept them all. I don't deny any of it. But when I made my statement, it was blanket. I could have been speaking about Italians, Irish, Polish, everything. But you jumped up. You're sitting on a hot seat.

Answer to question,
Militant Labor Forum,
JANUARY 7, 1965

Militant whites and blacks

MALCOLM: The brother wanted to know what practical steps could be taken to confront this unjust situation that exists here in New York and get some meaningful results. The one mistake that has been made in the struggle of the oppressed against the oppressor is that it's been factionalized too much—too many factions. You've got downtown factions, uptown factions, crosstown factions and some basement factions. Instead of them having any degree of coordination toward a common objective, usually they are divided and spend a lot of time either being suspicious of each other, or knocking at each other, or even outright fighting each other.

Whereas you have black people in Harlem who are militant, they don't go for white people downtown too much, no matter how militant they are. Now the blacks who come downtown and mix with the whites who are militant, usually don't even know how to talk to the blacks who are still uptown. I had to bring this out. I've noticed it from observation.

You have all types of people who are fed up with what's going on. You have whites who are fed up, you have blacks who are fed up. The whites who are fed up can't come uptown too easily because people uptown are more fed up than anybody else, and they are so fed up that it's not so easy to come uptown.

Whereas the blacks uptown who come downtown usually are the type, you know, who almost lose their identity—they lose their soul, so to speak—so that they are not in a position to serve as a bridge between the militant whites and the militant blacks; that type can't do it. I hate to hit him like that, but it's true. He has lost his identity, he has lost his feeling, and usually—play it cool, please—he usually has actually lost his contact with Harlem himself. So that he serves no purpose, he's almost rootless, he's not uptown and he's not fully downtown.

So when the day comes when the whites who are *really*

fed up—I don't mean these jive whites, who pose as liberals and who are not, but those who are fed up with what is going on—when *they* learn how to really establish the proper type of communication with those uptown who are fed up, and they get some coordinated action going, you'll get some changes. You'll get some changes. And it will take both, it will take everything that you've got, it will take that.

But how many sitting here right now feel that they could truly identify with a struggle that was designed to eliminate the basic causes that create the conditions that exist? Not very many. They can jive; but when it comes to identifying yourself with a struggle that is not endorsed by the power structure, that is not acceptable, where the ground rules are not laid down by the society which you live in and which you're struggling against—you can't identify with that, you step back.

Oh, when things get bad enough, everybody gets into the act. And that's what is coming—in 1965.

Answer to question,
Militant Labor Forum,
JANUARY 7, 1965

Marlene Nadle noted that Malcolm "considers all militant whites possible allies. He qualifies the possibility. And woven into the qualifications are the threads of the emotions running through Harlem."

MALCOLM: If we are going to work together, the blacks must take the lead in their own fight. In phase one, the whites led. We're going into phase two now.

This phase will be full of rebellion and hostility. Blacks will fight whites for the right to make decisions that affect the struggle in order to arrive at their manhood and self-respect.

The hostility is good. It's been bottled up too long. When we stop always saying yes to Mr. Charlie and turning the hate against ourselves, we will begin to be free.

Miss Nadle asked how he planned to get white militants to work with him when he was sending out slings and arrows at them.

MALCOLM: We'll have to try to rectify that.

[It would be difficult to get militant whites and blacks together.] The whites can't come uptown too easily because the people aren't feeling too friendly. The black who goes downtown loses his identity, loses his soul. He's in no position to be a bridge because he has lost contact with Harlem. Our Negro leaders never had contact, so they can't do it.

The only person who could is someone who is completely trusted by the black community. If I were to try, I would have to be very diplomatic, because there are parts of Harlem where you don't dare mention the idea.

From Marlene Nadle,
Village Voice,
FEBRUARY 25, 1965

Advice to a nonviolent heckler

A nonviolence advocate indignantly asked Malcolm if he thought the three civil-rights workers murdered in Mississippi were cowards. He interrupted the answer several times. He said he had been to Mississippi. A woman shouted a challenge to Malcolm about going there. While the questioner grew more heated and antagonistic, Malcolm remained calm throughout his reply.

MALCOLM: Sir, I have great respect and admiration for one who has the nerve to tie his own hands and then walk out and let a brute brutalize him. I have to respect him because he's doing something that I don't understand. What he's doing is beyond my power to even comprehend. It would be like putting handcuffs on me and putting me in the ring and telling me to fight Cassius Clay, or Sonny Liston, nonviolently. I don't think I could do it, and whoever could do it, you know—power to you. . . .

All I suggest is, and I don't suggest it as condemnation of COFO or SNCC—I know too many of them, they're brave students, men, and all that. All that I'm saying is— since your approach, as you say, is "tactical"—a tactical approach is designed to get certain results. It's designed to keep you alive. It's designed to bring you victory. Why, we just can't say victory has been brought about. We can't say that it is preserving life. . . .

I'm not criticizing you or condemning you, but I'm questioning your tactics. I'm questioning your tactics. [*Questioner speaks again*] No, no, if Schwerner could come back here and talk to you, or, what's the black one's name? Let me tell you something. I was over in Africa and I read what they did to Chaney. They said that they beat that black one to death; they shot the other two, but they said they beat every bone and every bone was broken. Now you know what? I think people who tell our people to be nonviolent are almost agents of the Ku Klux Klan. I don't think 1965 will be a very nonviolent year. Your year was '64.

I'm going down to Mississippi myself, I've been invited to go on down there, and Alabama and some of those other places, and you know—I just don't see nonviolence. [*Questioner speaks again*] You can go with me. [*Questioner speaks again. Chairman: "Can we have some order?"*] I don't blame him— he's excited. I would be excited too. [*Questioner continues*]

Now look here, brother, if you're going to be nonviolent in Mississippi, you should be nonviolent here too. I'll tell you why. It would be more "tactical" to be nonviolent with me than it would be to be nonviolent with the Klan. For a lot of reasons.

I don't want you to think I'm attacking COFO. I know James Forman, I saw John Lewis in Nairobi last summer, in Kenya, the land of the Mau Mau—he was over there in Zambia and other places. And they're all friends of mine.

As I said in my opening statement, I believe that the Mau Mau was one of the first and foremost of the liberation movements on the African continent. And in every instance on the African continent where the point was made, it took groups that were committed—committed to any means necessary to bring recognition and respect to their people. Whether it be on the African continent, or whether it be in Mississippi, Alabama, New York City, it takes groups of people, be they white or be they black, who are committed to any means necessary to preserve the lives and property of people when the law itself shows that it's incapable of doing its job.

In Brooklyn you have the Hassidic Jews who have formed vigilante committees. You have them in other parts of the country. No one thinks it's so wrong. Well, I say that all we need is a few. Only because of the type of oppression and tyranny and opposition we are confronted by, ours need to be invisible. You know what I mean by invisible—invisible. You never see them. You just feel them. Thank you.

Answer to question,
Militant Labor Forum,
JANUARY 7, 1965

On going back to Africa

Malcolm was asked how he thought Afro-Americans would be received by the Africans if they should go back to Africa.

MALCOLM: After lengthy discussions with many Africans at all levels, I would say some would be welcome and some wouldn't be welcome. Those that have a contribution to make would be welcome, but those that have no contribution to make would not be welcome; I don't think any of us, if we look at it objectively, could find fault with that.

And I believe this, that if we migrated back to Africa culturally, philosophically and psychologically, while remaining here physically, the spiritual bond that would develop between us and Africa through this cultural, philosophical and psychological migration, so-called migration, would enhance our position here, because we would have our contacts with them acting as roots or foundations behind us. You never will have a foundation in America. You're out of your mind if you think that *this* government is ever going to back you and me up in the same way that it backed others up. They'll never do it. It's not in them.

As an example, take the Chinese. You asked me about Red China. The Chinese used to be disrespected. They used to use that expression in this country: "You don't have a Chinaman's chance." You remember that? You don't hear it lately. Because a Chinaman's got more chance than they have now. Why? Because China is strong. Since China became strong and independent, she's respected, she's recognized. So that wherever a Chinese person goes, he is respected and he is recognized. He's not respected and recognized because of what he as an individual has done; he is respected and recognized because he has a country behind him, a continent behind him. He has some power behind him. They don't respect him, they respect what's behind him.

By the same token, when the African continent in its independence is able to create the unity that's necessary to increase its strength and its position on this earth, so that Africa too becomes respected as other huge continents are respected, then, wherever people of African origin, African heritage or African blood go, they will be respected—but only when and because they have something much larger that looks like them behind them. With that behind you, you will get some respect. Without it behind you, you can do almost anything under the sun in this society—pass any kind of law that Washington can think of—and you and I will still be trying to get them to enforce that law. We'll be like that Chinaman [about whom] they used to say, "He doesn't have a Chinaman's chance." Now you don't have a Negro's chance. But with Africa getting its independence, you and I will have more of a chance. I believe in that 100 per cent.

And this is what I mean by a migration or going back to Africa—going back in the sense that we reach out to them and they reach out to us. Our mutual understanding and our mutual effort toward a mutual objective will bring mutual benefit to the African as well as to the Afro-American. But you will never get it just relying on Uncle Sam alone. You are looking to the wrong direction. Because the wrong people are in Washington, D.C., and I mean from the White House right on down. I hope I don't step on anybody's toes by saying that. I didn't vote for him, so I can say it.

Answer to question,
HARYOU-ACT forum
for Domestic
Peace Corps members
HARLEM, DECEMBER 12, 1964

On black nationalism

QUESTION: How do you define black nationalism, with which you have been identified?

MALCOLM: I used to define black nationalism as the idea that the black man should control the economy of his community, the politics of his community, and so forth.

But, when I was in Africa in May, in Ghana, I was speaking with the Algerian ambassador who is extremely militant and is a revolutionary in the true sense of the word (and has his credentials as such for having carried on a successful revolution against oppression in his country). When I told him that my political, social and economic philosophy was black nationalism, he asked me very frankly, well, where did that leave him? Because he was white. He was an African, but he was Algerian, and to all appearances he was a white man. And he said if I define my objective as the victory of black nationalism, where does that leave him? Where does that leave revolutionaries in Morocco, Egypt, Iraq, Mauritania? So he showed me where I was alienating people who were true revolutionaries, dedicated to overturning the system of exploitation that exists on this earth by any means necessary.

So, I had to do a lot of thinking and reappraising of my definition of black nationalism. Can we sum up the solution to the problems confronting our people as black nationalism? And if you notice, I haven't been using the expression for several months. But I still would be hard pressed to give a specific definition of the over-all philosophy which I think is necessary for the liberation of the black people in this country.

From interview,
Young Socialist,
MARCH–APRIL, 1965

Describing an OAAU meeting in Harlem, Marlene Nadle wrote that "a man stood, rocked back on his heels, and very slowly said, 'We heard you changed, Malcolm. Why don't you tell us where you're at with them white folks?' Without dropping a syllable he [Malcolm] gave a black nationalist speech on brotherhood."

MALCOLM: I haven't changed. I just see things on a broader scale. We nationalists used to think we were militant. We were just dogmatic. It didn't bring us anything.

Now I know it's smarter to say you're going to shoot a man for what he is doing to you than because he is white. If you attack him because he is white, you give him no out. He can't stop being white. We've got to give the man a chance. He probably won't take it, the snake. But we've got to give him a chance.

We've got to be more flexible. Why, when some of our friends in Africa didn't know how to do things, they went ahead and called in some German technicians. And they had blue eyes.

I'm not going to be in anybody's straitjacket. I don't care what a person looks like or where they come from. My mind is wide open to anybody who will help get the ape off our backs.

From Marlene Nadle,
Village Voice,
FEBRUARY 25, 1965

The American ambassador

MALCOLM: I was speaking to the American ambassador in a certain country on the African continent. First thing he told me when I went in to see him, he told me, "I think you're a racist," and so forth and so forth and so forth. Well, I respected him because he spoke his mind, and once I explained my position, what I believed in and so forth, he told me this: He said, "You know, as long as

I'm on the African continent"—he had been an ambassador in a couple of other African countries, and an African head of state had told me that this man was the best ambassador that America had on the African continent; that's why I talked with him.

He said, "As long as I'm in Africa, I deal with people as human beings." He said, "For some strange reason, color doesn't enter into it at all." He said, "I'm more aware of the differences in language than I am that there is a difference in color: It's just a *human* atmosphere." He said, "But whenever I return to the United States and I'm talking to a non-white person, I'm conscious of it, I'm self-conscious, I'm aware of the color differences."

So I told him, "What you're telling me, whether you realize it or not, is that it is not basic in you to be a racist, but that society there in America, which you all have created, makes you a racist." This is true, this is the *worst* racist society on this earth. There is no country on earth in which you can live and racism be brought out in you—whether you're white or black—more so than this country that poses as a democracy. This is a country where the social, economic, political atmosphere creates a sort of psychological atmosphere that makes it almost impossible, if you're in your right mind, to walk down the street with a *white* person and not be self-conscious, or he or she not be self-conscious. It almost can't be done, and it makes you *feel* this racist tendency that pops up. But it's the society itself.

My suggestion would be that young people, like yourselves, many of whom are still in school and are more flexible in matters where you have not yet come to a conclusion, sit back and weigh the thing for yourself and analyze it. If you can ever find what it is in the very atmosphere here that brings out these things, then perhaps you might be able to save the country. You might be able to build a better society. But I have very much doubt that you can, I don't think that you can, change the generation that preceded you.

Answer to question,
HARYOU-ACT forum,
DECEMBER 12, 1964

The Red Chinese ambassador

MALCOLM: What do I think about Red China in relation to the Afro-American? Well, I think that it is good to have centers of power on this earth that aren't controlled from either Paris, London or Washington, D.C. I think whenever you have some power on the African continent or the Asian continent that can act in an independent way, it actually serves your and my purpose better. Because the only time this man gives you and me a break is when he has something on the outside of his house that he's worried about. Then he lets those on the inside of his house have a little more leeway than normal.

Plus, when I was in Ghana, I had an opportunity in May, and then again when I was in Africa a couple of weeks ago, to have dinner with the Chinese ambassador there. When I say the Chinese ambassador, I don't mean Chiang Kai-shek's ambassador—I had dinner with the Chinese ambassador that represents some 700 million people—and I found the man to be very intelligent, very well informed.

He acted more human than many of the Americans that I've met. And he was well informed on the problem here. He didn't sound racist, he didn't sound fanatic, he didn't sound unreal, he seemed to have a very objective picture in front of him, he didn't sound like he was anti-American, and he didn't sound like he was anti-white. In fact, he told me it was silly for a person to be placed, or allow himself to be placed, in the position of a racist.

Now, this is from a Chinese ambassador, who's projected by the American press as representing a country that strictly deals in racism. If he wanted to impress me, since he had heard I was a racist, because that's all they say I am, he should have been talking some of that racist talk to me. Instead, he was telling me that it's not wise and intelligent for a person to take the position of a racist because you can't defend it. And this is true. You can't take a racist position and defend it. No, you don't have anything to base it on.

Answer to question,
HARYOU-ACT forum,
DECEMBER 12, 1964

Nature of coming world showdown

PIERRE BERTON: There has been talk, I think by you, by Elijah Muhammad, about an Armageddon in the United States by 1984. I'm wondering if you still believe that, and why that particular date?

MALCOLM: Much of what Elijah Muhammad has taught, I don't think he believes in himself; and I say that and can easily defend it sitting opposite him. But where an ultimate clash between East and West is concerned, I think that an objective analysis of events that are taking place on this earth today points toward some type of ultimate showdown.

You can call it a political showdown, or even a showdown between the economic systems that exist on this earth which almost boil down along racial lines. I do believe that there will be a clash between East and West.

I believe that there will ultimately be a clash between the oppressed and those that do the oppressing. I believe that there will be a clash between those who want freedom, justice and equality for everyone and those who want to continue the systems of exploitation. I believe that there will be that kind of clash, but I don't think that it will be based upon the color of the skin, as Elijah Muhammad had taught it.

However, I do think you'll find that the European powers, which are the former colonial powers, if they're not able to readjust their thinking of superiority toward the darker-skinned people, whom they have been made to think are inferior, then the lines can easily be drawn— they can easily be lumped into racial groups and it will be a racial war.

From interview on
Pierre Berton Show,
JANUARY 19, 1965

Malcolm's last formal speech, "The Black Revolution and its Effect Upon the Negroes of the Western Hemisphere," was given February 18, 1965, to a capacity audience in the Barnard Gymnasium at Columbia University.

MALCOLM: We are living in an era of revolution, and the revolt of the American Negro is part of the rebellion against the oppression and colonialism which has characterized this era. . . .

It is incorrect to classify the revolt of the Negro as simply a racial conflict of black against white, or as a purely American problem. Rather, we are today seeing a global rebellion of the oppressed against the oppressor, the exploited against the exploiter.

The Negro revolution is not a racial revolt. We are

interested in practicing brotherhood with anyone really interested in living according to it. But the white man has long preached an empty doctrine of brotherhood which means little more than a passive acceptance of his fate by the Negro. . . .

[The Western industrial nations have been] deliberately subjugating the Negro for economic reasons. These international criminals raped the African continent to feed their factories, and are themselves responsible for the low standards of living prevalent throughout Africa.

From Columbia Daily
Spectator,
FEBRUARY 19, 1965

Linking the problem

HARRY RING: In the recent debate on the Congo in the United Nations, a number of spokesmen for the African nations condemned the U.S. intervention in the Congo and they likened the United States' role in the Congo to its treatment of the black people in Mississippi. One reporter at least—I believe from the *New York Times*—said that you were at least in part responsible for the African delegates taking this position.

MALCOLM: I have never taken responsibility or credit, you might say, for the stance taken by the African nations. The African nations today are represented by intelligent statesmen. And it was only a matter of time before they would have to see that they would have to intervene in behalf of 22 million black Americans who are their brothers and sisters.

And it is a good example of why our problem has to be internationalized. Now the African nations are speaking out and linking the problem of racism in Mississippi with the problem of racism in the Congo, and also the problem of racism in South Vietnam. It's all racism. It's all part of the vicious racist system that the Western powers have used to continue to degrade and exploit and oppress the people in Africa and Asia and Latin America during recent centuries.

And when these people in these different areas begin to see that the problem is the same problem, and when the 22 million black Americans see that our problem is the same as the problem of the people who are being oppressed in South Vietnam and the Congo and Latin America, then— the oppressed people of this earth make up a majority, not a minority—then we approach our problem as a majority that can *demand,* not as a minority that has to beg.

From interview,
Station WBAI-FM,
JANUARY 28, 1965

Moise Tshombe and Jesse James

MALCOLM: Imagine the United States saying Tshombe, the murderer, is the only one who can restore peace to the Congo. It's like saying Jesse James is the only one who can run the bank—therefore you should let Jesse James run the bank; and the only reason the bank is in trouble is because Jesse James was already in the bank.

Answer to question by
member of McComb
delegation,
JANUARY 1, 1965

Two minutes on Vietnam

MALCOLM: Address myself to Vietnam for two minutes? It's a shame—that's one second. It is, it's a shame. You put the government on the spot when you even mention Vietnam. They feel embarrassed—you notice that? They wish they would not even have to read the newspapers about South Vietnam, and you can't blame them. It's just a trap that they let themselves get into. It's John Foster Dulles they're trying to blame it on, because he's dead.

But they're trapped, they can't get out. You notice I said "they." *They* are trapped, *they* can't get out. If they pour more men in, they'll get deeper. If they pull the men out, it's a defeat. And they should have known it in the first place.

France had about 200,000 Frenchmen over there, and the most highly mechanized modern army sitting on this earth. And those little rice farmers ate them up, and their tanks, and everything else. Yes, they did, and France was deeply entrenched, had been there a hundred or more years. Now, if she couldn't stay there and was entrenched, why, you are out of your mind if you think Sam can get in over there.

But we're not supposed to say that. If we say that, we're anti-American, or we're seditious, or we're subversive, or we're advocating something that's not intelligent. So that's two minutes, sir. Now they're turning around and getting in a worse situation in the Congo. They're getting into the Congo the same way they got into South Vietnam. They put Diem over there. Diem took all of their money, all their war equipment and everything else, and got them trapped. Then they killed him.

Yes, they killed him, murdered him in cold blood, him and his brother, Madame Nhu's husband, because they were embarrassed. They found out that they had made him strong and he was turning against them. So they killed him and put Big Minh in his place, you know, the fat one. And he wouldn't act right, so they got rid of him and put Khanh in his place. And he's started telling Taylor to get out. You know, when the puppet starts talking back to the puppeteer, the puppeteer is in bad shape.

Answer to question,
Militant Labor Forum,
JANUARY 7, 1965

The Congo, Cuba and law

MALCOLM: They [the American government] put Tshombe in power. Never let them tell you it was an accident that Tshombe got in power. A very highly placed African official told me that one of the most powerful men in the State Department jumped on an airplane and followed an African leader all the way home over a year ago, begging him to use his influence to get other African heads of state to accept Tshombe as the prime minister of the Congo. This was out of Washington, D.C., where you and I send taxes. . . .

They put Tshombe there, because Tshombe was the only African who was criminal enough to participate in the scheme that the Western powers had of sending in Western troops after the so-called legal head of government would ask for them. You notice how they did this. They knew they would have to send Western troops over there to save the Congo for Western interests. But they had to have a man to make it legal who would call them in. . . .

By the way, if the United States justifies its entry into the Congo with its military forces simply because the head of state asks them, then Castro, who is the legal head of Cuba, was well within his rights to ask Russia to put missiles in Cuba. It's the same argument—if one is sovereign, both are sovereign.

But they don't use law—they use law for their interests. They don't go by law, international, federal, local—nothing!

They go by whatever is expedient to protect the interests that are at stake.

> *Answer to question,*
> *Militant Labor Forum,*
> JANUARY 7, 1965

The role of young people

QUESTION: In a recent speech you mentioned that you met John Lewis of SNCC in Africa. Do you feel that the younger and more militant leaders in the South are broadening their views on the whole general struggle?

MALCOLM: Sure. When I was in the Black Muslim movement I spoke on many white campuses and black campuses. I knew back in 1961 and '62 that the younger generation was much different from the older, and that many students were more sincere in their analysis of the problem and their desire to see the problem solved. In foreign countries the students have helped bring about revolution—it was the students who brought about the revolution in the Sudan, who swept Syngman Rhee out of office in Korea, swept Menderes out in Turkey. The students didn't think in terms of the odds against them, and they couldn't be bought out.

In America students have been noted for involving themselves in panty raids, goldfish-swallowing, seeing how many can get in a telephone booth—not for their revolutionary political ideas or their desire to change unjust conditions. But some students are becoming more like their brothers around the world. However, the students have been deceived somewhat in what's known as the civil-rights struggle (which was never designed to solve the problem). The students were maneuvered in the direction of thinking the problem was already analyzed, so they didn't try to analyze it for themselves.

In my thinking, if the students in this country forgot the analysis that has been presented to them, and they went into a huddle and began to research this problem of racism for themselves, independent of politicians and independent of all the foundations (which are a part of the power structure), and did it themselves, then some of their findings would be shocking. But they would see that they would never be able to bring about a solution to racism in this country as long as they're relying on the government to do it. . . .

QUESTION: What contribution can youth, especially students, who are disgusted with racism in this society, make to the black struggle for freedom?

MALCOLM: Whites who are sincere don't accomplish anything by joining Negro organizations and making them integrated. Whites who are sincere should organize among themselves and figure out some strategy to break down prejudice that exists in white communities. This is where they can function more intelligently and more effectively, in the white community itself, and this has never been done.

QUESTION: What part in the world revolution are youth playing, and what lessons may this have for American youth?

MALCOLM: If you've studied the captives being caught by the American soldiers in South Vietnam, you'll find that these guerrillas are young people. Some of them are just children and some haven't yet reached their teens. Most are teen-agers. It is the teen-agers abroad, all over the world, who are actually involving themselves in the struggle to eliminate oppression and exploitation. In the Congo, the refugees point out that many of the Congolese revolutionaries are children. In fact, when they shoot captive revolutionaries, they shoot all the way down to seven years old—that's been reported in the press.

Because the revolutionaries are children, young people. In these countries, the young people are the ones who most quickly identify with the struggle and the necessity to eliminate the evil conditions that exist. And here in this country, it has been my own observation that when you get into a conversation on racism and discrimination and segregation, you will find young people more incensed over it—they feel more filled with an urge to eliminate it.

I think young people here can find a powerful example in the young Simbas in the Congo and the young fighters in South Vietnam. . . .

From interview,
Young Socialist,
MARCH–APRIL, 1965

Working with other groups

HARRY RING: You've said that your attitude on many questions has changed in the past year. How about your attitude toward the established civil-rights organizations?

MALCOLM: I'm for whatever gets results. I don't go for any organization—be it civil-rights or any other kind—that has to compromise with the power structure and has to rely on certain elements within the power structure for their financing, which puts them in a position to be influenced and controlled all over again by the power structure itself.

I'm for anything that they're involved in that gets meaningful results for the masses of our people—but not for the benefit of a few hand-picked Negroes at the top who get prestige and credit, and all the while the masses' problems remain unsolved.

RING: But would you support concrete actions of these organizations if you feel they go in the right direction?

MALCOLM: Yes. The Organization of Afro-American Unity will support fully and without compromise any action by any group that is designed to get meaningful immediate results.

From interview,
Station WBAI-FM,
JANUARY 28, 1965

Marlene Nadle stated, "It's over the tactics of violence vs. non-violence—or, as Malcolm puts it, self-defense vs. masochism—that he and other civil-rights leaders disagree. This difference is what has prevented the unity that he feels is one of the keys to the struggle."

MALCOLM: It's not that there is no desire for unity, or that it is impossible, or that they might not agree with me behind closed doors. It's because most of the organizations are dependent on white money and they are afraid to lose it.

I spent almost a year not attacking them, saying let's get together, let's do something. But they're too scared. I guess I will have to go to the people first and let the leaders fall in behind them.

[That does not mean ruling out cooperation. I will try and stress the areas and activities where the groups can work together.] If we are going into the ring, our right fist does not have to become our left fist, but we must use a common head if we are going to win.

From Marlene Nadle,
Village Voice,
FEBRUARY 25, 1965

Actions worthy of support

HARRY RING: I noticed that last week a group of Harlemites, who had been without heat and hot water for over a week, went down to city hall and sat down in the mayor's office. A few days later, I read that the housing commissioner had decided that the city would make repairs on buildings that required it and bill the landlord. He made it known, and I had never known this before, that a law had been on the books for many years permitting the city to do this, that they had done it during the depression a few times, but it's never been used since. Now it seems to me that this action by these Harlem tenants brought this about. Do you think that effective gains can be made through this kind of action?

MALCOLM: Definitely. Whenever our people are ready to take any kind of action necessary to get results, they'll get results. They'll never get results as long as they play by the ground rules laid down by the power structure downtown. It takes action to get some action, and this is what our people have to realize. They have to organize and become involved in well-coordinated action which will involve any means necessary to bring about complete elimination of the conditions that exist—conditions that are actually criminal. Not only unjust, but criminal!

> *From interview,*
> *Station WBAI-FM,*
> JANUARY 28, 1965

QUESTION: How do you view the activity of white and black students who went to the South last summer and attempted to register black people to vote?

MALCOLM: The attempt was good—I should say the objective to register black people in the South was good, because the only real power a poor man in this country has is the power of the ballot. But I don't believe sending them in and telling them to be nonviolent was intelligent. I go along with the effort toward registration, but

I think they should be permitted to use whatever means at their disposal to defend themselves from the attacks of the Klan, the White Citizens Council and other groups.

From interview,
Young Socialist,
MARCH–APRIL, 1965

The John Brown school

MALCOLM: There are many white people in this country, especially the younger generation, who realize that the injustice that has been done and is being done to black people cannot go on without the chickens coming home to roost eventually. And those white people, even if they're not morally motivated, their intelligence forces them to see that something must be done. And many of them would be willing to involve themselves in the type of operation that you were just talking about.

For one, when a white man comes to me and tells me how liberal he is, the first thing I want to know, is he a nonviolent liberal, or the other kind. I don't go for any nonviolent white liberals. If you are for me and my problems—when I say me, I mean *us,* our people—then you have to be willing to do as old John Brown did. And if you're not of the John Brown school of liberals, we'll get you later—later.

Answer to question,
Militant Labor Forum,
JANUARY 7, 1965

His own mouth, his own mind

During the last month of his life, Malcolm made two speeches in the South, and was scheduled to make a third at a Mississippi Freedom Democratic Party rally in Jackson. The second was made on February 4, 1965, at the request of two Student Nonviolent Coordinating Committee members, to the young demonstrators in Selma, Alabama, where Rev. Martin Luther King was then being held in jail. A *New York Herald Tribune* reporter wrote that Malcolm's speech "clearly disturbed the people running the registration drive . . . The young crowd cheered [Malcolm] repeatedly, and for hours afterward other speakers tried to simmer off the steam that Malcolm had generated." Before the meeting, King's aides, Rev. Andrew Young and Rev. James Bevel, cautioned Malcolm against inciting incidents, causing violence, etc.

MALCOLM: Remember this: nobody puts words in my mouth.

> *From article by*
> *Alvin Adams,* Jet,
> MARCH 5, 1965

Three days before his assassination, Malcolm gave a two-hour interview which was reported the day after his death.

MALCOLM: I feel like a man who has been asleep somewhat and under someone else's control. I feel what I'm thinking and saying now is for myself. Before, it was for and by the guidance of Elijah Muhammad. Now I think with my own mind, sir.

> *From article by*
> *Theodore Jones,*
> New York Times,
> FEBRUARY 22, 1965

Index

Africa, 159
  identification in with U.S. Black
    struggle, 86–88, 106–8, 134–
    35, 185–87, 207–8, 277–78
  image of, 125–28, 216–17, 270
  industrialization in, 166–70
  leaders in, 108–9, 186
  liberation movements in, 110–
    11, 143–44, 164–65, 218
  religious and ethnic divisions
    in, 171–72
  strategic value of, 161–65, 170
  and ties with U.S. Blacks, 100–
    104, 196–98
  wealth of, 87–88
African bank, 169–70
African revolution, 21–22, 205–
  8, 219–20
  See also Africa, liberation move-
    ments in; Colonialism
Algeria, 22, 57, 91–92, 94, 97, 164
Allies, 49, 52–53, 122
  working with, 57, 62, 96–98,
    286–87
Americanism, 43, 221
American Revolution (1776), 20,
  23, 72–73, 150
Aswan Dam, 166–67

Babu, Abdul Muhammad, 120–
  21, 132, 135–38
Baldwin, James, 31
Bandung Conference, 17–19, 171
  See also Africa, liberation move-
    ments in; African revolution;
    Colonialism

Barnett, Ross, 222
Barnette, Aubrey, 229, 236, 238
Belgium, 164
Ben Bella, Ahmed, 94
Bernard, Stan, 229–30
Berton, Pierre, 252–53, 275–76
Bible, 149–50
Big Six, 30, 186
  See also Black leaders
Birmingham, Alabama, 28, 64
Black communities
  not controlled by Blacks, 260
  See also Harlem
Black leaders, 27–32, 36, 74, 100–
  101, 156, 186, 201–2, 215–16,
  220, 235–36, 263
  and Africa, 130, 223
  collaboration by with govern-
    ment, 37, 44–46, 80, 157–58,
    183–84, 196–98, 223, 260
  unity with, 100, 172–73, 283–84
Black Muslims. See Nation of Islam
Black nationalism, 36–37, 57–61,
  271–72
  and civil rights, 49–51
  and revolution, 23
  and separatism, 34–35
  See also Organization of Afro-
    American Unity; Separatism
Black nationalist movement, 70–
  71, 243–44
  See also Organization of Afro-
    American Unity
Black nationalist party, 61, 70, 261
Black revolution
  in Africa, 22

289

ALSO BY MALCOLM X

Malcolm X Talks to Young People

"The young generation of whites, Blacks, browns, whatever else there is—you're living at a time of revolution," Malcolm said in December 1964. "And I for one will join in with anyone, I don't care what color you are, as long as you want to change this miserable condition that exists on this earth." $12. Also in Spanish, French, Farsi, and Greek.

February 1965: The Final Speeches

Our revolt is not "simply a racial conflict of Black against white, or a purely American problem. Rather, we are seeing a global rebellion of the oppressed against the oppressor, the exploited against the exploiter." Speeches and interviews from the last three weeks of Malcolm X's life. $17

By Any Means Necessary

Speeches tracing the evolution of Malcolm X's views on political alliances, women's rights, intermarriage, capitalism and socialism, and more. $15

Malcolm X on Afro-American History

Recounts the hidden history of the labor of people of African origin and their achievements. $10

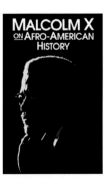

CAPITALIST CRISIS AND THE FIGHT FOR WORKERS POWER

Are They Rich Because They're Smart?
Class, Privilege, and Learning under Capitalism

JACK BARNES

Exposes growing class inequalities in the US and the self-serving rationalizations of well-paid professionals who think their "brilliance" equips them to "regulate" working people, who don't know what's in their own best interest. $10. Also in Spanish, French, Farsi, and Arabic.

The Clintons' Anti-Working-Class Record
Why Washington Fears Working People

JACK BARNES

What working people need to know about the profit-driven course of Democrats and Republicans alike over the last thirty years. And the political awakening of workers seeking to understand and resist the capitalist rulers' assaults. $10. Also in Spanish, French, Farsi, and Greek.

The Transitional Program for Socialist Revolution

LEON TROTSKY

The Socialist Workers Party program, drafted by Trotsky in 1938, still guides the SWP and communists the world over. The party "uncompromisingly gives battle to all political groupings tied to the apron strings of the bourgeoisie. Its task—the abolition of capitalism's domination. Its aim—socialism. Its method—the proletarian revolution." $17. Also in Farsi.

Is Socialist Revolution in the US Possible?

A Necessary Debate among Working People

MARY-ALICE WATERS

An unhesitating "Yes"—that's the answer given here. Possible—but not inevitable. That depends on what working people *do*. $7. Also in Spanish, French, and Farsi.

In Defense of the US Working Class

MARY-ALICE WATERS

Drawing on the best fighting traditions of workers of all skin colors and national origins, in 2018 tens of thousands of working people in states like West Virginia, Oklahoma, and Florida waged victorious strikes and won restoration of voting rights to former prisoners. Those who Hillary Clinton called "deplorables" have begun to fight back. $7. Also in Spanish, French, and Farsi.

"It's the Poor Who Face the Savagery of the US 'Justice' System"

The Cuban Five Talk about Their Lives within the US Working Class

How US cops, courts, and prisons work as "an enormous machine for grinding people up." Five Cuban revolutionaries framed up and held in US jails for 16 years explain the human devastation of capitalist "justice"—and how socialist Cuba is different. $10. Also in Spanish, Farsi, and Greek.

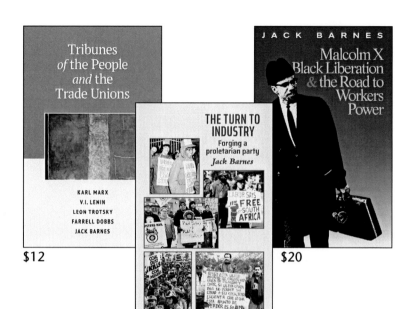

$12

$15

$20

Three books to be read as one . . .

. . . about building the only kind of party worthy of the name "revolutionary" in the imperialist epoch.

• A party that's working class in program, composition, and action.

• A party that recognizes, in word and deed, the most revolutionary fact of our time:

> That working people—those the bosses and privileged layers who serve them fear as "deplorables," "criminals," or just plain "trash"—have the power to create a different world as we organize and act together to defend our own interests, not those of the class that grows rich off exploiting our labor. That as we advance along that revolutionary course, we'll transform ourselves and awaken to our capacities—to our own worth.

Three books about building such a party in the US and throughout the capitalist world.

WOMEN'S LIBERATION AND SOCIALISM

Cosmetics, Fashions, and the Exploitation of Women
Joseph Hansen, Evelyn Reed, Mary-Alice Waters

How big business reinforces women's second-class status and uses it to market cosmetics, clothing, and other commodities, raking in profits. How the entry of millions of women into the workforce opens the road to emancipation—still to be won. $12. Also in Spanish, Farsi, and Greek.

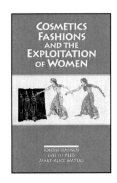

Woman's Evolution
From Matriarchal Clan to Patriarchal Family
Evelyn Reed

Assesses women's leading and still largely unknown contributions to the development of human civilization and refutes the myth that women have always been subordinate to men. "Certain to become a classic text in women's history."
—*Publishers Weekly.* $25. Also in Farsi.

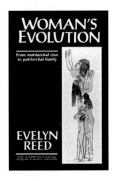

Abortion Is a Woman's Right!
Pat Grogan, Evelyn Reed

Why abortion rights are central not only to the fight for the full emancipation of women, but to forging a united and fighting labor movement. $5. Also in Spanish.

Communist Continuity and the Fight for Women's Liberation
Documents of the Socialist Workers Party, 1971–86

How did the oppression of women begin? Who benefits? What social forces have the power to end women's second-class status? 3 volumes, edited with preface by Mary-Alice Waters. $12

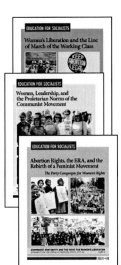

THE CUBAN REVOLUTION AND ITS IMPACT FROM AFRICA TO U.S.

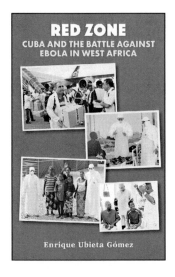

Red Zone
Cuba and the Battle against Ebola in West Africa
ENRIQUE UBIETA GÓMEZ

In 2014 three West African countries were hit by the deadly Ebola virus. Cuba's revolutionary socialist government provided what was needed most—and what no other country even tried to deliver. In a matter of weeks, more than 250 volunteer Cuban doctors, nurses, technicians, and public health specialists were on the ground providing care to thousands of desperately ill human beings and their traumatized families and communities. $17. Also in Spanish.

Cuba and Angola: The War for Freedom
HARRY VILLEGAS ("POMBO")

Cuba and Angola
Fighting for Africa's Freedom and Our Own
FIDEL CASTRO, RAÚL CASTRO, NELSON MANDELA

Two books that tell the story of Cuba's unparalleled contribution to the fight to free Africa from the scourge of apartheid. And how, in the doing, Cuba's socialist revolution was also strengthened. $10 and $12. Also in Spanish.

From the Escambray to the Congo
In the Whirlwind of the Cuban Revolution
VÍCTOR DREKE

Dreke was second in command of the internationalist column in the Congo led in 1965 by Che Guevara. He recounts the creative joy with which working people have defended their revolutionary course—from Cuba's Escambray mountains to Africa and beyond. $15. Also in Spanish.

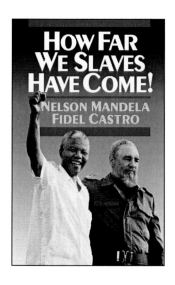

How Far We Slaves Have Come!

South Africa and Cuba in Today's World

NELSON MANDELA, FIDEL CASTRO

Speaking together in Cuba in 1991, Mandela and Castro discuss the role of Cuba in the history of Africa and Angola's victory over the invading US-backed South African army. That victory accelerated the fight to bring down the racist apartheid system. $7. Also in Spanish and Farsi.

Cuba and the Coming American Revolution

JACK BARNES

This is a book about the struggles of working people in the imperialist heartland, the youth attracted to them, and the example set by the Cuban people that revolution is not only necessary—it can be made. It is about the class struggle in the US, where the revolutionary capacities of workers and farmers are today as utterly discounted by the ruling powers as were those of the Cuban toilers. And just as wrongly. $10. Also in Spanish, French, and Farsi.

The Bolivian Diary of Ernesto Che Guevara

Guevara's day-by-day chronicle of the 1966–67 guerrilla campaign in Bolivia, an effort to forge a continent-wide revolutionary movement of workers and peasants and open the road to socialist revolution in South America. $23. Also in Spanish.

Che Guevara: Economics and Politics in the Transition to Socialism

CARLOS TABLADA

$17. Also in Spanish, French, and Greek.

The Jewish Question
A Marxist Interpretation
ABRAM LEON

At the opening of the 21st century, incidents of violent assault on Jews and anti-Semitism have begun spreading, fueled by today's capitalist crises. Across history—from antiquity to feudalism, to capitalism's rise and death throes of the past century—Jews have been targets of persecution.

Why is Jew-hatred still raising its ugly head? What are its class roots? Why is there no solution to the Jewish question without revolutionary struggles that transform working people as we fight to transform our world? $17. Also in Spanish.

The Fight Against Fascism in the USA
Forty Years of Struggle Described by Participants
JAMES P. CANNON

In 1939 some 50,000 people in New York City responded to a call by the Socialist Workers Party to answer a pro-Nazi rally of 20,000. "The question of how to fight fascism was answered in thunderous tones by the magnificent demonstration which raised the cry: Workers Defense Guards to crush the fascist danger!" $5

What Is American Fascism?
JAMES P. CANNON, JOSEPH HANSEN

Analyzes 20th century fascist currents in the US. "A fascist movement if it is to be successful must have a scapegoat on whom the petty bourgeois masses can vent their rage in place of the capitalists who deserve it," wrote Hansen about Father Charles Coughlin's anti-Semitic "Social Justice" movement in the late 1930s. "Coughlin like Hitler and Mussolini has selected the Jew." $5

FASCISM, AND THE WORKING CLASS

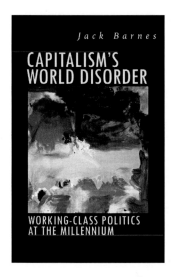

Capitalism's World Disorder
Working-Class Politics at the Millennium

JACK BARNES

"Fascism is a movement set in motion by the ruling class to maintain capitalist rule. Not a form of capitalist rule," says Barnes. "When workers understand what fascism really is, then the enormity of the responsibility to combat it becomes that much clearer." $20. Also in Spanish and French.

On the Jewish Question

LEON TROTSKY

"Now more than ever, the fate of the Jewish people is indissolubly linked with the emancipation struggle of the international proletariat," wrote Leon Trotsky. A selection of the exiled Bolshevik leader's writings from the 1930s. $5

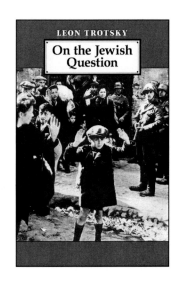

The Founding of the Socialist Workers Party
Minutes and Resolutions, 1938–39

JAMES P. CANNON

"The attack against Jews is a spearhead of the attack against the American working class," says a resolution adopted by the 1938 SWP convention. The party demanded that Washington "throw open the doors of the US to victims of the Hitlerite pogrom regime!" $23

WWW.PATHFINDERPRESS.COM

FROM THE DICTATORSHIP OF CAPITAL TO THE DICTATORSHIP OF THE PROLETARIAT

The Communist Manifesto

KARL MARX AND FREDERICK ENGELS

Communism, say the founding leaders of the revolutionary workers movement, is not a set of ideas or preconceived "principles" but workers' line of march to power, springing from a "movement going on under our very eyes." $5. Also in Spanish, French, Farsi, and Arabic.

State and Revolution

V.I. LENIN

"The relation of the socialist proletarian revolution to the state is acquiring not only practical political importance," wrote V.I. Lenin just months before the October 1917 Russian Revolution. It also addresses the "most urgent problem of the day: explaining to the masses what they will have to do to free themselves from capitalist tyranny." In *Essential Works of Lenin*. $17

Their Trotsky and Ours

JACK BARNES

To lead the working class in a successful revolution, a mass proletarian party is needed whose cadres, well beforehand, have absorbed a world communist program, are proletarian in life and work, derive deep satisfaction from doing politics, and have forged a leadership with an acute sense of what to do next. This book is about building such a party. $12. Also in Spanish, French, and Farsi.

Lenin's Final Fight

Speeches and Writings, 1922–23

V.I. LENIN

In 1922 and 1923, V.I. Lenin, central leader of the world's first socialist revolution, waged what was to be his last political battle—one that was lost following his death. At stake was whether that revolution, and the international communist movement it led, would remain on the revolutionary proletarian course that brought workers and peasants to power in October 1917. $17. Also in Spanish, Farsi, and Greek.

The History of the Russian Revolution

LEON TROTSKY

How, under Lenin's leadership, the Bolshevik Party led millions of workers and farmers to overthrow the state power of the landlords and capitalists in 1917 and bring to power a government that advanced their class interests at home and worldwide. Unabridged, 3 vols. in one. Written by one of the central leaders of that socialist revolution. $30. Also in French and Russian.

U.S. Imperialism Has Lost the Cold War

JACK BARNES

The collapse of regimes across Eastern Europe and the USSR claiming to be communist did not mean workers and farmers there had been crushed. In today's sharpening capitalist conflicts and wars, these toilers are joining working people the world over in the class struggle against exploitation. In *New International* no. 11. $14. Also in Spanish, French, Farsi, and Greek.

Defending
WORKERS' RIGHTS

Socialism on Trial
Testimony at Minneapolis Sedition Trial
JAMES P. CANNON

The revolutionary program of the working class, presented in response to frame-up charges of "seditious conspiracy" in 1941, on the eve of US entry into World War II. The defendants were leaders of the Minneapolis labor movement and the Socialist Workers Party. $15. Also in Spanish, French, and Farsi.

FBI on Trial
The Victory in the Socialist Workers Party Suit against Government Spying
EDITED BY MARGARET JAYKO

The record of an historic victory in the fight for political rights, including the 1986 federal court ruling against government spying and excerpts from trial testimony by SWP leaders Farrell Dobbs and Jack Barnes. $17

Cointelpro
The FBI's Secret War on Political Freedom
NELSON BLACKSTOCK

An in-depth look at the 1960s and '70s covert FBI disruption and counterintelligence program—code-named COINTELPRO. Contains reproductions of FBI documents released through the Socialist Workers Party suit against government spying. $15

BY THOMAS SANKARA

Thomas Sankara Speaks
The Burkina Faso Revolution, 1983–87

Under Sankara's guidance, Burkina Faso's revolutionary government led peasants, workers, women, and youth to expand literacy; to sink wells, plant trees, erect housing; to combat women's oppression; to carry out land reform; to join others in Africa and worldwide to free themselves from the imperialist yoke. $20. Also in French.

Women's Liberation and the African Freedom Struggle

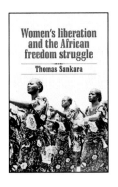

"There is no true social revolution without the liberation of women," explains the leader of the 1983–87 revolution in the West African country of Burkina Faso. $5. Also in Spanish, French, and Farsi.

We Are Heirs of the World's Revolutions
Speeches from the Burkina Faso Revolution, 1983–87

How peasants and workers in this West African country established a popular revolutionary government and began to fight hunger, illiteracy, and economic backwardness imposed by imperialist domination. They set an example not only for workers and small farmers in Africa, but their class brothers and sisters the world over. $10. Also in Spanish, French, and Farsi.

New International

A MAGAZINE OF MARXIST POLITICS AND THEORY

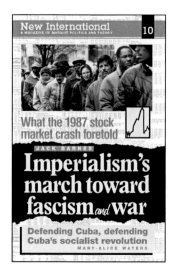

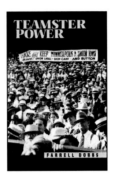